NO REGRETS

NO REGRETS

THE LIFE OF EDITH PIAF

CAROLYN BURKE

CHICAGO
REVIEW
PRESS

An A Cappella Book

This paperback edition first published in 2012 by
Chicago Review Press, Incorporated
814 North Franklin Street
Chicago, Illinois 60610

ISBN 978-1-61374-392-8

Published by arrangement with Alfred A. Knopf, an imprint of The Knopf Doubleday Publishing
Group, a division of Random House, Inc.

Owing to limitations of space, permissions acknowledgments can be found following the index.

Cover design: John Yates at Stealworks.com
Cover photo: Globe Photos, Inc.
Interior design: Iris Weinstein

Library of Congress Cataloging-in-Publication Data
Burke, Carolyn.
  No regrets : the life of Edith Piaf / Carolyn Burke. — Paperback ed.
    p. cm.
  Originally published: New York : Knopf, 2011.
  Includes bibliographical references and index.
  ISBN 978-1-61374-392-8
  1. Piaf, Edith, 1915–1963. 2. Singers—France—Biography. I. Title.

ML420.P52B85 2012
782.42164092—dc23
[B]

2012001255

Printed in the United States of America
5 4 3 2 1

For Georges Borchardt, and for Samuel Hynes

My songs are my life. I don't want to be nothing but a memory.

—EDITH PIAF

CONTENTS

PRELUDE

T hat kid Piaf tears your guts out," Maurice Chevalier was heard to say after watching the debut of the newcomer called "La Môme Piaf." It was not yet apparent that nineteen-year-old Edith Gassion (her birth name) would become one of the greatest vocalists of the twentieth century—the "little sparrow" whose gut-wrenching tones would come to represent France to the French and touch listeners all over the world, whether or not they spoke her language.

Piaf is often portrayed as a Gallic fusion of Billie Holiday and Judy Garland. Yet she was more feral than either and, like her friend Chevalier, more completely identified with *le petit peuple*—the "little people" to whose dreams she gave voice, whose adoration nourished her career from its inauspicious start in the Paris streets to her international fame: during her short life she would make ten tours of the United States, as well as numerous tours of Europe, Canada, and South America.

"Edith Piaf knocked my socks off," Joni Mitchell declared recently, "although I didn't know what she was singing about." Now, nearly five decades after Piaf's death, she is known worldwide as the prototype of the singer who takes listeners to the edge of their seats. Piaf fascinates music lovers as an icon of "complete vocal abandon," as the singer and recent Piaf interpreter Martha Wainwright put it—as someone whose "crackling emotion" washes over her audiences. Judging by the remarks of Mitchell and Wainwright, Piaf's importance to contemporary singers is based on their response to her sensibility, the way her songs create the kind of urgency that has never gone out of style.

Although Piaf's contemporaries felt her wholehearted generosity and visceral power, they also saw her as an emblematic figure who combined in her persona contradictory aspects of icons like Joan of

Arc and Thérèse of Lisieux, the singer's patron saint, even as she lived out the short, wayward life for which she became famous. That the diminutive star compared herself to Mary Magdalene—hoping to be forgiven for loving often because she loved greatly—astounds those of us who are not from Catholic countries.

Such comparisons were inevitable, given the paradigms for women during Piaf's youth in the 1920s, her hand-to-mouth existence in the 1930s, and her rise to fame over the next decades. Women were either whores or madonnas in the popular imagination. Piaf's many love affairs, as sensationalized in the press, evoked both archetypes, which in turn complicated her legend as the scrappy street singer who made her way out of the slums on the strength of her voice. Even now they may cause us to undervalue the musical intelligence with which she made her voice into a finely tuned instrument while nourishing her most enduring love affair, her intimacy with her audience.

Despite cultural differences, comparisons to Billie Holiday and Judy Garland have some merit. Piaf's legend appears to fit the template for successful artists who pay the price in their descent into suffering caused by drink, drugs, and, in the case of women, promiscuity. What is more, these three female vocalists, who died young after careers that were, to say the least, hectic, share an intensity, although Piaf's origins among the "dangerous classes"—the outcasts among whom she and her acrobat father eked out a living—suggest that she had more in common with Holiday than with Garland. The French street urchin and the black American each transformed the clichés of ordinary speech into a bodily communion; their transports produced in admirers an almost ecstatic response. (From the start, however, Piaf was claimed by the masses in her country—unlike Holiday, whose style endeared her mainly to white jazz-lovers until after her death, when black audiences finally accepted her.)

Piaf began as an interpreter of *la chanson réaliste,* the tradition of "realistic" song-stories about the downtrodden—often prostitutes or lovelorn women whose men desert them—but soon came to represent not only the French spirit as mirrored back to her compatriots but also the allure to the larger world of this fatalistic yet resilient stance. By the 1930s, an ideology of the "little guy" was in place in the French entertainment business. Chevalier and Mistinguett, his ever-popular former lover, were the golden couple of *music-halls* like the Folies Bergère, whose variety shows featured these insouciant icons of *je-m'en-foutisme*—the "I don't give a damn" response to adversity. Just below these venues on the show-business ladder came cabarets of varying repute, and beneath them the working-class dives that represented a promotion for a former street singer like Piaf. Her early repertoire gave audiences a certain view of society, one in which *la chanson réaliste* told the truth about working-class lives and piqued the curiosity of artists like Jean Cocteau, who went slumming in the poorer quarters in search of artistic vision.

Yet Piaf's origins, while fascinating in their own right, do not explain her appeal to all levels of French society and, after World War II, to music lovers around the world. She came on the scene in 1935 with a voice that was already a powerful brass instrument. Over the next few years, when she no longer had to project to street crowds, she refined it—bringing greater subtlety to the lyrics and bringing out their meaning with her hands, which swooped majestically or fluttered like moths as she sang.

Piaf's velvety vibrato and guttural "r"s soon became the marks of her style, whether she sang of everyday tragedies or performed the light, comic numbers that are less well known outside France. Choosing songs primarily for their lyrics, she soon performed them with the "proper French" diction she learned from her mentors, Jacques Bourgeat and Raymond Asso, who taught her to live more fully within each tune. From then on, as her musical intelligence developed, there was never a word out of place, never a false gesture even as she sang of great truths (or platitudes). Oddly, given Piaf's start as a spitfire, she perfected an art of sobriety, one that conveyed the rawness of deeply felt emotion yet retained a high degree of vocal purity.

It is not often noted that it was Piaf's sense of *métier,* the art of performance that comes with long experience, that underscored her poignant mix of vulnerability and defiance. "My song is my life," she wrote when applying to join the French songwriters' union. Yet the musical versions of her life that are still so completely identified with the singer were carefully selected, rehearsed, and polished for performance. Piaf played an active role in shaping all aspects of her recitals, from the accompaniments to the lighting to the order of each program. In the same way, she choreographed the publicity surrounding her appearances to cultivate her bond with the public that adored her and for that reason, she believed, should be allowed to know her own version of her unconventional life.

Since Piaf's death in 1963, she has never left the scene to which she devoted herself. Recordings, movies, theatrical presentations, biographies, and versions of her songs by others are too numerous to mention, except, perhaps, for Olivier Dahan's recent biopic, *La Môme* (*La Vie en rose* outside France), which gives a colorful account of her picaresque childhood. But this much-admired film also resorts to the familiar template for an artist's life—the trajectory from rags to riches with the emphasis on the sorrows (especially the addictive ones) that lead to the performer's downfall. Such commonly held myths do a disservice by thinning the texture of a life. What is worse, they perpetuate themselves in the public mind, causing us to distort the legend of the artist at the expense of her artistry.

The cliché of Piaf as self-destructive waif is too rigid to allow for her complex humanity. Its morality-play version of her life neglects or completely ignores her courage in World War II, when she defied the Nazis by sheltering Jewish friends and aiding the Resistance. In the same way, many accounts of her life say little about her mentoring of younger singers like Yves Montand and Charles Aznavour, preferring instead to shape her story by calling them "the men in her life"—each of whom gets a chapter, as if her existence had been organized around theirs.

Nor does this template elucidate her role as a lyricist. Piaf wrote nearly one hundred songs, which were set to music by trusted collaborators like Marguerite Monnot, with whom she formed the first female songwriting team. (According to myths still in circulation, Piaf had little affection for women, a reading of her life that ignores her close friendships with protégées, members of her entourage, and peers like Monnot and actresses Micheline Dax and Marlene Dietrich.)

Finally, myths about her life neglect Piaf's ongoing role as a muse who worked tirelessly with her collaborators. Her artistic family included both the musicians and songwriters with whom she devised melodies to embody her persona, and cultural figures like Jean Cocteau, who wrote plays for her, and the choreographer Pierre Lacotte, who created a ballet in homage to the star and to the city with which she is so completely identified. For it was in Paris that the diminutive sparrow became France's nightingale (Cocteau's phrase), then—following her recovery from near-fatal illness in 1959—its phoenix, its symbol of resurrection.

FITTINGLY, it was in Paris that I first heard Piaf's throaty tremor, in the maid's room I occupied in exchange for English lessons. Often, after climbing seven flights of stairs, I fell onto the bed and turned on the radio to hear her latest hit. In the fall of 1959, when I was studying at the Sorbonne and Piaf was pursuing what the press called her suicide tour, France was gripped by the Algerian War, then being waged in the casbahs of Algiers and the streets of Paris. Unclear about the issues but aware that bombs were exploding in public places, I retreated to my attempt to learn French by singing along with Piaf.

According to my teacher, her sharp diction and phrasing could not be improved upon, but she had learned them the hard way, having grown up with the *parigot* accent of the slums. This meant little to me, except that I was determined to get my tongue around those piquant sounds. Singing my way through her repertoire, I acquired a tolerable accent and a set of emotions I had not yet personally experienced, as if French culture had entered me viscerally by means of her music.

On my return to Paris in 1961, I learned that Piaf's phoenixlike revival had occurred earlier that year: she had found the strength to perform the inspirational "Non, je ne regrette rien," which was still resounding on the air. That winter I chanted her song as if it were the national anthem, doing my best to imitate her flurry of "r"s, her stress on the repeated negatives (the *nons*), her crystalline voicing of a stance that fuses acceptance with the will to survive. I did not fully grasp the song's reverberations in a time of unrest, yet felt its talismanic power along my pulse.

When I thought about Piaf's repertoire years later, it became clear to me that, unlike the tunes I had danced to as a teenager in the 1950s, *la chanson réaliste* treated songs as slices of life from the lower depths. These gritty stories dwell on the magnetic but often disappointing outcome of sensual experience, on the conflict between dreams of perfect love and their undoing, and, often, on resilience as the only response to life's woes. Because *chanson* lyrics were usually penned before their music, Piaf's tradition was closer to poetry—allowing the singer to depict an entire destiny, from promising start to tragic dénouement. Since the resurgence of interest in the art of cabaret in the United States and elsewhere, she is now seen as its foremost interpreter.

Starting work on this biography, I was pleased to learn that Piaf's melodies were again being sung by scores of interpreters in France and around the world: in Australia, where I spend part of the year; in Japan, where her acceptance of the ephemeral is embraced by a culture that values intimations of feelings; and in the many countries where each new singer with raw emotional power is compared with Piaf, the tradition's gold standard.

In 2006, I contacted L'Association des Amis d'Edith Piaf, a group of her admirers based in Paris, who introduced me to the scattered, often contradictory, sources available there and to their repository of Piafiana. My idea was to place her short, passionate life in its artistic and social contexts, while also exploring the myths that have grown up around it—an approach that will, I trust, reintroduce the singer to English-speakers for whom French culture seems ungraspably alluring, yet who find themselves moved by Piaf without knowing why.

I have been fortunate in having unparalleled access to sources that illuminate the multiple facets of her life, beginning with the recently released correspondence between the star and Jacques Bourgeat, her mentor, at the Bibliothèque Nationale de France, where I also consulted their extensive clipping files on her early years. While I was writing this book, more of Piaf's correspondence came to light: her letters to four of her lovers—Norbert Glanzberg, Takis Horn, Tony Frank, and Toto Gérardin—which help to situate her *amours* in the context of her career rather than the other way around. (Nonetheless, it has, at times, been a dizzying task to keep track of her many lovers.)

In France I was also introduced to collectors whose archives allowed me to see rare Piaf material, including home movies and recordings unavailable elsewhere, and to discuss with them our fascination with the singer whose identification with their country means that she remains very much alive there.

Synchronistic encounters with people who shared their memories and introduced me to others who had known Piaf or heard her sing made it seem that I was being drawn into her life—as in 2007, when I visited the former brothel in Bernay, the Norman town where she lived as a child, and attended a memorial to her in Père-Lachaise, her burial place, on the anniversary of her death. During the mass, which included Piaf's renditions of "Mon Dieu" and "Hymne à l'amour," I sensed that her songs often wed earthly to spiritual aspirations, that the religion of love espoused in them still reverberates for all who are touched by her credo. (At the next year's memorial, the priest referred to me as "*l'australienne, celle qui est venue de loin*"—the Australian, the one who came from far away—for the occasion.)

Over the course of the three years I spent completing this biography, I was often asked whether I had been inspired by *La Môme* and what I thought of it. Dahan's film allowed audiences around the world to feel the fierce purity of Piaf's voice, I replied. But it had been standing at her grave with her fans and relations that moved me to write a book in homage to the little star who taught me her language and, in the process, gave me a more generous view of her life, and of my own.

NO REGRETS

CHAPTER ONE

1915–1925

Edith Piaf's life began like a latter-day version of *Les Misérables*. A poor girl from the Paris slums, she grew up among the downtrodden souls who later populated her lyrics and, through their mythic resonance, shaped the scenarios of twentieth-century French culture. Her story is the stuff of working-class legend, its joys and sorrows the materials for her heart-stopping songs. From these impoverished beginnings, she kept her cheeky street sense and gaiety of spirit while reinventing herself as the chanteuse who reached across social, linguistic, and national divides to voice the emotions of ordinary people.

Though mythic, Piaf's childhood was no fairy tale. Because the few known facts about her inauspicious beginnings are entwined with the legends that she and others cultivated once she became famous, it is often impossible to separate fact from fiction—an ambition that is probably beside the point, since her art and legend nourish each other, circling back to the streets where she got her start. *Au bal de la chance* (1958) and *Ma vie* (1964)—accounts of her life dictated to others—must be complemented by interviews with Piaf and her friends to help us grasp the contexts for the legends that grew up around her.

Edith Piaf was born during the second year of World War I in Belleville, a defiantly independent village in the eastern heights of Paris that remained, long after its annexation to the city in 1860, a bastion of revolutionary culture. Unlike Montmartre, the city's other hilltop slum, Belleville did not possess a community of artists. With no

Picasso to celebrate the area and no bourgeois visitors in search of bohemia, the village was left to its plebeian ways. Maurice Chevalier, who grew up nearby in Menilmontant, called Belleville "the capital of the outskirts of Paris." Though the population was working-class, he wrote, it embraced all sorts: "A good honest fellow will live next door to the lowest pimp and respectable housewives line up behind street-walkers at the baker's."

A similar taint of promiscuity colors the tale of Piaf's infancy. "My mother nearly gave birth to me on the street," she supposedly told a journalist, who would later remove the word "nearly" to create the well-known tale of her entrance into the world shielded only by the woolen cape spread on the pavement by a quick-thinking policeman. Later in life, when asked whether she had really been born in the street, Piaf neither confirmed nor denied the story, letting people believe what they liked. "She didn't know very much about her childhood," the composer Henri Contet said, and she liked to entertain the accounts the press reflected back to her—as if by studying them she might glean enough to fill in the sketchy tale of her beginnings.

A document registered at the Mairie (or City Hall) of the twentieth arrondissement, the administrative center for Belleville, gives a somewhat more reliable account—that of the little girl's birth in the nearby Tenon Hospital. "On the 19th of December, 1915," it begins, "the delivery of Edith Giovanna, daughter of Louis Gassion, 'artiste acrobate,' 34, and his wife, Annetta Giovanna Maillard, 'artiste lyrique,' 20, took place at 5 a.m. in the rue de la Chine" (the address of the hospital). The document, signed by the nurse who assisted at the birth and two hospital employees—"in the absence of the father"—gives the couple's address as 72 rue de Belleville, the unimpressive building on whose steps her mother may or may not have gone into labor. Here the bare facts—the names, ages, and professions of the parents, their address, the time and place of birth—form the frame on which her story may be embroidered a stitch at a time.

Let us begin with the absent father, here identified as an "acrobatic artist." Louis Gassion, a handsome man with a fine figure, was just under five feet tall. A foot soldier in the trenches of eastern France when Edith was born, he would be away during most of her infancy. After the war, his repeated absences would be explained by his life as an itinerant entertainer and his love of *gros rouge* (cheap red wine): "It was the rotgut that kept him going," Piaf often said of her progenitor, whose diminutive stature she inherited (as an adult she measured four feet ten inches).

Louis Gassion had practiced his trade since childhood, having learned its tricks in the 1890s—when performers like Valentin le Désossé (the Moulin Rouge contortionist memorialized by Toulouse-Lautrec) entertained the masses. Piaf's father billed himself as a contortionist but never achieved Le Désossé's celebrity. Before the war he toured France with the Gassion family circus, which was based in Normandy under the direction of his father, Victor Gassion, an equestrian who also enlisted four of Louis's young sisters as trapeze artists. His mother, Louise-Léontine Descamps Gassion, presided over their large tribe. If any photographs of Louis's parents and their fourteen children were taken, none survive. Perhaps they were not sufficiently prosperous to record their lives in the manner of bourgeois families.

Louis's flirtatious manner more than made up for his size. Just before the start of war in 1914, he met Annetta at a fair outside Paris where she sold sweets and occasionally sang while her mother, a Moroccan Berber sideshow artist known as Aîcha, presided over her own attraction—a menagerie of trained fleas that she carried about in a matchbox. Annetta's official papers listed her father, an itinerant animal-trainer named Auguste Maillard, as deceased, and her mother (unlike the fleas) as having no fixed residence. Like other circus people, the Maillards had no place in the social order. Annetta may have sensed a kindred spirit in Louis, since her maternal grandparents had also been acrobats.

Annetta's marriage to Louis was one of many unions consummated hastily in wartime. The groom was stationed in Sens, south of Paris and beyond the reach of the enemy troops that decimated Senlis (a widely condemned act of German barbarity) two days after their wedding on September 4, 1914. Edith's December 1915 birth shows that the newlyweds had managed to be together the previous March. About this time they set up house in the rue de Belleville, around the corner from the sordid rue de Rébeval apartment where Annetta's mother, Aîcha, lived.

The effect of the war on daily life was inescapable. The most impoverished Bellevillois lined up for the *soupe populaire* (soup kitchen), which was for some their only nourishment. Annetta called her baby Edith in homage to the war heroine Edith Cavell, an English nurse executed by a German firing squad that October for having organized an escape route through Belgium for wounded soldiers. Though Piaf appreciated being named for a much-publicized symbol of resistance, she disliked her second name, Giovanna—her mother's gesture at passing on her lineage by giving her daughter her own middle name.

Of her maternal heritage, Piaf later wrote, "I've always thought that Fate led me to the very career that my mother dreamed of but could never manage, not through any lack of talent but because luck wasn't on her side." Annetta had had no choice but to follow in her parents' footsteps, Piaf believed. She sang in the streets while Aîcha looked after the baby, and soon took the stage name Line Marsa, an exotic sobriquet inspired by the Tunisian seaside resort La Marsa. Line's sultry manner suited her repertoire of drinking songs and torchy ballads—the kind of song called *la chanson réaliste*, which would make her daughter's name some years later.

Line would have found appreciative audiences in Belleville. Since the 1900s, the neighborhood had absorbed several waves of immigrants: first the Auvergnats, from the center of France, who delivered coal and cleaned chimneys; then Russian and Polish Jews fleeing pogroms (Belleville had the largest concentration of Jews in Paris); and, when Edith was a baby, Armenians and Greeks escaping the upheavals in their homelands. This mixed population of mechanics and craftsmen toiled in Belleville's many small workshops, turning out toys, tools, leather goods, shoes, mattresses, comforters, and any number of household items.

Successive generations of foreign artisans absorbed the locals' proud spirit. In revolutionary fashion they *tutoi*ed each other rather than use the *vous* of polite society, and expressed their solidarity in Belleville slang, a coded language reflected in the songs that Line and other *goualeuses* bawled out in the streets, the Café de la Liberté, the Vielleuse, and the other social centers specializing in *gros rouge*.

Differing accounts of Edith's childhood all emphasize the importance of *gros rouge* in both her paternal and maternal lineages. Though we cannot know for certain whether Aîcha dosed Edith's bottle with wine to make her sleep, it is likely that a fair amount of it was consumed in their household. Both men and women tippled to get through the day, especially during the war years, when food was scarce and heating almost unavailable. It is easy to imagine Line's choice to keep warm in the cafés while earning whatever their patrons could spare, rather than stay at home with her infant daughter. At twenty, she was more interested in becoming a singer than in being a mother.

Opportunities for enjoyment were not lacking in wartime Belleville. Tales of life there may be colored by nostalgia, but the area in those days is still recalled as a "miniature nation . . . whose insignia could have been the red paving stones, a giant bottle of *gros rouge*, a vegetable seller's cart, and an accordion." The shared experience of grinding poverty made residents all the more likely to live for the moment. All looked forward to the event that brought relief from the workweek, the rue de Belleville's Sunday fair, animated by vendors' cries in praise of their vegetables, smells of fresh bread and cuts of meat in the baker's oven, the tang of pastis emanating from café tables, and the scent of lilacs perfuming the hillsides in spring. Singers like Line plied their trade as customers made their way up the steep cobblestone street and, in a burst of generosity, granted their favorites some change.

The record does not say whether Louis came home from the war on leave, only that by the time he returned from the front in 1918, Annetta had left him and turned Edith over to Aîcha (later in life, Piaf would say that her mother left when she was two months old). Louis found their little girl sickly and malnourished. Aîcha, who made ends meet by cleaning apartments, had been spending her wages in the cafés and leaving Edith alone at home. In the different accounts of her removal from Aîcha's care, Louis, his younger sister Zaza (one of the retired acrobats), or both of them together rescued Edith and took her to Bernay, the conservative Normandy town where her Gassion grandparents had recently settled after turning the page on their lives as itinerant showmen.

The Gassions were not always wanderers. The family had lived in the Calvados region of Normandy since the seventeenth century, most often in Falaise, the birthplace of William the Conqueror. In the years just before Edith's birth, her grandparents had forsaken the circus for a more sedentary life in Caen, where they sold groceries, coal, and hardware. But their life as shopkeepers did not erase their notoriety. The neighbors gossiped; the taint of the circus followed them when they moved again to Bernay, where Léontine Gassion found employment as the manager of a *maison close*—a position on the fringes of a provincial society that deplored the brothel's existence while taking advantage of its services.

Edith's grandmother, known as Maman Tine, took the sickly child into this unusual household but never gave her the affection she craved. Perhaps she was too busy overseeing the arrivals and departures of the town notables who were her clients. Edith's health soon improved, except for an eye problem that impaired her vision, a state of affairs that made it possible to believe that she was unaware of what was going on.

Brothels like Edith's new home were called *maisons de tolérance*, their activities "tolerated" by the officials who regulated them and sometimes returned when off-duty. Its services were advertised by the lantern and the larger-than-normal street number that graced the façade of this three-story residence on the road to Rouen. The building's layout ensured visitors' privacy while also providing separate quarters for Maman Tine, Victor Gassion, and Edith. Clients came through the front door into a vestibule that led to the salon, where each night a player piano cranked out popular songs, and those who wanted to relax sipped absinthe or smoked their pipes.

Visits to *les filles* took place discreetly, in the small bedrooms on the second and third floors. Everyone behaved as if, apart from their nightly duties, "the girls" were boarders at a strange sort of finishing school, with Maman Tine as their headmistress. Taking up work as a *fille soumise,* or registered prostitute, subjected one to a high degree of discipline. It also meant taking a new name, usually from a list repeated from one *maison* to another—literary and operatic pseudonyms like Violette, Manon, and Carmen, or youthful-sounding diminutives ending in "-ette" (Yvette, Odette, Blondinette) that nourished clients' fantasies about the girls' willing "submission."

The inmates of such houses rose late, devoted what remained of the morning to their grooming, and spent the afternoon playing cards, gossiping, and smoking. A child would have been a welcome diversion, particularly for the women whose own children had been taken from them. One can imagine Edith's surrogate mothers fussing over her, especially once they realized that she could barely see. "I got used to walking with my hands out in front to protect myself," she said. "My fingers and hands were sensitive; I recognized fabrics by touching them, people's skin the same way. I would say, 'That's Carmen, that's Rose.' . . . I lived in a world of sounds."

One wonders how Edith interpreted what she heard at night or what she made of her new friends' working clothes, their scanty chemises and silk stockings. Although her eyelids opened only partway, she no doubt witnessed scenes in the salon, where the residents sat demurely until a client chose one of them and took her upstairs. "I always thought that if a man held out his hand to a woman, she had to accept and go with him," Piaf said years later.

On Tuesday, the residents' day off, they put on their most modest garb and, with Edith in tow, walked single-file behind Maman Tine to visit the coiffeur, the pharmacist, and other shops. This display of decorum did not change the townspeople's opinions of those they called *les filles perdues* (the lost girls), but it helped maintain a sense of order—just as the discipline at the brothel mirrored bourgeois home life. Residents were given registration numbers, as if they were in the army; they had to submit to sermons by the curé and visits by the doctor, who checked their health in compliance with state regulations.

Some time after Edith's arrival, the same doctor examined the child's eyes—whose color, a translucent blue, held tints of mauve and violet. He diagnosed her condition as acute keratitis, an inflammation of the cornea caused by the herpes virus or by bacteria. In our time, keratitis is treated with antiviral drops or antibiotics. Before these drugs were available, most patients recovered but some cases resulted in permanent damage, even blindness. Ointments were prescribed for Edith's symptoms—blurred vision, pain, and sensitivity to light. She was to rest, eat well, and cover her eyes with bandages.

After this approach failed to effect a cure, the women of the house took matters into their own hands. One day when the curé came to pray for divine intervention he found them telling their rosaries on Edith's behalf and invoking Saint Thérèse, the "Little Flower," whose cult in nearby Lisieux drew thousands of the faithful to her grave each Sunday. Hoping for the saint's intervention, Maman Tine organized pilgrimages to Lisieux for the entire household to pray for her granddaughter.

Piaf liked to tell the story of one of these trips, on a Sunday in August when she was six, she thought, though it is likely that it took place a year or two earlier. In this version of the tale, Maman Tine gave the girls the day off to visit the saint's grave like other worshippers. Ten days later, after their return to Bernay, the little girl announced that she could see. "Saint Thérèse performed a miracle for you!" she was told—an explanation that would comfort Piaf for the rest of her life. In the language of popular piety, she was a *miraculée,* someone who has been touched by a miracle.

Raymond Asso, Piaf's first composer, concluded after talking to her grandmother that this account was a work of fiction: Edith had regained her sight when the doctor removed the bandages; the household went to Lisieux to thank Saint Thérèse some time later. Piaf naturally preferred to believe that she had been singled out by the saint. When asked, much later, about her first happy memory, she replied, "The day I regained my eyesight!" From then on, she could enjoy life like other children. Yet, even after that day, according to Madame Taillère, a neighbor who washed bed linens for Maman Tine's household, "Edith's eyes were never wide open like yours or mine." To make up for this handicap, the prostitutes gave the washerwoman money to buy toys for Edith. "She was engaging, a little love," Madame Taillère recalled, "and they doted on her."

The child was also a favorite with this neighbor. Since the volume of washing required Madame Taillère's presence in the brothel every day, they were often together. Edith ran across the street to visit her easygoing friend and accompanied her to the *lavoir,* the communal washhouse down the hill, where a covered roof allowed washerwomen to work in all weathers. But although Madame Taillère lavished her affection on Edith, Maman Tine scolded the child for distracting her.

Bernay, built at the confluence of two rivers, abounds in streams running down the hillsides to the lowlands. Once Edith could see well enough to play outside, she would have sailed toy boats, chased the frogs that swim in the rivulets, and run up and down the steep stairways leading to the lowlands, where for a few years she attended elementary school. "She was a good student, she memorized everything she was given right away," her teacher recalled. Contemporaries remembered her because of her bad eyesight, the local historian said, but also because "the girl whose grandmother ran the town brothel was not likely to be confused with other pupils!"

Piaf said nothing about her brief education in her memoir *Au bal de la chance,* which omits these years except for the "miraculous" cure. Perhaps it was too painful to recall the taunts of classmates who threw stones at her and called her "the child of the devil's house." Perhaps she didn't recall these stories—which are still told in Bernay. Neighbors remembered stopping what they were doing when Edith began to sing. Some evenings, her grandparents took her to the Café de la Gare, where she was lifted onto a table to shouts of "Sing, little one, sing," a contemporary recalled: "Her voice was already unique, magical." Another Bernayan observed, "People knew that she came from a family of artists. You could tell even then that she would become someone."

It is tempting to think that Piaf's ability to look within herself for the essence of a song developed from these experiences. "When I wanted to understand, to 'see' a song, I would close my eyes," she reflected, after her eyesight, long since cured, allowed her to read music, compose, and accompany herself on the piano. Her memoirs often link clairvoyance with strong emotion or with her unshakable belief in the right to happiness. She was not religious by traditional standards, she said: "But my faith in something bigger, something stronger and more pure than what exists on this earth, that faith is immense. And I know that one only has to ask the 'world beyond' for signs, and it sends them, together with warnings and advice."

Edith was growing up in a time when the calendar of saints' days shaped the commonly held notion of divine providence at work in daily life. That her miraculous cure had taken place on August 25,

Saint Louis's day, would not have escaped the household's attention, for it was also Louis Gassion's saint's day, and for this reason doubly revered by Edith. Though Saint Thérèse was, in some way, her spiritual benefactor, she seemed to be working in concert with her beloved, though equally absent, father.

Legend has it that on a Gassion family outing to one of the Normandy beaches before Edith regained her sight, Louis appeared, the child heard his voice, and she exclaimed, "Papa!" It is more likely that she saw her father whenever his travels allowed him to visit Falaise, where she often spent weekends with her cousins. According to his sister Zaza, he strolled around Falaise with Edith, treated her to the local specialty, buckwheat crêpes, and showed her William the Conqueror's castle. Family members also visited Bernay. When Edith's cousin Marcelle spent Sundays there, the girls tried to get around their grandmother's objections to their socializing with the boarders: "We wanted to see [them], of course, but she would send us back to the kitchen."

It is also said that once Edith could see and consequently grasp the nature of the transactions in the household, the curé persuaded her grandmother and father that she must be removed from these evil influences. It is equally possible that Maman Tine told Louis that it was time he took responsibility for his daughter, and that, as an experienced busker, he knew that an endearing seven-year-old passing the hat would inspire generosity in his audiences. Whatever Louis's motivation, about this time he borrowed funds from his mother to buy an old trailer, signed with the Caroli Circus, and, with Edith in tow, headed for Belgium, where the troupe was booked on a lengthy tour.

Although many details are missing from the third phase of Piaf's childhood, what *is* known of her life after Bernay is, to say the least, picaresque. We must rely on the stories that she chose to tell much later, when summing up this period in interviews and her dictated memoirs.

Edith's playfulness survived in these new circumstances, even though her father proved a hard taskmaster. "Papa was not a tender man," Piaf said, "and I received my share of blows." Believing that her father did not love her, she tried to win his heart, and treasured the rare occasions when he kissed her. Piaf spoke of him admiringly, despite the blows: "Gifted athletically, extraordinarily agile and supple, . . . he meant to be his own master, going wherever he felt like going, taking orders from no one." Like other wanderers, Louis was temperamentally opposed to a settled existence.

Her recollections of their life together blend aspects of *Les Misérables* with elements of fairy tales. "I lived in the trailer and did the chores," Piaf explained. "My days started early, the work was hard, but I liked the constantly changing horizons of our vagabond life. It was a thrill to discover the enchanted world of 'the travelers,' the fanfares, the clowns' spangled costumes, the lion tamers' gold-braided tunics."

A snapshot taken on the steps of their trailer shows her father looking dignified in a shirt and tie, a younger girl, three attractive women (presumably performers), and a beaming, fashionably dressed Edith with thick, dark bangs—a reconstituted family of sorts in front of her new home. Aged seven or eight, she looks very much like her father, who presides over his female companions. Piaf's account of this time omits any mention of her original family—her mother and her little brother, Herbert, who was born in 1918 and was almost immediately handed over to the state social services when Line Marsa signed up for a singing engagement in Turkey.

The few children whose families traveled with the circus played together after their chores were done. During a game of hide-and-seek, Edith hid in the space between the lions' cages, within reach of their claws. After some time a search party, including her father and the lion tamer, found her and ordered her to tiptoe out without disturbing the beasts. "I was so afraid of getting punished that I made Papa promise not to beat me," Piaf told a journalist. Her father agreed, but once she was safe, he went back on his word.

Had Louis Gassion been able to control his temper, his career might have taken off, she believed. Calling himself an "antipodean" acrobat (he stood on his head) or a "cosmopolitan" contortionist (he traveled widely), Louis twisted himself into strange shapes—the head-seat (a head-to-buttocks backbend), the human knot (legs behind the neck), extreme splits, and perilous handstands—while awed audiences held their breath. With more care, Piaf thought, he could have joined the Medrano Circus, the home of the clowns and acrobats who, since the 1900s, had inspired artists like Cocteau and Picasso. (At this time, the Medrano already had a contortionist called the King of Vertigo: he maneuvered on a chair balanced in the neck of a bottle that was itself perched on a ten-foot pole.)

But Louis was not one to take pains, nor could he submit to discipline for long. Edith's time with the circus ended abruptly when her father walked out in a fit of anger, sold the trailer, and headed back to France with his daughter. "We kept on traveling," Piaf recalled, "staying in hotels instead of the trailer, and my father became his own boss. Mine too, of course."

The lives of itinerant entertainers are nearly impossible to document—they lived in defiance of social norms, a tribe of outcasts with its own rules and freedoms. The scenery changed as Gassion *père et fille* toured the country, yet one day was much like another. The high point was always Louis's performance. "Father spread his 'hanky' (his mat) on the ground, gave his spiel, and went through his routine," Piaf recalled. He told onlookers to show their appreciation to his daughter, who would pass among them before doing *le saut périlleux*. One day bystanders complained that saltimbanques were liars: the little girl had not done the perilous jump, as promised. Louis came up with a neat reply. Surely they didn't want the child, who was weak from the flu, to risk breaking her neck—they would be satisfied by hearing her sing.

At this point in telling the story of her life, Piaf forgot her evenings on the café table in Bernay. "I had never sung before," she said decades later. "The only song I knew was 'La Marseillaise.' " This patriotic choice can be seen as a reframing of her "first" performance, in the years when France was recovering from the Great War. But it is of interest to note that as a fledgling performer in 1936, Piaf told a journalist that she had sung "L'Internationale"—then the anthem of communist and socialist parties worldwide. Whichever song she performed that night, they took in twice as much money as usual.

From then on, Louis made sure that Edith sang at the close of each show. She learned several new songs, including the popular "Nuits de Chine." One wonders if audiences noticed the incongruity of a prepubescent child's crooning this racy fox-trot, which evoked opium-drenched delights in exotic settings: *"Nuits de Chine / Nuits calines / Nuits d'amour / Nuits d'ivresse"* (Chinese nights / Caressing nights / Sensual nights / Intoxicating nights"). Perhaps this strangeness only enhanced the song's appeal.

Piaf recalled only a few names and details of their travels in the next few years. At Lens, a town in northern France where they stopped on the way from Belgium to Normandy, the little girl spied a "rich child's" doll in a toy shop: "She held out her little porcelain hands to me. I had never seen anything so beautiful!" Since the doll cost the equivalent of their expenses that day, it was out of the question. Edith was astonished when her father presented it to her the next morning, their performance having earned enough for him to buy the doll before leaving town. "I understood that he loved me," she said, then added, "in his way."

At Le Havre, when Edith was scheduled to sing at a movie theater before the film, she awoke with a fever and a raspy cough. She stayed in bed all day but insisted on going on that night. Although her father was opposed to her endangering her health, she prevailed. "For people in our situation, it was worth making an effort for the take, however small. I sang, and afterward Papa gave me two big kisses on the cheek. I was startled and happy. He had never been so proud of his daughter."

On another occasion, a middle-class couple who were smitten with the child proposed to take her off Louis's hands. They offered him a hundred thousand francs—a very large sum—for the right to adopt her. "I'm not in the business of selling kids," she heard him say: "Why not make one of your own?" It is telling that Piaf situated this incident—to her mind, the proof that "he would never consent to being separated from me"—at Sens, the town that was the site of her parents' marriage.

During the time when Line remained in Turkey, Louis did not lack for companionship. "A handsome man, fickle, and an incorrigible womanizer, he was never alone for long," his daughter recalled. When people asked whether she had a mother, he always replied, "More than she needs!" Some of these temporary "mothers" were kind, she said, some less so, but none of them made her suffer: "Papa wouldn't have tolerated it." But, she allowed that some *had* been unkind. Of a certain Lucienne, Piaf said, "I still remember her thrashings, but that's because it was during her reign that I saw Papa cry for the first time"—an interpretation that lets Louis off the hook as being Edith's covictim. Perhaps the child found comfort in Saint Thérèse's promise that prayer could soften the hardest of hearts.

When Edith was ten, Louis formed a liaison with a woman named Sylviane who lived in Lyon. Their son died soon after his birth; Louis took Edith on tour, leaving Sylviane to mourn alone. Shortly after their return, Edith ran away. On the train, she told her fellow passengers that her parents beat her, and that she was escaping to her grandmother's in Normandy. A kindly woman pretended to be her guardian when the conductor came; Edith managed to get all the way to Bernay. "I had worked it all out," she told a journalist, whose reactions to this tale are missing, as are her reception at Maman Tine's and her father's mood when he came to retrieve her. Though the tale of her escape recalls the perils of Victor Hugo's Cosette, it is clear that the ten-year-old knew a great deal about travel, and even more about telling a story.

In Piaf's recollections of these years, Louis's liaisons seem like stops on an amorous *tour de France*. He had the seductive charm of those who get on by ingratiating themselves with others. Shrewd when it came to recruiting women, he placed advertisements in the regional newspapers: "Young woman wanted to look after child. Job includes enjoyable travel." Job candidates must have been struck by this diminutive father-daughter couple and may have wondered to what extent another person would be welcome.

A second Sylviane signed on in Nancy, when Louis and Edith were touring Alsace-Lorraine. This romance lasted long enough for Louis to bring his new partner to Falaise to meet his family. In the photograph taken that day, Edith looks about ten. She stands between Louis and Sylviane—who is identified on the back of the photo as "the girlfriend of the moment." Edith's expression implies a precocious sense that while domestic partners come and go, the love of father and child remains the lodestar of relationships.

By then she also knew what it took to survive. From her father she learned an entertainer's sense of timing, techniques for tugging on the audience's heartstrings, and the sort of patter likely to produce a good take. Her years with Louis were an education in "street smarts," a set of skills rarely acquired at school. Although she had just learned to read before leaving Bernay and would remain semi-literate until adulthood, she was adept at reading faces and judging an audience's—or a stepmother's—mood.

What was more, the Gassions' bohemian way of life had trained Edith to meet each situation as it arose, and to respect, or at least accept, all sorts of people. The years on the road with Louis offered a telling contrast to the mock respectability Edith had known in Bernay. Their hand-to-mouth life was the opposite of, though also the complement to, the bourgeois existence Piaf would never fully adopt, even long after her success. At heart she would always be a traveler—turning each of her many dwellings into a Gypsy caravan.

CHAPTER TWO

1926–1932

What did she recall of her years with her father? Piaf asked herself near the end of her life. "A new mother every three months: his mistresses, who were more or less kind to me, depending on whether my songs—I was already singing, and doing the collection—brought me money or catcalls."

Things might have turned out differently with more reliable mothering, she thought. "I had gone through a peculiar apprenticeship in life and love, which hardly disposed me toward romanticism. My mother had not been by my side to teach me that love could be tender, faithful, and sweet, so very sweet." Dictating these thoughts to a journalist friend, the aging Piaf did not reflect that it may have been this changing cast of maternal substitutes that made her cling to the idea of unconditional love—the tender, faithful, sweet affection that she sought for the rest of her life in her chosen companions.

⌐

Memory is selective, especially when one is retelling one's life to bring out its better moments. Piaf said nothing about the reasons for her return to Paris with her father, which occurred at some point in her early adolescence. The one anecdote that she did recall from this time is indicative. It associates her mother's reappearance in their life with a fleeting family reunion and a maternal kiss.

One evening, Louis took Edith, then about eleven, to a bistro in the raffish Faubourg Saint-Martin neighborhood, where entertainers gathered before their gigs at local cafés and cabarets. They were standing together at the bar when a woman with dark hair, thick bangs, and large earrings asked to embrace Edith. "My father doesn't allow me to kiss people I don't know," she replied. Smiling, Louis told her to go ahead: "You have my permission; that's your *maman*, the real one."

Although Piaf's recollection of this meeting is tantalizingly brief, her brother, Herbert, provided a few more details years later. Having recently returned from four years in Turkey, their mother had taken Herbert to live with her in Paris. An agent was handling Line's career; she turned up that night because she was singing in a club across the street. "While our parents talked, Edith and I played outside on the sidewalk. Then Mother took me away and my sister went with Father. That's all." Line had not, as Piaf told an interviewer, invited them to a restaurant, nor had she tried to reclaim Edith—instances of wishful thinking, Herbert implied, on his sister's part.

The details of Line's career are equally tantalizing. She returned to Paris in the mid-1920s, about the time when Edith and Louis settled there. According to Herbert, she found occasional gigs at cabarets like the Chat Noir or the Mikado in Pigalle, and the Monocle, a lesbian club, in Montparnasse, but more often performed in the *beuglants* (working-class dives), where her daughter would also belt out the melancholy ballads known as *chansons réalistes*.

The tradition of "realistic song"—a nostalgic, often sentimental, evocation of Parisian working-class life—dates back to before the Great War, when performers like Aristide Bruant and Eugénie Buffet entertained audiences with satiric or fatalistic lyrics that formed a counter-myth to bourgeois celebrations of the city. At the time Edith re-encountered her mother, Line was presenting herself as part of this still-vibrant tradition. No longer a lowly street singer, she also sang at the *bals-musettes* (dance halls), where workers, small-time crooks, and artists in search of inspiration mingled in the easy warmth of these establishments. Line may have had some success in her years abroad, which coincided with the twenties vogue for French culture in Turkey—from French bureaucracy to dances like the *java*, a light waltz, and *parigot* songs, belted out in the tough accents of a typical Parisian.

It is likely that Line knew Fréhel, the notorious *chanteuse réaliste*, who was also in Turkey during these years. Judging by Line's repertoire, which included songs first popularized by Fréhel, she modeled her act on that of the better-known performer—a savvy choice, even though Fréhel had long been famous for her drug-addled personal life. Line's return to Paris at the time when Fréhel was making her comeback there helped establish Piaf's mother as a *chanteuse réaliste* for those who could not afford to hear Fréhel at the *music-halls* (variety theaters) but came instead to dance at the kind of neighborhood joint where Line was singing the night of the Gassion family reunion.

One wonders whether Edith talked to her mother about their *métier*, whether Line shared with her daughter the secrets of their unpredictable trade. *Chanson-réaliste* lyrics, the most important part of the song, were usually sorrowful, the music in a minor key. Given that much of this material was in the same vein, it was important to choose songs that corresponded to one's "type," the persona a singer created for her audience. And since listeners liked to feel connected to their favorites, it was not enough to know your type: you had to play the part as if it meshed with your existence. It was said of the best interpreters of this tradition—Fréhel, Damia, and soon Piaf herself—that they sang the way they lived, their songs came from the heart. (The extent to which they consciously sustained this perception went unnoticed.)

If Edith had studied her mother's repertoire, she would have formed certain ideas about her. Line became known for her version of "La Valse en mineur," a dark Fréhel tune described as a *valse réaliste*. The lyrics evoke a neighborhood dance hall where young toughs spin their girls to the sounds of an accordion. Songs of this kind reflected the hopes of the working-class audiences that flocked to the *bals-musettes* for moments of happiness, at the same time hinting that such moments were all the more precious because of their brevity.

"La Valse en mineur" was bittersweet in its allusions to fleeting pleasures; "La Coco," another Fréhel song in Line's repertoire, was downright disturbing. The singer, in search of her unfaithful lover, consoles herself with champagne, morphine, and cocaine (the *coco* of the title), then, one night, finding him with another, stabs him in the heart. Since then she has only "*la coco*" to turn to: "*Je veux de la coco / Ça trouble mon cerveau / L'esprit s'envole / Près du Seigneur / Mon amant du coeur / M'a rendue folle.*" ("I want cocaine / It troubles my brain / My soul flies apart / Closer to God / The love of my heart / Has driven me mad.") This *noir* tale of love's (and cocaine's) ravages hinted at Line's addiction, a maternal heritage that Piaf would find hard to bear.

Not all *chansons réalistes* are as doleful as "La Valse en mineur" or as dark as "La Coco," but the actor Michel Simon, who began his career in a *bal-musette* where Line was performing, remembered her singing only the saddest songs in the repertoire. Her low, plaintive voice failed to please listeners, who wanted something brighter. Yet Line did not lack talent, Herbert Gassion believed. Within a few years' time, when Edith auditioned at one of the nightspots where Line had appeared, the manager said to come back when she could sing as well as her mother. Herbert concluded that Line was talented but unable to take advantage of what came her way.

His remarks are charitable, given that some time after the Gassions' reunion, Line again abandoned her son. The boy lived with family friends, then at the mercy of the welfare system, an experience that prompted him to enlist in the colonial army as soon as he came of age. Herbert would say nothing about his mother's many "mistakes" except that in later years, she was badly "adrift."

In addition to learning that Line was a drifter, Edith may have formed the opinion that mothers often abandon their children. About this time, Louis filed for divorce, giving as his residence Maman Tine's establishment in Bernay. The decree became final on June 4, 1929, when he was nearing fifty and Edith was thirteen. Still touring with her father on occasion (by this time, Louis may have found it hard to twist himself into knots), she met the last in the series of stepmothers who were more or less kind.

In 1930, on what may have been a farewell tour, Louis placed an ad in the Nancy newspaper and found a new partner, Jeanne L'Hôte, called Yeyette, who was only twenty, five years older than Edith. The new stepmother and stepdaughter moved to Belleville with Louis, higher up the hill, at 115 rue de Belleville, but not far from where Edith had lived as an infant. (If they learned of Aîcha's death on July 18, 1930, no mention was later made of it.)

Yeyette gave birth to Edith's half sister, Denise, on February 8, 1931, but refused Louis's offer of marriage, a puzzling decision given the stigma attached to status as a *fille-mère* (unwed mother). Edith ran away several times, only to be brought back by her father, who was her legal guardian. Yeyette was too busy with Denise to discipline her unruly stepdaughter, and Edith too attached to Louis to share his affections with his new family. She spent most of her time away from home.

Despite the locals' treatment of pretty girls who were not *en ménage* (shacked up) as fair game, the men of Belleville did not pose a threat. An unattached female was often the butt of innuendos designed as much to impress other men as to attract her attention, but Edith knew how to give as good as she got. Moreover, she did so in the piquant local slang and with a *titi-parisien* accent (a corruption of "good French" that marked one as working-class). This precocious knowledge stood her in good stead while she established herself as one of the "regulars" who sang in the streets and on weekends, at the *bals-musettes* that perpetuated the old traditions even as the village landscape was changing.

From the Gassions' apartment halfway up the hill it took barely fifteen minutes to amble down to Belleville's social center, the square at the bottom of the street. Popular tunes wafting from the cafés mingled with the outdoor musicians' waltzes and rumbas. Whenever the young accordionist Jo Privat, a local favorite, accompanied Edith, ragpickers hushed their cries to listen, and housewives dropped coins from their windows.

In the 1920s, the French working class rarely had access to records; songs were popularized mainly through the street singers' repertoires. It helped to come equipped for performances with *petit-format* sheet music to sell, the small-size scores printed by music publishers for this purpose. One day at a publisher's office Edith met a young music fan, Pierre Hiégel, who would become one of her impresarios. "I bought her coffee and a croissant, which was all I could afford," Hiégel recalled. "We stayed in touch for the rest of her life." He was awed by her ability to memorize a song after hearing it a few times, and even more by her intelligence: "Right after a real heartbreaker she would sing a few more subtle songs, the better to sock you in the guts with the next number!"

Edith soon became known in Belleville for her astounding voice, her saucy charm, and her give-and-take, the chaffing repartee that Parisians call *la gouaille*. She was often seen in the cafés—at the Vielleuse, where a statue of a woman playing the hurdy-gurdy on the roof welcomed customers, and the new star Berthe Sylva performed the latest *chansons réalistes*. In such settings Edith learned the songs that made up her first repertoire—whose lyrics bemoan woman's fate while celebrating affections nourished by wine, banter, and moments of joy. She was embraced because she sang as she spoke—with the *titi* accent of her neighbors.

The Belleville spirit, a blend of plucky defiance and fatalism, came out in force in the week before Bastille Day, when garlands festooned the streets and dance floors appeared in front of the cafés. Each evening, couples holding each other tight swayed to the *java* while leaning sideways to compensate for the slope of the street. It is easy to imagine Edith and her friends singing lyrics made popular by Fréhel and Berthe Sylva, tales of young women like themselves who had been seduced by swaggering charmers but saw the error of their ways.

On the nights leading up to the Quatorze (July 14), fireworks went off every few minutes; building façades turned blue, white, and red in the reflected light. The festivities continued long after midnight, as restaurants served late suppers of mussels *marinière* with fries. The sky grew bright again when the fire brigade marched up the hill bearing their torches. "Everyone kissed, everyone sang, no one, young or old, thought of sleeping," one of Edith's friends observed: "We weren't rich or educated . . . but how we laughed!"

By the winter of 1931–32, when she had turned sixteen, the Great Depression was making itself felt in France. Unemployment was higher than usual, with no safety net for the impoverished, and little hope for those who lacked either an education or middle-class manners. Edith managed to find a job in the posh sixteenth arrondissement, on the other side of Paris, at a creamery. After six days of wak-ing at 4 a.m. to make morning deliveries, and, one imagines, engaging in some insubordinate behavior, she was fired. She lasted only three days at her next workplace, another creamery, on the Left Bank, then made one more unsuccessful attempt at employment, in another of these establishments. Before leaving this job, she met an employee named Raymond, who also hoped to become an artiste. He taught her to play the banjo; they worked on songs to perform together with his girlfriend, Rosalie.

Their trio, "Zizi, Zézette, and Zouzou," featured Raymond on banjo and Rosalie crooning in the background, behind Edith's power-ful voice. Piaf often retold the improbable tale of their first outing. The three Z's were to appear at an army barracks in Versailles, where Edith (Zouzou?) had once performed with Louis. They booked a hotel room, ate dinner, and toasted the owner with a post-prandial rum—all on credit. When no one showed up at the barracks, the trio decided to forget the hotel. Hoping to find shelter, they went to the police station, only to run into the hotel-keeper and his wife. After much wrangling, the police chief talked the angry couple out of filing charges against the young performers, who promised to pay their debt after singing at a nearby base the following night. The appreciative audience there allowed them to keep their word. They again toasted the hotel-keeper, but Edith stuck out her tongue as they went out the door.

There is no record of the trio's performing again. They broke up after Raymond initiated Edith into sexual love. In their time together, Edith saw that she could summon her powers of invention when she found herself in a tight spot. With the confidence of a cocky sixteen-year-old, one whose radiance drew crowds even before her voice stopped them in their tracks, she decided to sing not just for Belleville, but for all of Paris. She would go it alone until she found company. Meanwhile, she was learning the bluesy songs popularized by Fréhel, Berthe Sylva, and her new model, Damia, known as "the tragedienne of song."

Whereas Fréhel was notorious for her confrontational manner (she regularly told audiences, "Shut your traps; I'm opening mine"), Damia had a more subtle performance style. Following Damia's example, Edith learned soulful tunes to balance the dark "realism" of her borrowed repertoire. She kept on belting out Damia's *parigot* songs, like "J'ai l'cafard" ("I'm bored"), which recalls "La Coco" in its allusion to "*Drogues infâmes / Qui charment les femmes*" ("vile drugs that harm / and women charm"). But she also sang one of Damia's greatest successes, "Les Deux Ménétriers" ("The Two Fiddlers"). This "macabre gallop" urges the dead to come back to life by loving unstintingly: "*Il vous faut aimer encore! / Aimez donc! Enlacez vous!*" ("You have to love again! / Start loving! Wrap yourselves around each other!") Edith's rendition of this stirring call to love echoed in the streets like an anthem for the poor, who had little but mutual affection to rely on.

Some time after the birth of Denise, Louis acquiesced to Edith's wish for independence on the condition that she remain in Belleville in a rented room, paid for with her earnings. Her father kept an eye on her through acquaintances like Camille Ribon, an acrobat whose specialty was standing on his thumbs. Ribon, who taught acrobatics to the neighborhood children, looked after Edith, though she showed no aptitude for his art. (He would be one of the old friends whom she helped to support once she became famous.)

Edith visited Ribon one day when a younger girl was going through her paces. Although a talented gymnast, the girl was plain, with narrow, darting eyes. They began talking. At fourteen, Simone Berteaut, known as Momone, worked in a factory assembling car headlights. Momone was impressed by Edith's tales of life on the street, and even more by her earnings. She sang only when she felt like it, Edith explained; she was her own boss. Momone should work for her, she said unexpectedly. She could take the collection, as Edith had done with Louis, since Edith earned enough for both of them.

"I was bowled over. . . . I'd have followed her to the ends of the earth," Berteaut would write in her spirited but misleading life of the singer, in which she presents herself as Edith's half sister. Later in life, Piaf called Berteaut her *mauvaise génie* (the evil spirit who brought out the worst in her) and omitted her from her memoirs. But at sixteen she was happy to find a friend who would do her bidding. When there were two of you, she told the younger girl, audiences took you seriously; if the sidekick had music to distribute, they didn't see you as beggars.

Madame Berteaut offered no resistance to the plan except to demand compensation for her daughter's wages. According to Berteaut, whose book is most reliable on their early years, Edith agreed to pay her room, board, and fifteen francs a day, to be turned over to her mother. An understanding was reached, and the young girl left home to become Edith's foil. No one seems to have reflected that their status as self-sufficient young women resembled that of the other sort of streetwalkers, the *filles* who figured prominently in the popular imagination and in Edith's repertoire.

The girls shared a room at the Hôtel de l'Avenir—a name that seemed like a good omen. She would become someone in the future, Edith told Momone, often stopping in churches to light candles and pray for guidance. But Momone, whose upbringing was that of a guttersnipe, was puzzled by Edith's faith in God and her devotion to Saint Thérèse. The younger girl's fixation on her "big sister," composed of gratitude, jealousy, and resentment, would warp her perceptions of their life together and her own role in Piaf's path to success.

Enchanted with their freedom, the friends rose late and took their time before going out. Edith had to drink coffee and gargle before performing, but once she was ready, she had "that same voice . . . the voice worth millions later on." She sang to be heard at a distance, her voice coming from her chest as well as through what musicians call the "mask"—the resonators in the head—which enhanced her *titi* accent and gave her the nasal tone common to singers needing to project over street noise.

Edith planned their itineraries according to the day of the week and the clientele. On weekdays, the take was good near the Champs-Elysées and in the sixteenth arrondissement, but on weekends residents there were too busy shopping to give freely. "Saturdays we'd hit the working districts," Berteaut wrote. "People there gave less at a time but gave more often. . . . They gave for pleasure, because they were happy, not just to be charitable."

To avoid arrest—street singing wasn't legal—the girls performed as far away as they could from police stations. When a large crowd gathered around them one day, the local policeman told Edith to move across the road. Then he asked her to sing his favorite—a fantasy of fleeting love called "Le Chaland qui passe" ("The Passing Barge"). Edith's rendition pleased him. Exclaiming that no one sang of love's transports the way she did, he gave her five francs.

On occasions when the girls were hauled off to the station, the police let them go after hearing Edith's heart-wrenching tales about their impoverished parents and their need to earn money. She was looking after her kid sister, she explained: with no training, all she could do was sing. (Being presented to the authorities as Edith's sibling no doubt planted the seed that resulted, decades later, in Berteaut's memoir.)

Edith also organized performances at the army barracks around Paris. Their mess halls were warm in winter; the soldiers warmed to the girls' nubile charms. Momone did gymnastics, Edith sang her more risqué songs, they met the men afterward in the local cafés. Though these flirtations made the girls feel "alive," they didn't count, Berteaut wrote: "You don't owe them anything. . . . You can joke and fool around as much as you please."

Edith continued to fool around until she fell in love with a young man named Louis Dupont, known as P'tit Louis. They met in a café in Romainville, a suburb northeast of Paris, where she was performing. Of this meeting she recalled: "He looked me straight in the eye, whistled with admiration, and with a regal flourish put a five-sou coin into my cup." For the next few days the pleasant-looking youth turned up wherever she was, then proposed that they live together. Louis joined Edith and Momone at the Hôtel de l'Avenir until the couple found an inexpensive furnished room.

With no kitchen facilities available, they ate from the tin cans that Edith heated on a hot plate. On Sundays they sat on the cheap wooden seats at the local cinema to watch Charlie Chaplin. Louis picked up the necessities for housekeeping on his jobs as a delivery boy, "cutlery or plates or saucepans that he'd stolen from shop displays or at cafés," Piaf recalled, as if this were the normal way to start life together.

Edith was sixteen and a half and Louis eighteen when she realized that she was pregnant. She and Momone continued their rounds, often running into Louis on his delivery route. In his view, she should not have been on the streets; sedentary work was more appropriate to someone in her condition, and it would allow them to get rid of Momone. Edith took a job at a boot factory, but when her pregnancy became obvious, the foreman said that he had to let her go. Years later, Piaf told interviewers that she stayed on awhile longer after softening up the foreman with a song. Her brief stint in the factory had shown that she was not meant to be a member of the working class.

Edith gave birth to a girl on February 11, 1933, at the Tenon Hospital, where she had been born seventeen years earlier. They named the baby Marcelle. P'tit Louis recognized his daughter (he and Edith were not married) and announced her arrival to his "in-laws," who came to the hospital with presents. When the Gassions learned that no one had thought to acquire a layette, they gave Edith her half sister's baby clothes. After Louis and Edith went to live with his mother in Romainville, Yeyette visited to show her how to care for the infant— soon known as Cécelle. (In Berteaut's version of the story, the young couple and Cécelle lived with her.)

It surprised Edith's family that she adored her daughter. "She went so far as to breast-feed her and was quite proud of herself," Denise Gassion recalled. "Her nursing rituals were like going to mass," she added, "with Edith, the high priestess of love, officiating. No one was allowed to smile." Berteaut told a different story: she and Edith fed Cécelle milk from bottles, which they rinsed but did not boil because they didn't know any better. Edith's real and pretend half sisters agreed that she returned to the streets within a short time, because her earning power was greater than P'tit Louis's, and because she missed the life.

"Edith wouldn't have left the baby behind for anything in the world," Berteaut explained. Still smarting from Line's having abandoned her in infancy, she continued to nurse Cécelle, trundling her all over Paris on the Métro. A young Belleville resident who saved coins to toss to her on Sundays recalled the ample bosom and powerful lungs of the little street singer: "She had a voice fit for a cathedral; it seemed to come from far away. . . . She just stood there, her feet planted on the pavement, and sang anything, from popular songs like Tino Rossi's 'Catarinetta' to masterpieces like 'Les Deux Ménétriers.' . . . The girl who came with her picked up the coins but 'my singer' never looked up. She just sang, as if inhabited by the music."

By the winter of 1933–34, Piaf was performing as "Miss Edith" in a trio with Camille Ribon and his wife. They toured the army barracks from Clignancourt in the north to Vincennes in the east, L'Ecole Militaire, and, this time under better auspices, Versailles. Despite Edith's earnings, P'tit Louis was not pleased. Perhaps his pride was hurt. "I felt that something was missing," Piaf said, "the protective strength of a man, a real man." Her companion was more like another child.

Edith's weakness for men in uniform made it almost inevitable that she would find someone with the strength she desired. Before a performance at the Colonial Infantry barracks (the branch that her brother, Herbert, joined), a handsome blond soldier asked if he might pay for his seat with a kiss. Edith agreed. "As for the kiss," she told him, "we'll see about that later, provided you behave yourself," Piaf recalled in the first account of their affair. That night, she fell in love and considered leaving Louis for this man, even though he often landed in the brig. Her soldier went AWOL the next day to see her; they discussed the hopelessness of their situation, and, after a night together, parted. "I was shattered," Piaf said, "mourning for the happiness I'd lost just when I'd found it." Their story was like a cheap romance novel, she said years later.

P'tit Louis may not have known about this man, but he soon realized that Edith no longer loved him. He pleaded with her to stay with him for Cécelle's sake. Edith's father and stepmother were called in. They tried to reason with her, but she had already decided to leave. "And when Edith decided on something," Denise wrote, "there was no point in trying to make her change her mind."

Soon she began exploring Montmartre, the raffish neighborhood where some of the performers she knew sang in clubs. With Momone, who came back at the first opportunity, she went to sing out of doors at the Place du Tertre and at the Lapin Agile, the cabaret where the *chanson-réaliste* tradition began. The chanteuse Rina Ketty, who befriended her there, was struck by the newcomer: "She interpreted those songs with such intensity that it hit you right in the gut. When she sang she was a great lady. Afterward it wasn't the same. She was surrounded by men, all drinking, smoking, having a good time."

One day, on the way down the hill from Montmartre to Pigalle, Edith and Momone met the owner of a nightclub, a woman named Lulu, who dressed like a man. After an audition, Lulu booked them to appear at the club, because, she explained, her customers liked girls who looked as if they had just stepped off the street.

This engagement gave Edith the idea that she might have a profession. By the 1930s, Fréhel, Damia, and Edith's new model, Marie Dubas, were all starring at the Paris *music-halls*. People often stopped in bars to hear their records; their posters decorated the city's thoroughfares. There was no reason why Edith could not become one of them—except that she would have to be discovered, which was more likely to happen in Pigalle than in Belleville.

P'tit Louis quarreled with Edith about her new job. In his opinion, Lulu's was a joint frequented by hookers and lesbians. He issued an ultimatum: she must refuse the offer, or their life together was finished. The choice was not difficult. Edith packed her belongings and with Cécelle, who was already a toddler, joined Momone in Pigalle.

CHAPTER THREE

1933–1935

By the time Edith moved to Pigalle, the artists who had lived there and in Montmartre before the war—Picasso and company—had mostly decamped to Montparnasse and other more respectable parts of Paris. Though Montmartre's bohemian past still drew tourists, especially foreign ones, visitors in search of local color were more likely to go slumming in the nightclubs that dotted the streets of lower Montmartre, as Pigalle was called—where small-time crooks, members of *le milieu* (the French mafia), and upstanding citizens intermingled. In the 1930s, when Edith was absorbing the area's louche atmosphere, Pigalle had already acquired mythic status as "the most intense chapter in the history of Paris's lower depths—but lower depths, unlike those of Belleville, that are inseparable from their suggestive setting."

P'tit Louis had been right about the high concentration of hookers in the area. Pigalle's many small hotels offered rooms by the hour as well as for the night. Edith moved, with and without Momone, from one alluringly named hotel to another. After some time at the Hôtel Eden, which had the advantage of a cheap restaurant next door, she settled at the Régence. It became her headquarters, the site of her education in local mores, and the place where she left Cécelle when performing at Lulu's. She soon learned that it was also a meeting place for *le milieu.*

As its proprietor's mannish dress implied, Lulu's welcomed women who liked women, along with a mixed clientele of prostitutes, crooks, and partygoers. Momone's juvenile form ("I didn't have any bosom or any behind," she wrote) appealed to Lulu's customers; they liked the slim, undernourished bodies of waifs like her and Edith. To enhance their ambiguous appeal, Lulu dressed them both in sailor costumes, though Momone often shed hers to perform gymnastics in the nude.

The two friends got on well with the hookers who waited there for clients, and with a sympathetic *garçon* who fed them the remains from customers' meals. But Lulu rarely kept their agreement about wages. If the girls were even five minutes late, she deducted ten francs from their salary. ("It's not easy to arrive bang on time without a watch," Berteaut wrote, "especially when you don't have any notion of time.") To make extra money, they "collected corks," which meant chatting with customers while they downed champagne, then presenting the corks at closing time—to be paid so much per bottle. Their nights often lasted until dawn. When Edith had the energy, she stumbled into the street to sing before going to bed. There she felt more like herself.

Piaf's memoirs are reticent about this period. *Au bal de la chance* (*The Wheel of Fortune*) omits the Pigalle years; *Ma vie* (*My Life*) reduces her time among the local pimps and prostitutes to a series of affairs, including one with the man who became her protector— though he offered a different type of protection from the sort she had imagined. But if Piaf preferred to forget the dark poetry of Pigalle, its smoky atmosphere colored her songs, the sulfurous repertoire for which she became known.

To pass the time at Lulu's, the pianist encouraged her to sing "C'était un musicien," a tango tune that could have been their theme song: "*C'était un musicien qui jouait dans une boîte de nuit / Jusqu'aux lueurs de l'aube il berçait les amours d'autrui.*" ("He was a musician who played in the nightclub / Until dawn lulling other people's loves to sleep." The song was popularized by a 1933 film with the same title.) The happy ending (a female customer falls for the musician) was exceptional in Edith's repertoire. Customers preferred fatalistic songs like "Comme un moineau," the better to savor the congruence between Edith's slender form and the tale of a prostitute who, "like a sparrow," is inured to the street: "*On s'accoutume à ne plus voir / La poussière grise du trottoir / Où l'on se vautre / Chaque soir sur l'pavé parigot / On cherche son pain dans le ruisseau.*" ("You get used to not seeing / The dusty gray sidewalk / Where revelers wallow / Each night on the Paris streets / You seek your living in the gutter.") Within a few years, composers would write similar songs just for her—evoking Pigalle's varied opportunities for oblivion and pleasure.

"There is nothing to see in Pigalle," a contemporary novelist wrote. The area bounded by the Place Blanche to the west and the rue des Martyrs to the east had no historic landmarks. But for the cognoscenti there was another reality behind its undistinguished façades. Pigalle had a tawdry allure for partygoers and thrill-seekers—"dark nights lit by flickering electric signs, the sound of rain and piano rolls, a hubbub, silence, dance halls, shadowy corners, neon lights, hallways"—the décor we associate with the film noir classics that were often set there.

Those who lived year-round in Pigalle were attuned to its delights. The Cirque Medrano had its headquarters on the prolongation of Pigalle's main axis, the Boulevard de Clichy. Picasso had often painted the Medrano's clowns and acrobats; locals drank with them after performances. The neighborhood became particularly animated in December, when a street fair lined the Boulevard de Clichy with fortune-tellers, shooting galleries, sideshows, merry-go-rounds, and stands selling French fries or sugary waffles. Strong men and sword swallowers performed there all year round; musicians gathered on the weekends in hope of a night's employment. One can imagine Edith greeting them on her way to Lulu's, or when she worked the street on her days off.

As emancipated but unprotected women, she and Momone were an anomaly—much like the *filles insoumises,* the unregistered prostitutes who made Pigalle notorious. Residents recognized the different types of whores, from the lowly *pierreuses,* who took all comers, to the *chandelles,* who stood like candles under the lamplights, and the *marcheuses,* who walked up and down the boulevards—the trade's aristocracy, because they had some freedom of choice. Working in Pigalle gave a woman cachet. Her pay was higher than elsewhere in Paris; compared with Belleville, Pigalle was a promotion.

Yet most of these women were controlled by pimps, many of whom came from the same poor neighborhoods. These men, known as *julots, harengs,* or *maquereaux,* affected a certain style. They strutted around Pigalle in the tight jackets and shiny leather pumps then in fashion in petit-bourgeois areas. Newcomers saw that to survive, they needed to distinguish among the local fauna and learn their codes. Edith's odd status attracted attention. Was she a *grenouille*, one of the many young women calling themselves singers who took up with strangers, or a part-time *michetonneuse*, an easy lay?

For a time her domestic life—sharing a room with Momone and Cécelle—was a safeguard. But before the locals could decide what to make of her, an event occurred that drove Edith to accept a more traditional form of protection. P'tit Louis showed up now and then, attempting to lure her back to Belleville. One morning when she and Momone returned from Lulu's, the hotel-keeper announced that her "husband" had come during the night and taken their baby. He left a message—if she wanted Cécelle, she must come home. She declined to do so but sent Louis money to pay for their daughter's care. "Edith never spoke of him again," Berteaut wrote. "We missed [Cécelle] at first. We didn't say so to each other, but there was an emptiness"—an emptiness that would haunt Piaf for the rest of her life.

The chronology of these events is unclear, but the void caused by the loss of Cécelle was partly filled by the man who became Edith's protector. (Piaf called this *milieu* big shot Albert in her memoirs; the locals used his gang name, Ali-Baba; Berteaut identified him as Henri Valette.) Their liaison, which may have predated Cécelle's departure from her life, perhaps explains why Edith did not go back to Belleville for her. And at eighteen she could not have understood that she was being drawn into a closed world, with its own codes and expectations.

Edith's life at the Régence blended imperceptibly into a situation from which it would have been almost impossible to escape. The hotel adjoined a tavern called Au Clair de la Lune, whose regulars—men like Valette, addicts, and homosexuals—made her their mascot. After Momone left (the details of their separation are not known), Edith spent her spare time at the tavern, where an orchestra played until 3 a.m. and Valette, flanked by his crony "Tarzan," presided over deals—mostly based on the earnings of their women. They dismissed *la nouvelle* as too scrawny; Valette changed his mind once she fell for his dodgy charm. When he said that she would have to work for him, Edith replied that working the streets her own way, she would earn the sums he required.

Her protector gave her a grudging respect and made her his accomplice. "I had to look out for dance halls where there were well-dressed women wearing necklaces and rings," Piaf recalled. Valette then showed up at these places in his best suit. "Since he was very good-looking and full of confidence," she continued, "he always succeeded in seducing his partner." These evenings ended in the alley, where he snatched the woman's jewels while Edith waited at a café. Later, she saw that her role gave him a hold over her: "It was the rule in the *milieu*. Men and women had to be compromised to keep them from escaping from the clutches of the crooks." Piaf's account is supported by the recollections of those who watched her struggle with the *milieu*'s mores.

At some point, when still besotted with Valette, she started singing at the Petit Jardin dance hall after the manager, who had heard her in the street, asked her to perform. On her first evening, the bandleader, the Gypsy guitarist Django Reinhardt, said that although his new pianist didn't know French, he, a "Kraut" named Glanzberg, would do his best to keep up with her. Her powerful voice made an impression, Glanzberg recalled, but he dismissed her as no more than an untrained street singer.

The Petit Jardin was a promotion from Lulu's. The dance hall served as the *milieu*'s headquarters and a meeting place for young thieves hoping to impress the bosses who planned deals there while awaiting the return of their protégées—but also for bourgeois who liked to go slumming. Accompanied by her friend Jo Privat, Edith sang lyrics that could have been written for the Petit Jardin's audience—like "Le Barbeau de Saint-Jean," a woman's lament for her lover: "*Il ne m'aime plus, ni moi non plus / C'est du passé, n'en parlons plus.*" ("He doesn't love me anymore, I don't love him either / It's a thing of the past, let's not talk about it anymore.") The patrons "had a soft spot for her," the writer Auguste le Breton, observed: "She knew how to project the songs that got under their skin, the songs inspired by these violent streets. . . . She gave off the odor of the street, of poverty, hunger, suicide." Hookers wiped their eyes when she sang; pimps greeted her when she came offstage.

One night le Breton, then an eighteen-year-old, went to the Petit

Jardin bar—where Edith was drinking wine. "Her shoes were down at the heel, but her shapely legs were sheathed in silk stockings, a jarring note given the rest of her." A hoodlum was amusing himself by getting her drunk. When the youth allowed that he would do better to buy her a meal, they began to fight. Le Breton pulled out a knife, his adversary brandished a gun, a *milieu* chief told the youth to take the singer elsewhere. "I left with the woman who would become the great Piaf, who, like myself, didn't even have decent shoes. We devoured ham sandwiches and beers at the Place Clichy."

Like le Breton, the Clair de Lune staff wondered why Edith accepted the codes of Pigalle. "It was a mystery to us," the bartender said, "why, for the sake of love, she would submit to a life full of disillusionment." (He did not reflect that her life with her father had predisposed her to having a boss who took her earnings and dictated her behavior.) Of her friendship with a young waiter, a country boy who was the butt of the local gang's taunts, the bartender recalled, "They understood each other's humiliation." One day Edith told Tarzan to leave the waiter alone. From then on the young man tried to help her, but on confronting Tarzan for his loutish ways with women, received a beating. Edith warned him, "Around here the strongest one always gets the last word."

Years later, Piaf recalled the "life-saving shock" she received when her friend Nadia drowned herself. Nadia's protector, who was one of Valette's henchmen, had threatened to beat her if she didn't work the streets. Nadia came to Edith in tears. She had tried to oblige but failed to entice any customers. A few days later, Nadia's body was found in the Seine. "I realized just how low I'd sunk," Piaf said. "That was the day when I decided . . . to escape from the *milieu*, to climb out of the depths on my own." (Though she spoke openly of the fate of female prostitutes, she did not mention the equally dangerous homosexual trade that flourished at the Clair de la Lune.)

Piaf's account of her attempts to leave Valette ring true even though they suggest scenes from a film noir. When he showed up at the Clair de la Lune after Nadia's death, Edith said that she did not want to see him again. A few days later, his cronies took her to his room. He could kill her, she told him, but she had made up her mind. To her amazement, "the tough guy threw himself on the bed and wept" and she "took the opportunity to disappear." But the story did not end there. Summoned to a café by her lover, she found him and his henchmen waiting. They threatened to shoot her unless she obeyed; she dared them to go ahead. A bystander deflected the shot; the bullet grazed her neck; Valette's honor was satisfied.

Edith became adept at being seen to honor the local codes of behavior while doing as she pleased. "I had a desperate, almost morbid, need to be loved," she reflected near the end of her life. Perhaps to convince herself that she *was* lovable after her experience with Valette, she took up with three men at the same time: "I acccomplished miracles to see all of them." But her memoir minimizes the reason for her feeling "ugly, wretched, all but unlovable"—the lasting hurt caused by her mother's abandonment of her, which would be revived by Line's reappearance in Edith's life just as she was making a name for herself in their shared profession.

Edith chose different stage names for different venues. She performed at La Coupole, Le Sirocco, Le Tourbillon (where she also swept the floor), and at a dance hall near the Place de la République where the great Damia went to hear the woman described as "a tiny little dame" singing the songs for which the older star had become famous. No longer calling herself "Miss Edith," she was by turns Denise Jay, Huguette Hélia, and Tania. Between engagements, Edith went back to singing in the streets, which may explain how Line, who also lived in Pigalle, learned that her daughter had joined her there.

It would have been heartbreaking to run into her mother in these circumstances. Line sang at low dives whose customers ignored her; she was paid in glasses of wine. When not performing, she eked out a living selling herbs in the markets. Once she knew how to find Edith, Line turned up at her hotel to ask for money. Edith gave her what she could, although her earnings were unpredictable and she had to pay the woman who looked after Cécelle while Louis worked. The Clair de la Lune's bartender watched Line play on Edith's need for love: "When she tried to reason with her mother, they quarreled and her mother hurled curses. . . . To calm her, her daughter would get another glass of wine, which didn't help. Then the mother would start crying and complaining. Matters only got worse."

Edith's friends wondered how she kept going in the face of such trials—her complicated affairs, her distressing rapport with Line, the loss of Cécelle to P'tit Louis. "She took strength from her love of singing," one of them wrote. "She never dared to hope for success, just to be able to live and to keep singing." Edith sometimes mentioned her "secret," the inner strength that helped her to cope with what fate had dealt her. Her admirers took this secret to be her reliance on her talent: like most people over the course of her life, they knew nothing of her other secret, her spiritual belief.

Piaf's devotion was a private matter. Few saw beyond the medal of Thérèse de Lisieux that she wore around her neck—a common practice in Catholic France. Fewer still knew that between street performances she often slipped into nearby churches to pray. Her faith in Saint Thérèse never wavered. According to Danielle Bonel, Piaf's confidante in later years, "she prayed to her to find peace, beauty, lightness of spirit, joie de vivre. . . . To feel safe, she needed the protection of a supernatural power." But she rarely went to mass, preferring her private devotion to institutionalized ritual.

Edith's faith was tested when Cécelle became ill in the summer of 1935. P'tit Louis came to her cabaret to tell her that the two-year-old had meningitis, then considered incurable. She had been rushed to the Children's Hospital, on the Left Bank, for a lumbar puncture—a treatment that required a waiting period to see if the patient would survive. Thinking back to this time, Piaf said, "For eight days I believed in miracles." On July 6, she walked all the way from Pigalle to the hospital in time to see Cécelle open her eyes. She spent the night praying to Saint Thérèse, but learned the next morning that her daughter had died.

Accounts differ about what took place that day. Piaf remembered being alone with her sorrow; Berteaut claimed to have accompanied her to the hospital and back to Pigalle, where she put Edith to sleep by drugging her with Pernod. (Momone probably came back into Edith's life after she left Valette.) Their immediate task was to find money to bury Cécelle. After Edith's friends took up a collection, ten francs were still lacking. In Piaf's version, that night she was accosted by a man who asked what it cost to go to bed with her. Without thinking, she replied, "Ten francs." He took her to a hotel room, where she burst into tears and told him why she had accepted his offer. "I saw that he felt sorry for me, that he would let me go without demanding what he'd paid for. It's in memory of that unknown man that I've helped others whenever I could, without asking anything from them."

In Berteaut's account, the man got what he paid for but gave Edith more than the paltry sum she requested. Piaf corroborated this version in an interview with Jean Noli, the journalist who helped her write *Ma vie* toward the end of her life. The truth would shock readers, he thought. Why not say that the man had felt sorry for her? "You're right," Piaf is said to have replied. "It's better that way, more moral." Piaf also told Noli that she had Cécelle's coffin blessed at Saint-Pierre de Montmartre, the small church in the shadow of Sacré-Coeur, and, with P'tit Louis, buried their daughter in a pauper's grave at the Thiais Cemetery.

"It was a very dark moment in our lives," Berteaut wrote, "one of the rottenest times we ever went through, . . . but to tell the truth, it didn't last long." In Berteaut's recollection of that summer, when Edith was nineteen and she was seventeen, they just stopped thinking about Cécelle: "We were only kids, and we didn't give it another thought."

Momone may have forgotten the little girl, but Edith never stopped thinking about her—though she rarely mentioned her name. Near the end of her life, Piaf told the photographer Hugues Vassal that, had Cécelle lived, she would be thirty and have children of her own. Although the little girl hadn't been baptized, Piaf was sure that she had gone to heaven. "She must have been a big help to my guardian angel," Piaf joked, "because where I'm concerned he's had quite a time!" Then she asked Vassal if he was a believer. "You must have faith," she told him, "because when you bring life into the world, at that moment you also sign a death sentence."

CHAPTER FOUR

1935–1936

P iaf recalled the years from 1933, when she left Belleville, to 1936, when she began extricating herself from Pigalle, as an endless walk—one punctuated by intermittent gigs, countless street songs, and many narrow escapes from both the *milieu* and the authorities.

She did not attend to the political scene, except perhaps to notice that Parisians had fewer coins to spare and that soup kitchens' lines were growing longer. By 1933, 1.3 million Frenchmen were unemployed. In 1935, the week after Edith buried Cécelle, an alliance of four hundred thousand members of the Radical, Socialist, and Communist parties marched through Paris on Bastille Day, calling for "bread, peace, and liberty." The following spring, under Léon Blum, the leftist Popular Front government accorded major reforms to the working classes.

But the topics of the day—workers' rights, the growth of right-wing groups modeling themselves on Hitler's Brownshirts, the rise of anti-Semitism, the Third Republic's wobbliness—were of little concern when what mattered was just getting by. Having grown up outside established social structures, Edith did not identify with the working-class ethos of social betterment through class struggle. As a girl of the streets, she knew that her only chance to transcend them would depend on her determination and talent.

Leaving Belleville had allowed Edith to imagine another way of life, though, like most people she knew, she was almost penniless—in part because she spent whatever she earned right away. Yet she was sure that her luck would change. "People have the wrong idea about Edith," Berteaut wrote of this time. "She wasn't sad. She loved to laugh. She used to split her sides all the time, and what's more, she was sure she'd make it." She would put "this stinking poorhouse" behind her.

⌐

In these years, the music business was being transformed in response to the availability of records and radio broadcasts featuring well-known singers. Although working-class fans of *la chanson* could not afford tickets to the Folies Bergère, where stars like Mistinguett, Maurice Chevalier, and Josephine Baker performed, music came to them in the city's open-air theaters—street markets, *bals-musettes,* outdoor fairs. Some found the time to visit the record shops on the boulevards, where one could hear one's favorite songs in a sound booth, as Edith did in order to learn popular lyrics. But this form of enjoyment was limited to those who could pay for it, as were radios and gramophones, which were too expensive for working-class families.

Since Edith could not read music, she relied on her ability to memorize songs. When she performed this "borrowed" material (often without sheet music), "the pianist who accompanied her played however he felt like playing," Berteaut recalled, "and Edith would sing without paying much attention to him. The surprising thing is that it worked out anyway." Although an untrained singer, she surely sensed that speeding up or slowing down the tempo as she did (the technique called "rubato") served to enhance a song's emotional qualities, and that her intense, velvety vibrato suited her repertoire. She knew everything instinctively, her friend Rina Ketty observed: "Her songs expressed all she had suffered in childhood. At the end of her life she had more technique, more *métier,* but she couldn't have given any more of herself, since she gave her whole heart from the beginning."

It was this quality—giving everything she had—that led to Edith's first engagement outside Pigalle. For the rest of her life she described her discovery at nineteen in mythic terms—"Fate took me by the hand to turn me into the singer I would become."

One gray day in October 1935, she and Momone decided to work the area near the Arc de Triomphe, in the rue Troyon. As Edith warbled "Comme un moineau" ("Like a Sparrow"), passersby may have reflected that its image of a poor hooker—"*Elle est née comme un moineau / Elle a vécu comme un moineau / Elle mourra comme un moineau*" ("She was born like a sparrow / She's lived like a sparrow/ She'll die like a sparrow")—suited the singer's waifish appearance. A well-groomed bystander with silvery hair declared that she would ruin her voice if she kept belting out songs that way. When Edith said that she sang in order to eat, he introduced himself as Louis Leplée and asked her to audition at his cabaret, le Gerny's. Leplée gave her five francs and an appointment a few days later.

After checking out le Gerny's, an elegant nightspot near the Champs-Elysées, Edith and Momone spent the night celebrating in a Pigalle bar. When Fréhel arrived, they announced their good fortune to the older singer, who said to be careful. Leplée might "inveigle" them into something underhanded, like white slavery. Having decided that Fréhel was jealous, Edith went to the audition, her flyaway bangs slicked down with soap and her one black skirt spot-treated for the occasion. Berteaut recalled, "We were so petrified we couldn't talk."

It would not have been obvious that le Gerny's portly impresario was himself a habitué of Pigalle. The nephew of the successful music-hall artist Polin, Leplée had performed at the Liberty's Bar, on the Place Blanche, with his partner, "Bobette"—a duo that flaunted their sexual orientation. A few years before taking on le Gerny's, Leplée had run the basement club at the Palace Theater in Montmartre, to which district he still came to find young men at homosexual hangouts. That these places were linked to the *milieu* only enhanced their allure. That they were also dangerous—clients were sometimes victimized by their lovers—was seen as a fact of life by those who liked rough trade.

Leplée's underworld connections were not apparent to Edith when she came to his club. She noted his elegant manners and "the tender blue of his eyes"—marks of distinction in a man, where she was concerned—as well as his limp, from a war injury. Above all, she was impressed by his kindness. "I put all my heart into my songs," she recalled, "not so much to get an engagement, which seemed unlikely, as to please the man who had shown an interest in me and with whom I now felt a mutual trust and sympathy."

After hearing her, Leplée asked whether she could start on October 24 at forty francs a night. He had two requirements: she was to learn some new songs, and wear something more presentable. Edith accepted on the spot, promising to finish the sweater she was knitting. (Piaf continued to knit throughout her career, but most projects were never completed.)

Her stage name came as an afterthought. She wasn't Russian, so Tania wouldn't do, Leplée reflected; neither would Denise Jay or Huguette Hélia. She must have a name to match what he felt as he watched her. A true Paris sparrow, she should be called La Môme Moineau, but that name was taken. Why not use the slang for sparrow, which was *piaf*? The singer remarked years later, "I was baptized for life."

Like the experienced showman he was, Leplée knew how to make the most of his protégée. He would present her not as a glamorous chanteuse but as herself: the contrast between her childlike mien and her assaultive vibrato would move audiences as it had moved him. The songs he chose for her, *réaliste* classics about the "dangerous classes" from which she came, would play up her origins and undernourished form. "Nini peau de chien," a Montmartre classic, portrayed its heroine's life on the streets as a poor girl's fate; "La Valse brune," an insinuating prewar waltz tune, wrapped its *"chevaliers de la lune"* (crooks who prowl by night) in the poetry of dark corners; "Si petite" voiced the *états d'âme* of a woman who tells her lover that she feels so small in his arms. Edith was to rehearse each afternoon with Leplée's pianist; the house accordionist, Robert Juel, would arrange the accompaniment to suit her.

By the twenty-fourth Edith knew her repertoire but had not completed her sweater, which lacked a sleeve. Dismayed by her appearance, Leplée found a solution with the help of Maurice Chevalier's wife, the actress Yvonne Vallée, who was in the audience that night. Vallée gave Edith her white silk scarf for good luck and to distinguish her from other *réaliste* singers, who draped their shoulders in red ones.

"I was dressed like a pauper but she paid no attention to that and treated me . . . like an artiste," Piaf said years later.

Nearly paralyzed with stage fright, she made the sign of the cross while Leplée told the audience that he had found his new attraction in the street. "Her voice overwhelmed me," he continued. "I am presenting her to you as she was when I first saw her: no makeup, no stockings, in a cheap little skirt."

Edith came onto a stage lit by harsh orange spots, the "in" color of the moment. Standing motionless to hide her bare arm, she launched into the most theatrical of the songs Leplée had chosen for her, "Les Mômes de la cloche"—about the feral girls who "drag their soiled hose and love stories along the boulevards": "*C'est nous les mômes, les mômes de la cloche, / Clochards qui s'en vont sans un rond en poche, / C'est nous les paumées, les purées d'paumées, / Qui sommes aimées un soir, n'importe où.*" ("We're the poor girls, the poor kids / We roam around broke, / We're the rejects, outcast girls, / We're loved for a night, it doesn't matter where.")

It was as if a guttersnipe had invaded the inner sanctum where sophisticates like Chevalier, Vallée, and the aviator Jean Mermoz sat drinking champagne. Yet as the guests, electrified by her voice, put down their glasses, Edith sensed that she held them. She threw up her arms at the end of the song; the scarf fell from her shoulders. There was silence, then wild applause and shouts of "bravo." "That kid sings straight from the guts," Chevalier cried.

She finished her repertoire in a trance. "You really had them," Leplée kept saying. "You'll have them again tomorrow and every other day." Mermoz, a French national hero who was said to love poetry, offered her champagne and, on another night, bought the contents of the flower seller's basket to show his appreciation—the first time Edith had ever received flowers. "These courtesies, from someone like Mermoz, astonished me," Piaf said years later.

Still, the young performer lacked confidence. "When I think of the way that I sang in those days, I have to confess that my 'talent' was of an extremely dubious nature." She knew that certain patrons came to gape at her as if she were a specimen, that some thought her vulgar. Her ignorance of conventions made her doubt herself. "You're doing fine," Leplée assured her. "When you recognize your shortcomings you can do something about them. It's a matter of determination and hard work."

She did not immediately take his advice. With Momone in tow, Edith returned to the Pigalle bars, where Fréhel listened scornfully as she raved about her new friends. Edith was no one until composers wrote songs just for her, Fréhel said; this lucky break would not last unless she made her name with recordings. The denizens of the Clair de la Lune were also skeptical about Leplée, but Edith insisted that he was like a father to her—he was helping her take herself seriously.

Two of Leplée's friends asked to meet Edith as soon as they heard her sing. The first, a middle-aged man named Jacques Bourgeat, had fallen in love with her voice and wanted to help her career. An autodidact who spent his days in the Bibliothèque Nationale, Bourgeat wrote poetry when he was not studying French history. "Jacquot" would become Piaf's mentor, confidant, and spiritual guide. He often walked her from her hotel to le Gerny's and home again, reveling in the piquancy of her slang. Because the feeling was mutual—Edith admired the way he spoke—he began teaching her proper French and gave her Baudelaire's poems, which they read aloud to each other. When she asked Bourgeat to write lyrics for her, he composed "'Chand d'habits," a *réaliste* number about an old-clothes peddler that would have suited the classic film of Paris street life, *Les Enfants du paradis*. With Bourgeat's support, Piaf recalled, "I felt that I was on the path to success. Helped by my true friends, I was happy."

Through Leplée she also met Jacques Canetti, whose influential program, *Radio-Cité*, was broadcast on Sunday mornings. A few days after her debut at le Gerny's, she began appearing on this popular revue. "I felt a sense of compassion for the poor little thing," Canetti wrote, "and at the same time, enormous admiration for this burning fire, this voice that came from her heart rather than from her head." When listeners began phoning to find out who she was, Canetti had her perform each Sunday for the next twelve weeks. By November, La Môme Piaf was such a sensation that newspapers sent reporters to le Gerny's to interview her.

She was "a singer who lives her songs," *Le Petit Parisien* declared.

Their critic told readers to "imagine a pale, almost ashen visage" with "a sort of secret, pathetic nobility." La Môme Piaf was poorly dressed, he wrote, and didn't know how take a bow: "In fact, she doesn't know anything. But she sings. This girl of the streets gives to her street songs the same poignant, piercing, sweetly poisonous poetry as is found in Carco's novels." Recognizing the literary dimension of her perform- ance, its nostalgic poetics of Paris life, he predicted that within the year she would be singing in New York.

Another critic noted La Môme's awkwardness onstage: she seemed "embarrassed at being so small." But then there was her voice: "the color of oysters . . . that indescribable voice, which is both harsh and ample, ordinary and unique . . . still childlike and already full of despair, that voice that hits you in the stomach just when you're not thinking about it." He could not explain why it was so moving to hear her sing an old chestnut of Parisian folklore like "Les Mômes de la cloche," since she did nothing "except to be really little, really thin, poorly coiffed . . . and to have that voice."

Edith slept late and spent afternoons at the music publishers in the attempt to build her repertoire. But despite her good reviews, publish- ers were reluctant to entrust their new tunes to someone who had not made a record. At best she could perform those that were not under contract to better-known singers. One afternoon, in the studio of one of the few publishers willing to help, she listened to the popular soprano Annette Lajon run through a song about a sailor that sounded like one of Edith's brief affairs. Called "L'Etranger," it would become the prototype for Piaf's love songs in the future: "*Il avait un air très doux, / Des yeux rêveurs, un peu fous, / Aux lueurs étranges. . . . / Il s'en allait je ne sais où.*" ("He seemed gentle / He had dreamy eyes, a little crazed, / With strange lights in them. . . . / He drifted away, I don't know where.") Edith memorized the song while Lajon rehearsed and performed it that night at the club. When Lajon showed up there a few days later, she forgave Edith, despite her annoyance.

On December 18, the day before her twentieth birthday, Edith made her first record with Canetti, at the Polydor recording studio. For her debut he chose "L'Etranger" (no longer under exclusive contract), "Les Mômes de la cloche," and two songs in *parigot* slang that evoked

*Edith Giovanna Gassion (on the right), with her cousins
Marcelle and Mauricette (on chair), c. 1919*

GASSION

CONTORSIONISTE-ANTIPODISTE

L'HOMME QUI MARCHE LA TÊTE A L'ENVERS

Poster advertising Edith's father: "Gassion, the antipodean contortionist,
the man who walks upside down," late 1920s

POUR QU' ÇA VOUS ATTACHE

Chanson Réaliste

créée par LINE MARSA

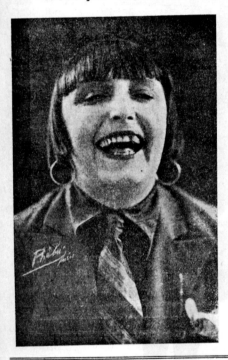

Son Répertoire

LE BON MARTEAU
C'EST UN MALABART
LA COCO
LA DERNIÈRE CIGARETTE
FILLES DE JOIE
LES INQUIETS
MON TOUR DE JAVA
RÉDEMPTION
TON OMBRE
TU AS BESOIN DE MOI
VALSE EN MINEUR
Y' EN A QU'UN

Chant seul . . . . *l fr.*
Chant et Piano . . . *6 fr.*

PAROLES ET
MUSIQUE DE **TRÉMOLO**

MARCEL LABBÉ, Éditeur, 20, Rue du Croissant, PARIS-2ᵉ

*Sheet music presenting Edith's mother, Line Marsa,
with her* chanson réaliste *repertoire, late 1920s*

*Edith performing at around age eight (c. 1923), when
known as "Miss Edith, Vocal Phenomenon"*

*Street scene in Bernay, where Edith lived with her
Gassion grandparents in a discreetly run brothel*

Belleville, where Edith sang after settling in Paris with her father in the mid-1920s

Louis Gassion, Edith (age ten), and Louis's then girlfriend

Edith on Louis Leplée's lap in his nightclub, le Gerny's, at the start of her career, October 1935

Edith, now known as La Môme Piaf, preparing to go onstage at le Gerny's, 1936

Edith being questioned by the police after the murder of Louis Leplée on April 6, 1936

LE PLUS GRAND
HEBDOMADAIRE
DES FAITS DIVERS

9ᵉ Année — Nᵒ 390
1 fr. 50
Le jeudi 16 PAGES
16 AVRIL 1936

DIRECTEUR :
Marius LARIQUE

DÉTECTIVE

Les Quatre Tueurs

RENIÉ PAR SES COMPAGNONS DE VICE, LOUIS LEPLÉE N'EUT QUE DES FEMMES, LA MOME PIAF ET LAURE JARNY, POUR PLEURER A SES OBSÈQUES. Pages 2 et 3, les révélations de Marcel **MONTARRON**.

Special issue of Détective *on the Leplée affair, "The Four Killers," shows an unconsolable Edith at his funeral*

Raymond Asso, Edith's songwriter-lover, and his protégée perusing sheet music, c. 1938.
Her version of Asso's "Mon Légionnaire" and other songs she inspired
restarted her career after the Leplée scandal.

Edith and her close friend Marguerite Monnot (with whom she would co-write some thirty songs), studying one of their compositions in 1950

Petit format *sheet music for "C'était un jour de fête," a love song written by Piaf and Monnot in 1941*

In her first film role (La Garçonne, 1936), as an entertainer at a lesbian nightclub, Edith croons "Quand même," whose title recalls Sarah Bernhardt's motto.

Edith examines a score with René Bergeron (center) and Jean-Louis Barrault (right) in Montmartre–sur–Seine (1941); the film popularized four of her songs composed with Monnot, including the bluesy "L'Homme des bars."

Jean Cocteau and Edith in a publicity shot for Le Bel indifférent, *the one-act play he wrote for her and Paul Meurisse*

This special issue of the tabloid Voilà, "The Stars Go to the Front," heralds the plans of French entertainers, starting with Piaf, to entertain the troops at the outset of World War II.

*An unknown friend, Edith, the composer Norbert Glanzberg, and
Andrée Bigard enjoy life in the Unoccupied Zone, c. 1942.*

*Edith shares conditions with French prisoners of war in Germany, August 1943,
during a trip that resulted in some of them escaping thanks to plans organized by
the Resistance and executed in secret by Piaf and her secretary, Andrée Bigard.*

the cheeky atmosphere of the *bals-musettes* (the sort of song that foreign audiences rarely heard once Piaf became famous, because of their argot and lack of fit with her "tragedienne" persona). "She was relaxed and full of fun" at the studio, Canetti observed: "she felt at ease and understood immediately what needed to be done."

The same month, she performed in a film version of Victor Marguerite's scandalous novel *La Garçonne,* about a middle-class woman who forsakes an arranged marriage to experience life in Pigalle—where she frequents lesbian bars like Lulu's, the occasion for Edith's cameo role. Dressed in satin evening pajamas and surrounded by female admirers, Edith crooned "Quand même," a sultry apologia for vice: *"Le bonheur quotidien / Vraiment ne me dit rien / La vertu n'est que faiblesse / Qui voit sa fin dans le ciel / Je préfère la promesse / Des paradis artificiels."* ("I don't give a damn / For ordinary joys / Weakly the virtuous ones / See their end in heaven / I prefer the promise / Of artificial paradise.") A provocative part in a film with stars like Marie Bell, Arletty, and Suzy Solidor meant that Edith was on her way.

In the meantime, she was happy to go on singing at le Gerny's, which gave her an income and a loving relationship with Papa Leplée, her name for her protector. They confided in each other about the recent deaths of her daughter and his mother; they found emotional strength on visits to the Thiais Cemetery, where both were buried.

On a more practical note, the critics' observations about La Môme's stage clothes prompted Leplée to take her shopping at the couturier Tout Main, where they ordered a simple black dress, the style she would wear throughout her professional life. When he sent her back to publishers in search of new songs, this time their positive response led to her recording eight more numbers for Polydor, including another celebration of the underclass entitled "Les Hiboux," and "Fais-moi valser," whose lyrics implore the woman's lover to grant her one last waltz before leaving forever.

Leplée worried about Edith's carousing with the lowlife types who waited for her at the stage door and accompanied her to Pigalle, where she treated them to whatever they wanted. (Since nightclubs had to pay tribute money, he no doubt knew that she too was under the *milieu*'s protection.) If, as Berteaut writes, Leplée shared Edith's attraction to sailors, legionnaires, and apprentice hoodlums, he also knew that such associations, however stimulating, would not further his plans for her future.

One wonders how much she told him about having been turned over by Henri Valette to her new lover, Jeannot, the ex-sailor with whom she shared a room. He was a patient man who put up with Edith's whims—including her insistence on buying him pointy-toed patent-leather shoes that looked stylish but were a size too small. "He was a simple, honest fellow," a friend recalled. "He loved her for her own sake." Another of her lovers, a jealous thug named René whom she rejected in favor of Jeannot, followed her for years and may have exacted protection money. He was, Piaf wrote, "incapable of forgiving or forgetting."

Knowing the code of the *milieu*, Leplée had reason to be concerned about La Môme's safety, although he paid less attention to his own. The impresario often befriended the better-looking hoodlums who turned up at the club. He offered Jeannot a tuxedo so he could come to le Gerny's, but Edith's lover said that he preferred his blue-and-white-striped top and sailor cap. "She had difficulty attuning herself to this new world in which she found herself," a friend observed, "but she kept on trying even when it seemed impossible."

At Edith's first gala appearance—a charitable event at the Cirque Medrano on February 17, 1936—it must have seemed as if she were fulfilling her father's dream of appearing there. The evening, a benefit for the widow of a famous clown, brought together well-known actors, athletes, and circus performers. The little singer was thrilled to see her name on the program in letters the same size as those of her "comrades" Maurice Chevalier, Mistinguett, Fernandel, and Marie Dubas. She and Leplée formed an odd couple, "he, very tall and elegant in his well-cut evening clothes, and me, very small, very 'Belleville-Ménilmontant' in my sweater and knitted skirt." After her performance, Leplée declared, "You're a tiny thing, but you'll be fine in the greatest locales."

Her next booking, he announced on April 5, would take them to Cannes for a charity ball to benefit street urchins—an occasion that no doubt seemed appropriate. Yet, while he looked forward to showing her the Riviera, he felt a sense of foreboding—having been unsettled by a bad dream. Edith tried to talk him out of his dejection. She promised to go to bed early that night to be fresh for a radio broadcast the next day but ignored his advice and after her performance at the club made the rounds of Pigalle.

Edith was startled to hear a new voice when she phoned Leplée in the morning to change the time of their appointment. She must come to his apartment immediately, the man said, using the formal *vous* rather than the familiar *tu* with which Leplée adressed her. On hearing her name, the policeman who let her into the building followed her upstairs. The door was open. Leplée had been shot through the eye; he was dead. Decades later, Piaf recalled the shock: "How can I describe the feeling of total emptiness, of unreality, that left me senseless, unable to move or respond to a world that had gone to pieces in a second?"

Suddenly she was a suspect in a murder case. The police interviewed everyone from le Gerny's, starting with her. They questioned her for two days about her background, her relationship with Leplée, her ties to the petty criminals of Pigalle. Under pressure, she reluctantly gave the names of her lovers, including Valette and Jeannot, but kept insisting that she knew nothing. The police verified her alibi and let her go. But she was to keep them informed of her whereabouts.

Following Edith's release, the media refused to let her off the hook. *Détective*, a popular scandal sheet, ran photos of the grief-stricken singer at Leplée's funeral, along with their analysis of the case. "The man in the street doesn't know about Louis Leplée," the journalist Marcel Montarron wrote, "but he does know about 'La Môme Piaf,' whose name and voice have already been heard on the airwaves." Since the authorities had found nothing to implicate her, he guessed that blackmail, racketeering, or a combination of the two had motivated the murder, given the "special nature" of Leplée's preferences.

What *Détective* did not say was that, three years earlier, Leplée's friend Oscar Dufrenne had been brutally murdered at the Palace, the *music-hall* in Pigalle where Leplée had run the club. The murderer, identified as one of the men posing as sailors who picked up clients like Dufrenne and Leplée, was never found. When Leplée met the same fate, the police investigated Piaf's entourage but were unable to find a lead, despite Leplée's housekeeper's description of the four young men who entered his apartment the night of the murder, tied her up, and accosted her employer. The men, presumably known to the victim, must have expected a handsome payment, the journalist suggested, but when the weapon they brought to scare him went off accidentally, a case of blackmail turned into a murder.

La Môme Piaf remained in the headlines while the investigation dragged on. The four men were never found. The newsreel *Éclair-Journal* tracked her down in its attempt to sensationalize the affair. Despite her stylish gloves and fur collar, Edith looked terrified. Asked why she had given her friends' names to the police, she replied, "I had to say who I'd been with or they'd have thought I was protecting someone." When the interviewer questioned her about how well she had known Leplée, she sobbed, "My friends are gone. I have no one. Leave me alone."

Edith pulled herself together some days later for an interview with Montarron for another popular magazine, *Voilà*. Having become interested in her when researching his piece for *Détective*, he planned to do a human-interest story—one that would show readers that, though she came from Belleville, she was not one of the immoral creatures she sang about. "La Môme Piaf" appeared in *Voilà* on April 18, with photos of sparrows and of the little singer, her dark dress adorned with a white bow at the neck—an ironic touch, given the cigarette in her mouth.

Edith trusted Montarron enough to invite him to her hotel room and introduce her *"petit homme"*—Jeannot—stretched out on the bed in his sailor's blues. When the journalist took the couple to a restaurant in view of Sacré-Coeur, it reminded her of singing there with Cécelle in her arms. "She died eight months to the day before Monsieur Leplée was killed," Edith said, as if their deaths were linked in her mind, or as if she was already adept in giving the press the kind of stories they wanted. They did not discuss the case, except to tell the story of her discovery by the impresario. Leplée was still protecting her, Edith added; he had asked friends to look after her in case anything happened to him. Club owners were approaching her because of her notoriety. Everyone wanted an *"artiste à sensation."*

That night, she began singing at Chez O'Dett, on the Place Pigalle, where the young producer Bruno Coquatrix had booked her for two months. (Coquatrix lent her the money for a new black dress with sleeves, to cover her scrawny arms, and with pockets, to hide her hands.) O'Dett's was a comedown from le Gerny's, where she had earned more than twice as much per night. The main attraction, a drag show, drew customers from the artistic world and the homosexual elite, who were usually sympathetic. But when Edith came onstage, she faced hostile stares. "I might as well have been singing psalms," she said. "I wonder if they'd have noticed the difference. They hadn't come to hear a singer; they'd come to see 'the woman in the Leplée affair.' "

One night, an older man stood up to lecture a member of the audience who had greeted her songs with disapproving whistles. Not only was it unfair to judge someone whose innocence had been proved, he said, but it was bad taste to whistle in a cabaret: "If she's good, applaud, and keep your nose out of her private life." The audience began to clap; "then, as he joined in, the applause was for me," Piaf recalled. Hoping to put Pigalle behind her, she did not renew her contract at O'Dett's.

Edith's resolve to concentrate on her career may have been strengthened by the absence of Momone that spring. The police had picked up Edith's "evil spirit" after Leplée's murder and, on learning her age, sent her to a school for wayward girls. Without her accomplice (Berteaut said that, as Piaf's "demon," she deliberately encouraged her vices), Edith turned to her few remaining friends—Robert Juel, Jacques Bourgeat, and Jacques Canetti.

Juel continued to accompany her on the accordion while also acting as her bodyguard, a service that must have been reassuring when she sang at another Pigalle venue, the Ange Rouge—a particularly dangerous club, thanks to the presence of the Corsican mafia. "Jacquot" Bourgeat helped her find peace of mind by having her read the classics of philosophy, though it is hard to see how she could assimilate Plato in such volatile circumstances. Bourgeat, who loved her gaiety, enjoyed playing the role of Edith's professor: "She was attentive, a good student, but mainly she wanted to listen."

It was Canetti who allowed Edith to imagine a new life by having her record songs that would make her a bankable asset. In May, accompanied by a full orchestra, she cut four new tunes for Polydor. Although the violins bothered her at first, she adjusted to the new sound. Around this time, she met the composer Raymond Asso, whose lyrics for one of these songs, "Mon Amant de la Coloniale," evoked an affair between a man in the French colonial army and the woman he leaves behind—taking advantage of the vogue for love-'em-and-leave-'em tough guys. Also through Canetti, Edith joined a traveling company called La Jeune Chanson 1936, which performed at Paris *music-halls* in May and June, then made its own *tour de France* during the summer.

While the Jeune Chanson troupe traveled around the country, French workers were enjoying their first state-sanctioned paid holidays, a Popular Front innovation that helped fill the theaters. But such revolutionary measures (the Blum government also agreed to salary increases, shop representatives, and collective bargaining) made no impression on the young singer, judging by her memoirs. "She never even thought about changing the world," Piaf's most reliable French biographers observe. "Her desire was to seduce it, to conquer it, and, more precisely, to escape from the one from which she came."

In August, Edith wrote to Bourgeat from Lausanne, where the troupe was performing at the Maison du Peuple. Having had to replace her lost identity card, she had in the process understood that she needed to put her life in order. "I'm no longer with Jeannot, or Georges, or Marcel, or Jacques," she told him. "I've decided to be serious and work hard to please my dear old Papa Leplée." She hoped to disentangle her life from the *milieu:* "I'm completely disgusted by all that. I'm going to keep my dough for myself." Promising to learn good French (the letter is full of mistakes), she swore "on Monsieur Leplée's ashes" to reconnect with her father, who could take charge of her, and, for company, with Momone. To close this eighteen-page screed, she called Jacquot her "wildflower," doodled a sparrow with an envelope in its beak, and signed it "didi." (In the bulk of their cor-respondence, she is his "Piafou.")

Edith found it impossible to keep her promises when Momone was released and joined her in Pigalle. The singer went back to O'Dett's, despite the pay, since she had both of them to support. In September, she had engagements at two of the better *music-halls*, the Alhambra and the Trianon, and in October, through Fernand Lumbroso, an associate of Canetti's, at the Broadway Theater in Brussels. She no doubt performed the tunes she had recorded that spring, Asso's "Mon Amant de le Coloniale" and "Il n'est pas distingué," sung in the per-sona of a streetwise accordionist called "Zidor" (a nickname for "Isidore"?), whose dislike of the current German leader turns this comic number into satire: *Moi, Hitler, j'l'ai dans le blair / Et j'peux pas le renifler.* ("I can't stand Hitler / He gets up my nose.")

But Edith was less concerned with the mounting European crisis than with making her way. In November, Lumbroso booked her and Momone, her presenter, for a week in Brest. Edith was to open at a the-ater before the main attraction, a film entitled *Lucrezia Borgia,* a histor-ical drama, which, however well acted, was unlikely to attract the town's most vocal residents, the sailors quartered there. Momone called Brest "an impossible dump" except for the sailors—"you had as many as you needed." Their presence at the theater, where they defended Edith by picking fights with other members of the audience, and the singer's nightly carousing prompted the manager to take action. After he rang her producer, an angry Lumbroso summoned her back to Paris.

Earlier that year, Edith had sought out Asso, who had made an impression on her when they met at a music publisher's. After playing Asso's latest song, "Mon Légionnaire," the pianist introduced her to the lyricist, a tall, thin man with a big nose and an edgy manner. Though Edith said that this song did not suit her, Asso watched as she sang another of his compositions: he was moved to tears. Later that year, when Marie Dubas's recording of "Mon Légionnaire" became a hit (the song consecrates the 1930s myth of the Foreign Legion), Edith felt as if Dubas had stolen what was hers. The lyrics seemed to echo her adventures with men in uniform.

That year, she and Asso often crossed paths in Pigalle. He thought that he could write for her but noted her lack of discipline: "She was a wild thing, . . . unwilling to accept any limits on her freedom." Edith had turned to him when afraid that life was closing in on her, and one night, after the murder of Leplée, took refuge in his hotel room. She trusted the lyricist but would not comply with his demand that she lead a more orderly life and break with Momone, the "devilish girl . . . who followed her around like her shadow."

In December, Lumbroso gave Edith one last chance, a booking in Nice, at the basement club of Maxim's Restaurant. On the train to the Riviera, she shared her third-class compartment with a young man who held her hand while she dozed on his shoulder. At Marseille, two detectives handcuffed the man and, to Edith's distress, hauled him off the train.

Berteaut, who joined her in Nice, recalled their stay as a continuous party, including drinking contests with the American sailors in port. Edith's memories are more somber: "My situation wasn't great. . . . Not having much money is annoying but it's not a disaster. Losing your taste for life is far worse, and I was almost there. With the death of Leplée, I lost everything, the guidance that I so badly needed and, above all, an affectionate, irreplaceable friend." She was on the Riviera at last but under circumstances very different from those she had imagined with Leplée. To celebrate her twenty-first birthday, she and Momone downed a bottle of wine.

"I've been doing a lot of stupid things," Edith wrote Asso from Nice. She asked whether he would send her his new songs; he said that he would not think of it unless she changed her way of life. The day after her return to Paris, in January 1937, she phoned him in desperation. She would have to return to the streets unless he took charge of her, she said; Asso replied that he had been waiting for this opportunity for over a year. "Take a taxi and come right over," he added. To Piaf, his response marked a turning point. Years later, she said of this moment, "I was saved."

CHAPTER FIVE

1937–1939

I f Leplée had fostered Edith's talent by nurturing her self-confidence, Raymond Asso would become her Pygmalion—or, as some have said, her Svengali. Piaf believed that Asso taught her to be human. "It took him three years to cure me. Three years of patient affection to teach me that there was another world beyond that of prostitutes and pimps. Three years to cure me of Pigalle, of my chaotic childhood . . . to become a woman and a star instead of a phenomenon with a voice that people listened to as if being shown a rare animal at a fair."

In retrospect, Asso saw himself as Edith's *dompteur*—the tamer who breaks a wild creature of its need to scratch and bite. Only when totally exhausted, he said, "could she submit to a *dompteur*'s authority." She was an uncut diamond, he continued. His role had been "to facet her, which wasn't always easy. Her scrappy street spirit often took over. If she hadn't had that extraordinary desire to sing, to become good, I would never have succeeded."

The lyricist saw that his protégée had to be retrained. Edith sang as she had always done, her hands glued to her sides, her body stiff and unmoving, her few gestures awkward or repetitious. Worse, to Asso's way of thinking, her accent was vulgar, and she was deaf to the lyrics: "Distorting the words, she deformed the most basic rhymes; she sang magnificently but without grasping the meaning." With him she would learn to adapt her diction and phrasing to each song, and to build her career with the disciplined approach that the French call *métier*.

Yet to say that Asso remade Piaf is to underestimate the singer's role in her own transformation. Though she stood like a statue onstage, she was no Galatea, nor did she simply submit to his unlikely Svengali. Aware of what Asso had to offer, Edith sought him out when she was ready to work with him, then struggled to keep her independence while being retrained—like a Parisian Eliza Doolittle. After Piaf's death, Asso reflected on his role, which had gone beyond teaching her to pronounce words properly: "My work was to offer moral and physical guidance to a little creature who—because she had lacked the tenderness I gave her and the trust I inspired in her—would never have been more than an odd little thing on her own." Yet her talent was so great, he confessed, that anyone in his shoes would have done the same.

Soon after Edith went to live with Asso at the Hôtel Piccadilly, the lyricist began severing her ties to the lowlife types whose influence got in the way of her career. Their hotel, just down the street from the Place Blanche, was too close to familiar haunts and temptations. In March 1937, they moved up the hillside to the Hôtel Alsina, a spot that encouraged a loftier perspective, which was especially useful once she returned to singing at O'Dett's. Asso made a list of all those who were not to visit their refuge—chief among them, Momone and Louis Gassion, who came around whenever he was short of funds. (Momone found work in a Belleville grocery store and made a marriage of convenience; Louis waited each week for Asso to bring him his share of Edith's earnings, his old-age pension.)

Edith called her mentor Cyrano because of his sharp wit and beaky nose, but also because he wrote the kind of world-weary verse that she admired. Although the lanky ex-soldier was an improbable person to effect her transformation from street urchin into artist, Edith believed in him. She loved the luminous blue of his eyes, the sensitivity hidden beneath his swagger, his way of stroking her hair and crooning "*ma petite fille*" when their lessons exhausted her. He called her Didou, a nickname that suggests his almost paternal feelings for her.

At thirty-five, Asso exuded an odd glamour. Like Edith, he had fended for himself since the age of fifteen. He had been a shepherd, a smuggler, a *spahi* (a native soldier in the French colonial army), a ghostwriter, and, lately, a lyricist whose songs had begun to be recognized. He often collaborated with the pianist Marguerite Monnot, who had composed the music for "Mon Légionnaire"; soon she and Edith also became friends. In 1937, Asso gave Edith two of his favorite songs, "Le Fanion de la légion" ("The Foreign Legion's Pennant," music by Monnot) and "Mon Légionnaire" for her next recording session—when the vogue for music with doomed romances in exotic settings was at its height. In time, Piaf came to believe that Asso had written "Mon Légionnaire" for her. The quintessential song of its era, this colonial fantasy portrayed a woman's one-night stand with the soldier who leaves her to pursue his fate in the "hot sands" of the Sahara: *"J'sais pas son nom, je n'sais rien d'lui, / Il m'a aimée toute la nuit, / Mon légionnaire! / Et me laissant à mon destin / Il est parti dans le matin / Plein de lumière. . . . / Mon légionnaire!"* ("I don't know his name, don't know anything about him, / He made love to me all night, / My legionnaire! / Leaving me to my fate, / He went off / In the bright morning light. . . . / My legionnaire!")

Even though Asso's "pocket tragedy" (Jean Cocteau's phrase) seemed to evoke Edith's past, it was also linked in her mind to the first person to record the song, Marie Dubas—whose successful career she hoped to emulate. But before Edith would be ready to sing in the *music-halls* like Dubas, Asso insisted, she had a great deal to learn. Her table manners had to improve if she was to feel comfortable in society; she had to dress as elegantly in daily life as she did onstage. Edith often rebelled when he showed her how to hold her knife or said to wait for the right moment rather than blurt out what was on her mind. Yet she knew instinctively that these essentials of *savoir-vivre* (good breeding) would help to shape her image—the "personality" that Asso kept talking about. Quarrels over such things as posture at the dinner table alternated with lessons in French poetry once Edith accepted him as her mentor, the man to complete the process she had begun with Jacques Bourgeat.

Still, her relations with Asso were more fluid than the teacher-pupil model suggests. When Edith told him stories about her past, the lyricist took notes in order to use his protégée's life as his sourcebook.

Some have called Piaf his "creation," but one can also see her as the muse who inspired many of his best songs. Their partnership confounds fixed ideas of muse and artist: they alternated in these roles with each other. Just as Edith enabled Asso to write lyrics that he would not have composed without her, so, with his support, she honed her craft to perform these songs on the larger cultural stage. Over the three years they lived and worked together, their contentious collaboration would nourish both partners' creativity.

In March, Asso took his protégée to watch Marie Dubas sing at the A.B.C., the city's leading song palace. By the end of the set, Edith was dumbstruck; her eyes brimmed with tears. "Now do you understand what makes an artist great?" Asso asked. From then on, whenever she had a free evening, Edith went to the A.B.C. to study Dubas's expressions, the way she shaped a song with gestures, her ability to provoke tears and laughter, the ease with which she modulated from one rhythm to another to reach an emotional climax. Above all it was the audience's love for the star that moved her: "All these people, their faces full of expectation, formed one single heart together. . . . I too wanted the public to love me like that."

The A.B.C.'s location—down the hill from Pigalle, on the Boulevard Poissonière—gave it the respectability lacking in joints like O'Dett's. The director, a canny Romanian named Mitty Goldin, had chosen the theater's name so that it would come first in directory listings; by 1937, he was booking all the best-known performers—Dubas, Fréhel, Damia, Tino Rossi, Suzy Solidor, and Lucienne Boyer. Asso tried repeatedly to get Edith a booking there, but Goldin resisted. In his view, she was inexperienced and had a bad name because of the Leplée affair. Undeterred, Asso courted the impresario until he agreed to give her a chance—as one of the acts preceding Dubas, the main attraction.

On March 26, her hair coiffed and her black dress enlivened by a white lace collar, Edith came onstage as an accordionist played her theme song, "Les Mômes de la cloche." She was to close the first part of the program with five songs. To mark a contrast to the familiar tune that had introduced her, she launched into one of Asso's compositions, the bittersweet "Un Jeune Homme chantait" (the tale of a man who goes off singing after taking a young girl's virginity). Next she sang a comic number and three more Asso songs: "C'est toi le plus fort" (a woman's confession that she allows her lover to be "the stronger one"), "Browning" (a noirish tale of a Chicago-style hoodlum in which she gleefully rolled the "r" in the man's name), and "Le Contrebandier" (a stirring tune that claims its smuggler hero as "a sort of poet"). When the audience refused to let her go until she sang "Mon Légionnaire," Goldin re-raised the curtain. Edith kept coming back to take her bow; Asso declared victory.

The critics agreed that La Môme was now a star. She had made "astonishing progress," *Le Figaro* noted; when evoking the poorer districts, "she was quite simply remarkable." More poetically, *Paris-Soir* wrote, "The frail street flower no longer wilts on the Parisian stage. Hav[ing] gained in strength and knowledgeability . . . she has become a very great success." To the left-wing journalist Henri Jeanson, Edith's was "the voice of revolt." Listening to her rousing rendition of "Le Contrebandier," he added, "I felt as if I were crossing the border under the nose of the authorities."

To Maurice Verne, a critic of popular culture and a friend of Fréhel's, La Môme's performance brought to mind Colette's saucy prewar heroine Claudine. "Here is the miraculous resurrection of Claudine's short hair, her white collar . . . her black dress resembling a schoolgirl's uniform." To suit her "metallic" voice, she needed songs written just for her to tell certain kinds of stories: "*réaliste* portraits of working-class life, gray with the soot of factory chimneys and abuzz with tunes picked up from bistrot radios." Years later, Piaf recalled in her memoirs, "Asso wrote songs like this for me; direct, sincere, without literary pretensions . . . as welcoming as a handshake."

～

Despite her triumphant A.B.C. debut, Edith could not afford to rest on her laurels—particularly since Asso had accepted a low fee in order to get her a booking there. Starting on April 16, the day after her A.B.C. engagement ended, she sang at O'Dett's and the Sirocco; then, in May, went on tour to Aix-les-Bains; Lille, Belgium; and, over the summer, eight French watering spots, where she performed in the casinos. After a month's rest, she appeared in several of the large Parisian cinemas that featured live attractions before the film. Her September gig at the Belleville Cinéma would have brought back memories; in October, after falling ill during a gig in Le Havre, she would have recalled leaving her sickbed as a child to perform there. Asso arranged Edith's bookings, planned her repertoire, and accompanied her on tour—the better to play his role as *dompteur*—but also because he loved her.

For the next two years, Edith recorded only her lover's compositions, showing the gratitude she felt toward the man who had "saved" her, though she was already chafing under his discipline. In 1937, she recorded three of Asso's songs from her A.B.C. debut along with his latest ballad, "Paris-Méditerranée"—inspired by her tale of the man in the train on whose shoulder she had slept until the police took him away. Asso imagined their brief encounter from her perspective: "*Dans une gare ensoleillée / L'inconnu sautait sur le quai. / Alors des hommes l'entourèrent / Et, tête basse, ils l'emmenèrent / Tandis que le train repartait.*" ("In the sunlit station / The stranger jumped onto the platform. / Then some men surrounded him / And took him away, head hanging, / As the train took off.") When the man raises his hands to bid her adieu, she sees the sun glinting off his handcuffs and hears the train's piercing whistle in the background.

That autumn, Edith took charge of details when she could, changing the words of a refrain when recording Asso's songs or, in performance, finding the gestures for each of her numbers. By November, it must have been clear to him that his Didou had grown up. She was ready for her return engagement at the A.B.C., an event that would mark another turning point. At Asso's insistence, Edith would no longer be billed as La Môme. On opening night the orchestra played "Les Mômes de la cloche"; then the mistress of ceremonies made an announcement: "La Môme is dead! You are about to hear Edith Piaf!" Wearing her beguiling black dress and white lace collar, Edith demonstrated her range by performing songs as different from each other as a saucy *java* in working-class slang, "Correqu' et réguyer" ("Correct and Regular"), and the intense, patriotic "Fanion de la légion."

The critics were quick to applaud her name change and her repertoire. "The 'môme' was charming," *Le Journal* wrote. "But Edith Piaf—and the general public's triumphant welcome for every one of her songs—that's something else. She's an artist, a great artist." Though rebaptized Mademoiselle, Edith had lost none of her fieriness onstage, another critic observed: "She seemed to be standing on a barricade, the better to hurl invectives against social injustice." Carried away by his rhetoric, he continued, "She is, by turns, poverty-mistreated, a low whore rebelling against her condition, a convulsive kid clawing the police who grabbed hold of her."

After her final appearance at O'Dett's in December, Edith celebrated Christmas 1937 by singing at the circus in Rouen. One wonders whether she found time to visit the Gassion household in nearby Bernay, or to tell her father about her circus gig after returning to Paris for a New Year's Day radio broadcast. From then on, she kept busy with an almost uninterrupted round of radio programs, recordings, cinema appearances, and casino tours until her third engagement at the A.B.C., from April 15 to May 4, 1938.

Now that Edith was a rising star, Goldin gave her second billing on the program, before his new attraction, the jazzy, lighthearted Charles Trenet. Surprised that the La Môme had turned into an artist, *Comoedia*'s critic praised "her perfect diction and air of knowing a great deal for her age." He hoped she would stay true to herself as one "who belongs to the race of Fréhel."

Two days after her A.B.C. booking ended, Edith began an eight-week engagement at the Lune Rousse cabaret, which earned more enthusiastic praise. "Edith Piaf has worked very hard since her debut," Roger Feral wrote; he hoped that she would not become too professional or lose her spontaneity. To Paul Granet, "her beautiful masklike face resembles the mask of Greek tragedy, but one that is animated and exalted, that reflects every emotion and passion moving through the soul of this highly sensitive artist." In June, when she did double duty at the Européen *music-hall*, Louis Lévy confessed that, although he had formerly seen La Môme as "just a miniature girl of the streets," he had changed his mind because of the singer's sobriety and intelligence: "This time I was completely won over."

If one stops to measure the distance Edith had come since her discovery by Leplée, one realizes that it had been harder, not to say more unlikely, to make the transition from joints like O'Dett's to the *music-halls* than to move from street singing to the cabarets. By working nearly nonstop for the past three years, she had won over the critics and the general public. In a sense, she came on the scene as the last *chanteuse réaliste*, when a predominantly female radio audience still preferred her fatalistic songs to upbeat musical trends influenced by American-style swing and jazz.

Yet one can also see Piaf's popularity in relation to a persistent myth celebrating the fringes of society—the crooks, pimps, whores, and other fallen women who were the dramatis personae of her music. Harking back to a familiar view of the past, her songs updated the tradition of urban poetry, a kind of popular epic in which misfortune must be endured—at least by its female characters, since its male ones, the soldiers, sailors, and other adventurers, all disappear, leaving their women to lament or, on occasion, shake their fists at Fate. Piaf's way of seeming to rise above her hard-knock life may have been the reason that she was asked to sing at an anti-Franco rally that year, at the left-wing Palais de la Mutualité, on the Left Bank. Told to avoid songs that glorifed militarism, she belted out patriotic airs until the audience, composed mainly of pacifists, called out for everyone's favorites, "Le Fanion de la légion" and "Mon Légionnaire."

If Asso's tragic legionnaire resonated in the popular imagination, the woman of easy virtue who gave herself to him was an equally evocative, and nostalgic, trope. Again inspired by Edith's past, Asso gave this figure his full attention in his next song for her, "Elle fréquentait la rue Pigalle"—which harked back to the *réaliste* obsession with prostitutes: "*Ell' fréquentait la rue Pigalle, / Ell' sentait l'vice à bon marché, / Elle était tout' noire de péchés / Avec un pauvr' visage tout pâle. / Pourtant y'avait dans l'fond d'ses yeux, / Comm' quelqu' chos' de miraculeux / Qui semblait mettre un peu d'ciel bleu / Dans celui tout sale, de Pigalle.*" ("She hung out on the rue Pigalle, / She smelled of cheap vice, / She was black with sin / With a poor pale face. / Yet there was something in her eyes / Like a miracle / That seemed to put a little blue / In the sooty sky of Pigalle.")

Asso's tale of a whore with a heart of gold ends badly when the man who tries to free her from the trade abandons her. The woman re-affirms the status quo by returning to Pigalle—though the little singer who seemed to be the incarnation of this character was already attempting to flee from its streets. A historian notes, "Critics who acclaimed Piaf's renewal of the repertory of French Song were hear-ing a new voice rather than new themes, a re-identification of the singer and the words." In time, she would escape from Asso's limited vision of her potential. But for the next eighteen months, Edith accepted her Cyrano's benevolent tyranny.

After her triumphant Bastille Day show in the provincial town of Tulle (in Corrèze, central France), the couple took a brief vacation at the Château de Lafont in Chenevelles. This estate belonged to the family of Edith's new pianist, Max d'Yresnes, whose mother received paying guests. Engagements in Geneva, Deauville, Ostende, and Brussels took up the rest of the summer until it became obvious that, having worked continuously since the New Year (sometimes with two gigs a day), Edith needed a rest.

Asso arranged for her to return by herself to the château in Septem-ber. The political situation had been tense since Hitler's annexation of Austria in March. When it became clear that he planned to do the same in the Sudetenland, two and a half million Frenchmen, all those under the age of sixty, were mobilized. Meanwhile, the Popular Front gov-ernment had collapsed. The new government, under Edmond Dal-adier, temporized, while Neville Chamberlain sought peace at any price with Germany.

Since Asso controlled all aspects of Edith's career, including the purse strings, she wrote to ask him for funds to buy fabric for a dress, adding that the seamstress would charge very little to make it. In another letter, she expressed her lack of ease with her hostess, who treated her like a child, and her concern for the future, her own and that of France. "What news of the war?" she asked. "If things go badly, I won't have a penny, no one to take me in. I'd be in bad shape. I spoke a lot about this at dinner yesterday. No one said a word. I'm really disgusted with the people here."

She had only her faith to rely on, the simple spirituality to which she turned when in crisis. One day at church she prayed to the figure of Jesus on the cross: "I cried a lot and then I talked. I said to him, 'Don't let this war happen.' Then I looked at his feet, his hands, his face full of suffering. Finally, I thought about everything he had endured without holding it against anyone." Still, she was afraid—of the poison gas the Germans were said to be stocking, "afraid of Paris, of everything . . . a huge anxiety in my heart." She blamed herself for her misery and that of the world. "God gave me everything and I'm destroying my own happiness. . . . The earth is full of filth like me. That's why there are wars."

Asso's letters did not always bring the comfort she sought. Edith's vulnerability is evident in her reply to one that denounced her faults. "My dear love," she wrote, "how much it must have cost you to write such awful things. But you're right, I'm stupid. I always told you I was, and you tried to convince me that I was intelligent. Besides, the fact that I did all those dumb things before I met you only proves my lack of intelligence. It's time I made amends to all the people I hurt through the years. . . . But you're going too far to say all the things you said in your letter. I hate myself, I have no confidence in myself whatsoever." (She nonetheless found the strength to say that she disliked Max d'Yresnes's music for Asso's latest song. "I told him so," she wrote, "and he didn't like it at all.")

Edith returned to Paris on September 30, the day that Daladier signed the Munich Pact, which appeared to have purchased peace by ceding the Sudetenland to Hitler. The French gave Daladier a hero's welcome and went back to work under the illusion that war had been prevented. For the next few months, the Germans mobilized to occupy Czechoslovakia while the French censors kept worrisome news out of the papers.

Edith began preparing for two important engagements—top billing at the Européen from October 21 to 27, and, the following week, at the

Bobino Theater in Montparnasse. Asso hired a young woman named Suzanne Flon (soon to be a well-known actress) as her secretary, though Piaf later joked that Suzanne's real job was to keep an eye on her.

The actress appreciated her charge's gaiety. Each day, when she arrived to find Edith doing her exercises, the singer dictated several lines of the songs she had begun composing, and Suzanne typed them with two fingers. Edith was also writing a novel about a working-class woman's life, which did not go beyond the first few pages. When her new friend left to pursue her acting career, Edith gave her an auto-graphed photo of herself that read, "For Suzanne, who doesn't type very well, who isn't a very good secretary, but whom I love very much just the same."

Even though Edith's schedule of recording sessions, radio pro-grams, and singing engagements left little time for friendship, she found relief from Asso's watchfulness with his collaborator, Mar-guerite Monnot. Piaf later called the woman she nicknamed Guite "my best friend and, of all the women in the world, the one I admire the most." In her view the musician was "the living incarnation of the art." It was all the more remarkable that, having been a child prodigy who gave piano concerts throughout Europe, Monnot had abandoned her classical career to write songs like "L'Etranger," which had brought them together. Guite's tales of her upbringing—her parents both taught music; friends came to their house each night to play and sing—would have enchanted Edith, who admired those who grew up with a knowledge of the arts. But their friendship was complicated by Guite's artistic partnership with Asso in these years, when they were creating the repertoire that built Piaf's reputation.

After her successful engagements at the Européen and the Bobino that autumn, Edith recovered sufficiently from her self-doubt to ask Asso about the terms of her contracts—a matter she had, until then, left to him. He took her questions as a sign of her desire for greater freedom. Manipulating her feelings of gratitude, he pleaded for one more year of obedience—after which she could go her own way. "I think you would be wrong to want to free yourself completely," he told her, "but I will accept what you decide."

During this time Edith turned to Jacques Bourgeat for advice. She found respite with him outside Paris, in the Vallée de Chevreuse, where the two friends often spent weekends walking, reading, and sitting in companionable silence. "Far from the noise, far from the world," Bourgeat wrote, "with only a pile of books for company . . . an old man and a young girl recall memories and measure the paths they have trod. It's a time devoted to study. From the writings of Sainte-Beuve they learn about those great figures of French literature who came to the region, whose spirits linger there"—Ronsard, Molière, Baudelaire, Rimbaud, Verlaine. "Even Plato has followed the hermits there, with his *Apology* and *Banquet* under his arm," Bourgeat continued. "What a noble company! And how dear those evenings before the fire we build to gaze upon while Piaf draws from these books the treasures of knowledge."

By the end of the year, when Edith turned twenty-three, it may have struck her that, unlike Bourgeat, Asso asked more than he gave in return. In his own account of this period, the composer had become her "moral jailer"—talking her into submission to his regime by claiming that it was for her own good. Years later, he said that he had "committed professional suicide" to devote himself to Edith. She remained faithful to him, despite the tensions in their partnership. But by the spring of 1939, when Edith was again performing almost nonstop, his vision of her as his creation had become too constraining.

Reviewing Piaf's April engagement at the Européen, the critic Léon-Martin said that her place in the music world was now established. He noted the presence in the audience of groups of mobilized soldiers on leave. Perhaps they saw themselves in Asso's characters, his devil-may-care legionnaires. Though there was not yet a distinctive Piaf sound, audiences liked programs in which Asso's *réaliste* songs and evocations of exotic lands were interspersed with lighter numbers that showed off Piaf's talent as a *comédienne* and, as her tone became less nasal, the increased richness and roundness of her voice.

Edith's Cyrano was mobilized in August, when she was singing in Deauville. While Asso joined his unit in the French Alps, she continued her tour to Ostende, Brussels, and back to Deauville, by which time the Germans and the Soviets had concluded a Nonaggression

Treaty. On September 1, Hitler invaded Poland. On September 3, Great Britain and France declared war on Germany. As France entered the period known as *la drôle de guerre*—the funny, or phony, war— Edith continued to sing the songs that Asso had written for her. But she had turned the page on their relationship, perhaps without even knowing it.

CHAPTER SIX

1939–1942

For the rest of the year, the French pretended that nothing much had happened. Germany was not ready for combat, they insisted; in the event of an invasion, France would be safe behind the reinforced Maginot Line. Parisian nightspots, which had closed for three weeks following the declaration of war, reopened in late September. "We understood that terrible things were happening in Poland and Austria," Maurice Chevalier recalled, "but Parisians don't really care about anything but Paris." He added, "I guess we feel that we are doing our share by giving laughter and gaiety to the nation."

Piaf's war years began with engagements at Le Night Club, an American-style cabaret near the Arc de Triomphe, and the Européen, in the Place Clichy, where soldiers on leave called out for their favorite songs. On October 29, before her Night Club gig, she did a benefit with Charles Trenet in aid of the first French prisoners. Though she claimed not to know much about politics, songs like "Le Fanion de la légion" (which glorified the French Foreign Legion, symbolized by their flag) seemed to take on new meaning in the phony war. But, like Chevalier, she was just doing her share. "My job is to sing," she insisted, "to sing whatever happens!"

As rumors of peace settlements circulated, only to be denied the next day, Edith kept in touch with Asso. Describing her December opening at the Etoile-Palace in a letter, she praised his new composition, "Je n'en connais pas la fin" ("I Don't Know What the End Will Be," an ironic title given the political situation). "It's better than anything you've done till now," she wrote. "It'll be my big hit." Above all, she was stunned by her own success: "a full house every night."

Edith's letters did not mention the changes in her life since Asso's mobilization. Unable to tolerate being alone, she got back in touch with Momone, who moved into his room at the Alsina. The two friends began carousing and carrying on all night in Pigalle after Edith's performances—until she met the man who would take Asso's place and, as he had done, remove her from Momone's influence.

Late one evening, the entertainer Paul Meurisse went to Le Night Club, near where he was performing, to have a look at the former Môme Piaf. Knowing her reputation as a *réaliste* singer with a street-wise accent, he was impressed by the silence: "not a word," he noted, "not even the clink of bottles, the sound of the maître d' filling glasses." All eyes were on the little figure at the end of the room: "Through the magic of her voice, she turned these customers into spectators. They were enchanted." As was Meurisse. "She was radiant, as if she had stepped out of an El Greco painting," he continued. When Edith turned up beside him at the bar, they began a flirtation that led to their polishing off a bottle of champagne at his *garconnière*.

Meurisse was so smitten that he wanted to move in with her, despite the great differences in their backgrounds. "Edith Piaf doesn't live at Paul Meurisse's," she protested. The son of a banker who had broken with his family after winning a singing contest, the dapper twenty-eight-year-old joined her and Momone in Pigalle, then quickly found a solution for himself and Edith—a furnished apartment near the Arc de Triomphe.

The couple moved in together, engaging a cook (it was unthinkable for Edith to prepare meals) and a secretary (whose main job was to open correspondence). From then on, she would forsake the rougher parts of Paris for the *beaux quartiers,* the fashionable areas near the Champs-Elysées where she had once sung for the spare change she received from well-heeled passersby.

Meurisse was not the only spectator to be enchanted by Edith that season. In November, a Spanish journalist wrote an account of Le Night Club's beguiling songstress: "She makes her way among the tables and steps onto the stage without a smile or a bow. . . . Her voice, full of a gravity that becomes profound, raises the curtain on scenes that are highly picturesque, but terribly sad." Though she seemed about to burst into tears, Piaf remained silent at the end of each number while the audience clapped wildly. In his view, Asso's songs suited her because they shared "the realism of a tormented life, of loneliness, of an errant, unprotected destiny."

In private, Edith showed a great deal more joie de vivre than onstage, Meurisse noted. Social opposites, they were astonished to find themselves together but shared the same desire to laugh. An occasion presented itself during their first week at the Alsina, when Piaf heard a familiar knock at the door. Asso was in Paris on leave; Meurisse just managed to slip into Momone's room. His memoirs restage this scene as French farce, giving Edith the classic line "*Ciel! Mon mari!*" ("Heavens! My husband!"), and crediting Asso with the last laugh—the next day, the jilted composer came to his rival's club to say that he should not leave telltale cigarette butts in the ashtrays. Asso "withdrew without any fuss," Meurisse wrote, underestimating his predecessor's hard feelings.

Meurisse also recalled Edith's delight as she toured their new apartment. She had seen bourgeois dwellings before, but never had one to herself, with a dining room, a large bathroom, guest rooms, and a grand piano in the salon. "I won't have to go to the composers' any more," she exulted; "they can come to me!"

The couple made efforts to adapt to each other. Although Edith liked to ridicule middle-class propriety, she accepted customs like letting the man pull out her chair or help her into her coat. Meurisse exercised tact when teaching her not to mistake a finger bowl for a palate cleanser. Her more outrageous gaffes made them laugh, especially when she repeated them deliberately, to thumb her nose at stuffy guests. "It wasn't so much that *le savoir-vivre* was imposed on her," Meurisse wrote; "rather, that she imposed herself on *le savoir-vivre*."

Meurisse was awed by Piaf's professionalism. She rehearsed all night without complaint. "She would laugh and begin again," he recalled; songwriters had to keep up with her. If a novice had a glimmer of an idea, she refused to let him go until it came to fruition. "Over and over, she interrupted meals to force the writer back to the piano. . . . I never saw Piaf in a bad mood because hours and hours of work hadn't produced anything." But she was pitiless when a song was not quite right: "In her work, as in her life, her ability to put the past behind her went beyond anything a dictator might have attempted." The one exception to her dictatorial ways was her friendship with Marguerite Monnot, whom she admired "as one admires perfection."

Meurisse was pleased when Piaf broke her contract at Le Night Club to join him at his cabaret. She also took on the role of artistic mentor, doing so as mercilessly as Asso had done with her. Her lover's routine was "shit," she told him. Given Meurisse's character—aloof and patronizing—he should try for a comic effect by underscoring the contrast between his silly songs and his natural hauteur with grandiose orchestral settings. "Idiotic words supported by orchestrations meant to be played in cathedrals" broke the rules, but it worked. Meurisse credited his success to Piaf's musical intelligence.

By the new year, Edith was contemplating changes in her own routine. She already knew the Russian-born composer Michel Emer, whose songs for Lucienne Boyer and Maurice Chevalier had been well received, although Edith thought them too sentimental. Emer turned up late one night in February 1940 with a tune that he had composed for her: having just been mobilized, he had to join his unit the next day. Piaf listened to the first stanza—*"La fille de joie est belle / Au coin d'la rue là-bas / Elle a une clientèle / Qui lui remplit son bas."* ("The lady of the night is *belle* / Over there on the street corner / She has a clientele / Who keep her pockets full.") She knew right away that she wanted the song (which would become "L'Accordéoniste") for her next engagement at the Bobino Theater.

Emer's tale of the prostitute whose dream of starting afresh ends with the death of her lover (an accordionist turned soldier) resembled Asso's songs for Piaf yet marked a new, more deeply expressive, stage in her performances—an opportunity to coordinate voice, hands, and stage presence to underline the song's pathos. That night, because Emer had not thought how she was to perform the final lines, *"ARRETEZ! / Arrêtez la musique!"* ("STOP! Stop the music"), she made him stay until they found the solution. The orchestra would stop abruptly and she would sing them a cappella.

Emer prolonged his departure to see Piaf introduce his song on opening night, February 16. After several numbers by Asso and Monnot, she launched into "L'Accordéoniste." With the first refrain—"*Ça lui rentre dans la peau / Par le bas, par le haut / Elle a envie de chanter . . . / . . . C'est une vraie tordue de la musique*" ("[The music] gets under her skin / From her head to her toes / She feels like singing . . . / . . . She's just nuts about music")—she ran her hands up and down her slender form. Until then, Piaf had held her hands at her sides. Now they enacted her possession by the music, her abandonment to it. With a minimum of gestures, she sketched the *fille de joie*'s bliss, then her unbearable sorrow.

Piaf's intensity is still palpable in recordings of 'L'Accordéoniste," especially the wrenching sob of the last lines. "The response was delirious," Emer recalled. Piaf asked the composer to come onstage and introduced him as a soldier about to go to the front; the crowd applauded all over again. He and Piaf became close friends; he would write many of her favorite songs. "Her kindness to me was outstanding," Emer said years later. Though she was despotic in rehearsals, she would always go out of her way to help him.

At twenty-four, the diminutive singer already had a commanding presence—often too commanding, especially when she broke all the dishes during an argument to provoke a reaction from her lover. (Meurisse bought more china at the Galeries Lafayette, knowing that Edith was likely to smash it as well.) "Living with him changed the way I looked at life," she told a reporter. "His indolent courtesy was so completely different from all the rogues I had known in Montmartre . . . that I soon fell in love with his face, that of the favorite child. It bore no relation to my old ideas of the perfect man but opened the doors to a world of refinement, whose existence I had never imagined."

Still other doors opened for her. One evening Madame Raoul Breton, the wife of Piaf's music publisher, asked her to dinner to meet Jean Cocteau, at his request. The "prince of poets," who often sought new energy in popular art, was as entranced with Edith as she was with him. By the end of the meal they were addressing each other with the intimate *tu*. A friendship began that evening that would last the rest of their lives.

Piaf was a being of "regal simplicity," Cocteau wrote. On first hearing her, he was stunned "by the power emanating from that minuscule body," and by her eyes, "the eyes of a blind person struck by a miracle, the eyes of a clairvoyant." Edith was flattered to have the leader of the artistic avant-garde enamored of her; she admired his elegance, his erudition, his wide-ranging artistic gifts. That winter, Cocteau often visited Piaf and Meurisse after their gigs at the cabaret. The poet was "at the summit of art and intelligence," Meurisse wrote. "To know him was to enter the realm of magic." Since Cocteau equaled Molière in Piaf's opinion, she asked him to write a song for her, as she had done with Bourgeat: surely men of learning who wrote poetry would also be good at songwriting.

Cocteau would instead produce a one-act play for two actors based on Piaf's relations with Meurisse, whose icy calm suggested the title, *Le Bel Indifférent*. Originally conceived as a *chanson parlée* (a "spoken song"), the play is a monologue directed at a "handsome, indifferent man" by the lover he ignores—Piaf's role. "A magnificent gigolo on the verge of no longer being so," he reads his newspaper while she becomes increasingly desperate because of his lack of response. When she promises to do everything he wants, he walks out, slamming the door.

After befriending the couple, Cocteau rewrote an earlier draft of the play, one of his many dramatic works on the theme of unrequited love, to take advantage of Piaf's reputation. He made the female character a cabaret singer in a little black dress and called for a realistic set, a hotel room of the sort she had inhabited in Pigalle. Her persona inspired the playwright to realize his "dream theater," he wrote—"a play that disappears behind the actress, . . . who seems to improvise her role each night." At first Edith was unsure how to hold the audience for the thirty minutes it took to declaim her monologue. But, though the role was a challenge, Cocteau was delighted: "She executed it with the ease of acrobats who exchange their trapezes in midair." The play opened on April 20. "Mademoiselle Piaf is excellent!" *Marianne* exclaimed. "Her acting is both passionate and precise," *Le Figaro* noted. Piaf was "magnificent," according to *Les Nouvelles littéraires*, whose critic could not resist saying that she came by her tragic air naturally.

Meurisse did not record his feelings about playing opposite his lover, except to say that not speaking for half an hour made him tense. His habitual sangfroid was further tested when he was mobilized after only six performances, and Piaf declared that he was better at acting than at singing.

Le Bel Indifférent ran until May 14 with another actor in the male role. By then the Germans had occupied the Low Countries, and northern France was under assault. Following a Red Cross benefit at the Bobino and a return engagement there, Edith left for two weeks in Provence while Hitler's troops marched on the capital. Soon a million Parisians were fleeing before their advance. She returned to Paris on June 12—two days before the victorious Germans hung a huge swastika from the Arc de Triomphe and marched in formation down the Champs-Elysées.

After the fall of Paris, all places of entertainment closed. Following the announcement of the armistice on June 17, France was divided into Occupied and Unoccupied zones, with three-fifths of the country under German rule and a pro-German regime in Vichy. Those who could leave Paris did so as soon as possible.

Edith made her way to Toulouse, where Meurisse was stationed. Finding her old friend Jacques Canetti among the horde of refugees, she asked him to find her a gig. Hotel rooms cost a fortune; she needed cash. Soon she was sharing the stage at a movie house with her lover. For the next two months Meurisse accompanied her on a tour of southern France, the first of the many tours of the *zone libre* (Unoccupied Zone) that Piaf would make during the Occupation. It took them to Perpignan (where they ran into Cocteau), Montpellier, Toulon, Nîmes, Béziers, and Narbonne. By September, she had had enough of touring. Refusing to be intimidated, she declared to her lover, "Krauts or no Krauts, the capital of France is Paris."

They arrived in Paris on September 17 to find most public buildings draped with swastikas. From their lunch table at Fouquet's, they watched a German officer on horseback lead a company of soldiers to the Place de la Concorde. "It was a terrible shock," Meurisse recalled.

"We pretended to be indifferent, but although we already knew that we had lost, we understood at this very moment that with defeat comes humiliation."

It became apparent that Paris was now on German time—one hour earlier than in the past. The next day, when the couple began rehearsing for a joint engagement at L'Aiglon, they learned that all programs had to be submitted to the Propaganda Staffel (censor). To maintain an air of normality, the cabarets, cinemas, and theaters had been reopened by the occupiers, who were astounded by the the Paris audiences' defiant chic—their way of showing that their spirits would not be cowed.

"At this time, the occupiers had clean hands," Meurisse wrote. "We would soon see the arrival of the other sort." In this context, Piaf's songs evoked prewar Paris, *Aujourd'hui* observed: "the sharp wind blowing round the corners of poorly lit streets, . . . the touching images of her rhymes, tales from despairing penny novels." Her girl-of-the-streets persona helped audiences reimagine the city that had, until recently, been theirs.

Piaf's official return, a gala at the Salle Pleyel, took place later in September. More nervous about appearing at this prestigious theater than about the Germans, she felt "excessively fearful," she explained: "Standing there for an hour in my schoolgirl's mourning dress . . . trying, without artifice, interlude, or trickery—with only sixteen popular songs—to please all those strangers who came just for me, seemed such a hopeless task, one at which I was so likely to fail, that before going onstage, I told myself that the organizer was crazy." Once onstage, she went into a trance; the hour passed quickly. She ended with "Le Fanion de la légion," its vision of the besieged garrison that holds out against the enemy stirring thoughts that France too would one day "cry victory." The audience gave her a standing ovation.

"Edith Piaf has more astonishments in store," *Paris-Soir* wrote of this concert. "She possesses the best quality an artist can have—sincerity." This tribute from a newspaper with strong collaborationist leanings may have made her feel that she need not worry about the censors.

For the rest of the year, Piaf performed without incident at L'Aiglon, the A.B.C., and the Folies Belleville—until December 6, opening night of the A.B.C.'s winter revue. Edith went onstage after a singer whose servile attack on the English, intended to please the German officers present, unsettled the audience. She began with "Le Fanion." The audience held their breath as she evoked the legionnaires' defiance of "*les salopards*" ("the bastards"); when she turned to face the Germans, the crowd erupted in condemnatory whistles—the song's iconic flag again stirring thoughts of victory over the swastika. The next day, the Kommandantur ordered her to remove "Le Fanion" from her repertoire.

All forms of cultural expression were now being vetted by the Germans. Giving in to the pressure for self-censorship, the Society of Authors, Composers, and Editors of Music (SACEM), which handled song rights, blocked disbursals to Jewish composers even before the Germans could tell them to do so. Works by Jewish songwriters were also *verboten* on the radio. Three of Piaf's songs were prohibited: "Mon Légionnaire" and "Le Fanion" for their references to a unit of the French army, and "L'Accordéoniste" because its author was Jewish. (By then Emer had gone into hiding.) When Edith's friend Pierre Hiégel, the popular radio host, accidentally played her 1936 satire "Il n'est pas distingué," listeners were stunned to hear her intone, "I can't stand Hitler." The censors took note but did nothing.

Though Piaf detested the occupiers, she had to go on singing—to earn her keep, and because she could not do otherwise. "On the one hand," her friend Henri Contet explained, "she felt an instinctive hatred of the Krauts. . . . On the other, she was hardly bothered by the Occupation." Her loathing for the Germans kept her from making the compromises that would call other singers' careers into question; she was relatively undisturbed, because the occupiers meant to maintain the appearance of normality by distracting the French with uncontroversial entertainment.

At the same time, the situation changed dramatically for Jewish Parisians. Starting in the autumn of 1940, the Germans issued a series of decrees defining Jewish identity and ordering all Jews to register at the Préfecture de Police. Overnight, Jewish shops were marked with signs indicating their owners' origins; soon many business and cultural activities, ranging from banking to attendance at the Conservatory of Music, were *verboten* for Jews.

Through the spring of 1941, Edith kept busy with appearances in Paris and the provinces. Feeling the need to refresh her repertoire, she missed her composers, who either had been called up or were seeking refuge in the Unoccupied Zone. Among the songs she recorded in May, the passionately felt "Où sont-ils mes petits copains?" was unusual because it spoke of war's impact on friendship, but even more so because Piaf penned the lyrics and had them set to military music by Monnot: "*Où sont-ils tous mes copains / Qui sont partis un matin / Faire la guerre? / Où sont-ils tous mes p'tits gars / Qui chantaient, 'On en r'viendra / Faut pas s'en faire.'*" ("Where are all my pals? / They left one morning / For the war / Where are all those dear guys / Who were singing, 'We'll be back / Don't worry.'") The missing *copains*—they hail from all over Paris—form the throng imagined in the final line, "*Le voilà! Les voilà!,*" an up-tempo vision of prewar life. By comparison, Piaf's bluesy "J'ai dansé avec l'amour," also set by Monnot, mimes a dancing couple's embrace in its swaying rhythms—a song that could be aired on the radio without complaint from the censor.

When the film director Georges Lacombe asked Edith to star in *Montmartre-sur-Seine,* about a flower girl who becomes a singer, the opportunity to perform her own songs onscreen proved irresistible. She and Monnot collaborated on the score, which includes "J'ai dansé avec l'amour," and two romantic waltz tunes, "Un Coin tout bleu" and "Tu es partout." Obtaining a role for Meurisse did not improve their deteriorating relationship. He criticized her interpretation of the heroine, Lily—who falls in love with her accompanist though he is enamored of someone else. When Meurisse said that she had made fish eyes in a love scene, Edith exploded. Their fight ended only after he sat on her and both burst out laughing.

Another cast member, the young Jean-Louis Barrault (whose character admires Lily in vain), took a more favorable view: "Everything she did or sang touched the heart." Edith could have been a fine actress, he thought: "She was extremely sensitive, which I understood since we both came from modest backgrounds." Looking back, he admired her integrity, the way "she remained 'Piaf' for the rest of her days, following her infallible instinct."

Montmartre-sur-Seine summed up Piaf's prewar life by capitalizing on her reputation as a street singer who beguiles audiences from all backgrounds, even those suffering from class resentments. In a nostalgic sequence filmed on a bridge over the Seine, she croons the lilting "Tu es partout" to the unresponsive hero (played by Henri Vidal); in the next scene, the scenario underscores the modesty of Lily's (and Edith's) background by having her peddle sheet music to the crowd in her *titi-parisien* accent. "Je ne veux plus laver la vaisselle," another of her songs composed with Monnot, was omitted from the film because of its insubordinate tone, which was enhanced by Monnot's rising lines and tempo: "*Je ne veux plus vider les poubelles / Je veux qu'on m'appelle Mademoiselle.*" ("I don't want to empty the garbage / I want to be called Mademoiselle.") Piaf's lyrics, which read like a declaration of independence by a *réaliste* heroine, marked the start of her attempt to distance herself from that tradition's emphasis on the squalid side of life, its *misérabilisme*.

Henri Contet, then a journalist sent by *Paris-Midi* to visit the film set, failed to see how anyone could resist her. The pavement might be cardboard, he wrote, but "this false street set became real as soon as she sang." (Paul Meurisse, on the other hand, seemed unemotional.) Contet pondered the film's "complicated, tortuous" plot, the hero's lack of interest in the singer. "But after all," he concluded, "isn't real life, the way we live it, often more complicated, difficult, and heartbreaking than the passions that are invented for us?"

Contet, a handsome blond with an elegant air, was attracted to Piaf, who was still living with Meurisse. That autumn, he wrote several more articles about *Montmartre-sur-Seine*. In "Edith Piaf Weeps for Her Lost Love," Contet's narrative restages the scene when her impassive lover leaves her. "What to do," he wrote with tongue in cheek, "console her? But how? I thought of all those songs to which the star gave her own tears, her immense heart, the admirable strength she can find in herself." Half jest, half confession, Contet's article impressed its subject. After reading his poems, she gave him a nickname, Riri, and asked him to write a song for her—the start of yet another complicated, difficult relationship.

Montmartre-sur-Seine opened in Paris in November 1941. By then Piaf had begun another tour of the Unoccupied Zone, where life was freer despite the Vichy government's attempts to enforce its credo, "*Travail, Famille, Patrie.*" The pro-Nazi newspaper *Je suis partout* declared that even though the film was untainted by the presence of Jewish artists, it nevertheless inflicted on audiences "that little person with cavernous eyes, a macabre big head tucked into her hunched shoulders." Other pro-German mouthpieces described her in similarly anti-Semitic language. "Piaf should have stayed a working-class singer peddling songs on street corners," *Révolution nationale* ranted. "Miraculously, she avoided such a fate thanks to the snobs who took her up." But, having had the effrontery to show herself onscreen, she was now "the perfect incarnation of our decadent epoch."

If Edith had learned that she had become the personification of non-Aryan-ness, she would, no doubt, have burst out laughing—"that laugh that never left her," Paul Meurisse observed, "even at the most tragic of times." Her lover went with her to Lyon, the first stop on their joint tour: she was again accompanied by Norbert Glanzberg, the German pianist with whom she had worked while singing with Django Reinhardt in Pigalle. She and Meurisse performed at Toulon, Nîmes, and Marseille before his return to Paris for another engagement. Piaf was at loose ends, as was Glanzberg, but for different reasons.

Having made his way to the *zone nono* (French slang for the *zone non occupée*) Glanzberg, who was Jewish, knew he had to watch his back—especially in a place like Marseille, where thousands of refugees awaited passage out of the country. In October, at the louche Café des Artistes, he had met the Corsicans who ran show business on the Riviera. One of them, the impresario Daniel Marouani, had hired him to accompany Piaf on her tour, starting in Lyon.

Within a short time, Glanzberg joined her entourage—the musicians and handlers, driver, cook, and secretary who functioned as her court, and whose expenses she paid. At twenty-five, Edith commanded such high fees that she could fill her hotel rooms with flowers and treat friends to black-market items like champagne. Glanzberg remarked years later, "She knew that because of the way she abused her health for the sake of her career, she wouldn't have much time to enjoy what she earned." (He seemed unaware that she had never acquired bourgeois habits like putting away funds for one's old age.)

Piaf and her new pianist shared little but a love of music and a gift for survival. Glanzberg, a classically trained composer who became an accompanist and songwriter after fleeing to Paris, scorned French popular music and the cabarets of Pigalle, where he had earned his living in recent years. Once the SACEM blocked access to his French song rights, Edith became his lifeline. But in his opinion she did not measure up: a scrawny little thing who lacked good manners, she sang like a fishwife. (Her intelligence and sense of humor nonetheless impressed him.) Still, at each performance, when Glanzberg worried that his features would betray him, he gained strength from her presence: "When Edith leaned on the piano, the better to create that intimacy that bound her to the music, to her music, I was seized by a mysterious, enchanting power." In those moments, he was sure that nothing bad would happen.

Because Edith had a horror of being alone, her entourage was expected to stay up late with her. One night, when Glanzberg was preparing to leave, she dismissed the others and told him to stay since it was after the curfew. "What could I do? It was Edith Piaf or Adolf Hitler," Glanzberg ungallantly told a journalist. He did not love her, but made the best of the situation—a little less than a love affair, a little more than a fling.

Paul Meurisse, tipped off by a mutual acquaintance, was sufficiently upset by the news of their affair to come to Monte Carlo, where Edith was performing in March 1942. When he knocked on the door of her hotel room, it was "*Ciel! Mon mari!*" with the roles reversed. The next day, Meurisse assumed an outraged air without quite pulling it off, because his wife-to-be was waiting for him in Paris. Had he and Edith loved each other? "We were opposites," he wrote. "I could easily believe that each of us wanted to astonish the other." (About this time, Piaf astonished a local journalist named Léo Ferré: the singer was "without any question a tragedienne," he wrote, "whose profoundly human art comes from the depths of her heart." In 1945, when Piaf encouraged Ferré to become a songwriter, he moved to Paris. Within a few years, he had become known for his settings of French poetry, and by the 1950s, he was a noted composer and performer.)

Over the next two years, Norbert Glanzberg's career improved dramatically. His association with Piaf led to other engagements, with singers like Charles Trenet and the Corsican crooner Tino Rossi, but at the same time, the *zone nono* became more dangerous. Once the Vichy government excluded Jews from most professions, Glanzberg's name could no longer appear on programs. He became Pierre Minet, relying on a fake French passport obtained through Rossi's network, though his German accent was likely to betray him at any moment.

Edith's concern for her clandestine lover is evident in the nickname she gave him— *"Nono chéri"* or "darling Nono"— and in her correspondence. "I'm worried about you," she wrote him during a separation. "I drink only water and tea, go to bed at midnight, and sleep all night long. Everyone says I look well. It must be love!" Moreover, she was improving as a singer thanks to his high standards. Aware of the increased risk for Jews in Marseille, where the Germans conducted daily searches, she arranged for Glanzberg to take shelter nearby, on a farm that belonged to her secretary, Andrée Bigard, known as Dédée—whose family did their utmost to help Edith's Jewish friends (at her request, they would also shelter the young film director Marcel Blistène).

When Glanzberg's hiding place became too dangerous, Piaf prevailed on a new friend, the Countess Pastré, to hide him at Montredon, her château near the lonely *calanques* (coves) on the coast near Marseille. Lily Pastré was a music lover who maintained good relations with the authorities, some of whom attended concerts at her château. What they did not know was that, at various times, the countess sheltered some forty Jewish composers and musicians as part of a secret artistic network. Delighted to learn that Glanzberg was classically trained, she took him under her wing, along with the superb classical pianist Clara Haskil, whose failing vision she saved by organizing a clandestine operation in the château's basement. Piaf came when she could; visitors heard her rehearsing upstairs in one of the Pastré children's bedrooms.

But even at Montredon, one had to be careful. Every morning Glanzberg left to hide in the cove where the countess left provisions, unaware that Edith was paying for his protection (Lily had to obtain ration cards and supplies for each new boarder). In November, when the Germans invaded the south, he fled to Nice under the protection of Rossi's Corsicans. Edith continued to pay for his support, often sending Dédée to look into his welfare while also helping other Jewish friends.

That year Edith wrote a song whose title, "Le Vagabond," hints at thoughts of escape from the grimness of life under the occupation. "*J'ai l'air comm' ça d'un' fille de rien / Mais je suis un' personn' très bien*," it began. "*Je suis princesse d'un château / Où tout est clair, où tout est beau.*" ("I may look like a poor girl / But I'm really someone / A princess in her château / Where all is clear, all is *beau*.") The princess thinks of her troubadour lover and of joining him on the road: "*Et c'est mon coeur qu'il écoute / Notre amour dans le vent / Nous sommes vagabonds / Nous chantons nos chansons.*" ("He hears my heart / Our love is in the wind / Vagabonds / We sing our songs.") A dream of freedom in hazardous times, its vision improved upon the reality of childhood travels with her father.

"Whatever people say or imply about her," Dédée Bigard wrote of this time, when she became Piaf's confidante as well as her secretary, "she was a woman of great purity." And, it should be said, one whose support of friends created ties that would outlive their years of angst and vagabondage.

CHAPTER SEVEN

1942–1944

While Edith toured the *zone libre* the summer of 1942, conditions worsened in the north, especially for Jews. Since May they had been made to wear a yellow six-pointed star with the word *Juif* stitched in black letters. Newspapers ran campaigns on the "Jewish peril." An exhibition presenting Jews as cheats, criminals, and sexual deviants drew thousands of Parisians before its successful tour of the country. People whispered about raids, but few knew of the Nazis' plans to arrest some thirty thousand Parisian Jews until two days after Bastille Day, when the combined forces of the gendarmerie, the mobile guard, and the police herded their victims to the Drancy internment camp, northeast of Paris.

By then, although some non-Jews wore yellow stars in protest, most Parisians were more concerned with food shortages, power cuts, and the difficulty of getting anywhere because of minimal public transport. To supplement the diet obtainable with ration coupons, those who could afford it turned to the black market for butter, eggs, and cheese. *Marie Claire* told readers how to stay healthy by balancing menus, assuming they could find the ingredients, and offered "easy recipes for difficult times"—a substitute for wine made of pea pods, a soup composed of nettles. Riding a bicycle would keep one fit, the magazine explained, and since it was impossible to get stockings, backs of legs could be painted with a dark line.

"Edith Piaf is coming back to us," headlines announced in October. Her reappearance in the capital after more than a year's absence was the singer's way of showing solidarity with her fellow citizens. When she and Dédée stepped off the train, "all of Paris was waiting at the station," she wrote to Glanzberg. "It was wonderful!" she continued. "I had to give a press conference at lunch, as if I were a princess!" She could not admit that he failed to return her affection, but her dream of love had come true on a different scale, with her overjoyed reception by the adoring crowd.

The press treated Piaf's opening night as the event of the season. She came onstage with renewed self-assurance for her reunion with the public that had been awaiting her. After a few standards from prewar days, she sang all new songs, including Emer's "Le Disque usé"—a risky choice in that it ended with Edith's imitating a broken record, but even more so because the composer was Jewish. (What was more, its heroine, another poor girl waiting for her lover, maintained a proud, haughty stance—"*fière et hautaine*"—that could be taken as a kind of resistance.) The program also featured Edith's compositions, including "Je ne veux plus laver la vaisselle" and "Le Vagabond," whose dream of escape inspired rapturous applause. She took a greater risk by performing "Où sont-ils mes petits copains?" with the stage lit in blue, white, and red—the colors of the French flag. The next day, she was summoned to the Propaganda Staffel and told to replace the lights with a neutral spot.

Journalists treated Piaf's A.B.C. engagement as her homecoming. The very genre of song had returned, a critic noted, "in the person of the one who created it." Piaf's was "the best *tour de chant* since Yvette Guilbert, Damia, and Yvonne George," another wrote—and one that eschewed the current vogue for talky introductions and other forms of "trickery." She simply came onstage and sang "straight from the heart."

Similarly, *Paris-Midi* praised the star's ability to imbue old material with a new nobility—"a purity of intention, breadth, and sobriety." The A.B.C. program showed "her perfect command of the 'Piaf style,'" now more moving than ever. One wonders what Edith made of the "Piaf style," whether she laughed at the idea or took it as a tribute to her professionalism. "She no longer looks like a child," another critic wrote. Her program showed "an intelligence that no longer owes

everything to 'nature,' that from now on knows exactly what it wants."
At a time when singers rarely wrote their own songs, Piaf's creative
zeal was exceptional. Yet few understood the extent to which the matu-
rity evident in her programming had been shaped by her collaboration
with her composers—Asso, Monnot, and Glanzberg, who was still in
hiding in the *zone libre*.

Edith soon concocted an unlikely plan for her Nono—to bring him
back to Paris, where he could hide in Monnot's apartment. In November, when the Germans occupied all of France, she told him, "I'm terribly afraid after what's happened. I can't come because I can't get a
laissez-passer. . . . I beg of you, don't make mistakes that could have
dire consequences." He was her *"seul amour,"* she assured him, but, as
Glanzberg knew, *"seul"* was an elastic term in her vocabulary. What
he did not know was that she had resumed her affair with Contet.

Buoyed by her success at the A.B.C., and with fourteen of her own
songs in her portfolio, Piaf applied to the SACEM for professional status as a lyricist but failed the test—a composition on a set theme, "the
train station." Contet tried to make up for this setback by writing the
lyrics for "C'était une histoire d'amour," a slow, swingy tune that
declared his affections. Admitting that love stories like theirs were not
likely to last, the song ended on a resigned note: *"Il faut toujours que
quelqu'un pleure / Pour faire une histoire d'amour."* ("Someone always
has to cry/ To make a love story.") Piaf recorded the song with a male
singer echoing her acceptance of this proverbial sentiment at the end.
Over the next few years, Contet would write a number of songs that
gave a more complex dimension to the "Piaf style." Because his lyrics
explored their stories' undercurrents, they were more ambiguous than
the *réaliste* classics with which she was identified, and for this reason
did not always find favor with the critics.

When Piaf's A.B.C. engagement ended in November, her next concern was to arrange for housing. Contet loved her but would not leave
his wife; Piaf could not bear to be alone. Her decision to rent an apartment near the Place de l'Etoile where discreet afternoon visits could be
arranged offered a solution that was not without charm, since it was on
the third floor of a high-class brothel. The proprietor, Madame Billy,
was on excellent terms with the occupiers. In addition to being well

supplied with food and drink, her establishment had heat, a luxury in the harsh winter of 1942–43. Life there would reinvent the conviviality of Maman Tine's on a grand scale.

Piaf invited Momone, who resurfaced whenever the star was alone, to join her. Momone introduced herself to Madam Billy as Piaf's "guide fish," but the madam formed the opinion that she was "more of a piranha"—an impression confirmed when Momone stole five pairs of her alligator pumps to sell in Pigalle. Momone and the madam maintained a wary truce once the two friends moved in; Billy was relieved when Dédée Bigard joined them. Edith's well-brought-up young secretary—"the anti-Momone"—was a good influence, the madam thought, gently showing Edith how to behave.

Since Billy's kitchen served meals at all hours, Edith often had lunch there—nearly always the same dish, steak covered with garlic. She drank little except for peppermint sodas and spent much of her time practicing at the grand piano in the salon. When neighbors complained about after-hours concerts, the German patrol knocked on the door but backed down on hearing the singer's name. "They all knew her," Billy recalled, and they often stood outside to listen. "Edith didn't give a damn about the Germans, . . . or about the risks we ran." As an entertainer, she had a pass that let her come and go freely; one of her fans, a Lieutenant Weber, told her to phone if there was any trouble.

Most afternoons, Marguerite Monnot arrived on her motorbike to work with Edith. The composer seemed oblivious to their surroundings except to note that the building was warm. Although she often showed up the day after appointments, Guite would come immediately when Edith phoned at 3 a.m. and stay at the piano until dawn. Once, she turned up on a new motorbike, fretting that it was someone else's, but when told to return it to where she had found it, said she had no idea where that was. She wasn't absentminded, she explained, just thinking about other things. Guite understood Edith perfectly: both women dreamed of finding the passionate romance celebrated in their songs.

Piaf spent her whole life yearning for a great love, Contet mused years later. Once she concluded that he was stringing her along, Edith took another lover—the young man named Yvon Jeanclaude who had sung backup on "C'était une histoire d'amour." Contet learned that he had a rival when he arrived at Madame Billy's one afternoon to find that Edith could not receive him. He turned the situation into a wry song entitled "Le Brun et le blond": depicting himself as the blond with a dark-haired rival for the same woman's affections, he gave the blond man the last word, the note he leaves when he decides that he has had enough. (In performance, Piaf raised one hand to her eye to signify tears, an economical but effective gesture.) She added the song to her repertoire along with Contet's darkly poetic "Coup de grisou," the tale of a coal miner's failed romance, and "Monsieur Saint-Pierre," a saucy prayer to heaven's gatekeeper.

Edith became Contet's muse and mentor in spite of their amorous ups and downs. He should not think of imitating Asso, she counseled; since his light touch did not suit the dark mood of *réaliste* song, he should follow his instincts. Pleased with the subtle direction his songs were taking, she was inspired to write several of her own, including two bittersweet glances at old *amours,* "J'ai qu'à l'regarder" and "C'était si bon"—a jazzy fox-trot that ends on an affirmative note with Piaf's rising glissando on a single word to her man—"*oui.*" Yet at times Contet's domestic commitments enraged her. One freezing day during the Christmas season, when he remained at his own home, Edith took off her clothes and stood on the balcony, supposedly to punish herself for sleeping with a married man.

Even so, Contet kept writing for his tumultuous muse, often with Monnot setting his lyrics in the kind of close collaboration that Edith enjoyed with members of her artistic family. Contet would continue to write for her long after the end of their affair. "We writers, what were we after all?" he said years later. "Our words stammered and stuttered; she turned them into cries and prayers." Though she was often tyrannical with collaborators, Edith was always inspiring: "Her enthusiasm compensated for all the rest. . . . You ended up writing what she wanted."

Piaf considered Contet a modern-day Ronsard, but she liked to distinguish between her two favorite lyricists. Emer wrote songs that spoke to the people; Contet gave her more subtle texts with refrains that one could hold on to. She sang works by both men during her engagement at the Folies Belleville in January 1943. *Comoedia*'s critic, who followed her career closely, found Emer's "De l'autre côté de la rue" and Contet's "Le Brun et le blond" rather difficult for audiences accustomed to more direct fare, though in his view these two songs opened her repertoire to "nuances of feeling . . . with mysterious, almost magical, notes."

From the censors' perspective, Piaf's show the following month at the Casino de Paris was only too direct. The manager illustrated her songs by projecting images onto a screen behind her and sending dancers with oversized accordions onstage as she sang Emer's "L'Accordéoniste." Though the critics did not complain about these changes in her normally minimalist staging, the Propaganda Staffel made strong objections to her singing songs by a Jewish composer. When Piaf refused to remove Emer's work from the program, she was banned from singing until April. In the interim, Suzy Solidor, who was on good terms with the occupiers, took her place. Lieutenant Weber could not help. Piaf was persona non grata.

⌐⌐

Though Piaf's habitual gaiety was not in evidence during her five weeks of enforced rest, Madame Billy did her best to humor her. Given her experience of all types, Billy got on well with everyone except for Momone. Something of a snob, the madam preferred Edith's well-known guests, Jean Cocteau and his lover Jean Marais, and the actors Michel Simon, Marie Bell, and Mary Marquet, of the Comédie-Française. In turn, these prewar celebrities were amused by Billy's trade in what was commonly called "horizontal collaboration."

While at Madame Billy's, Piaf hired a Vietnamese chef named Chang to cook for her entourage. "What marvelous evenings we spent with her," Billy recalled. "Her own happiness consisted in pleasing others." On some nights she sang for her guests or recited the classic French poems she had learned by heart. She charmed Mary Marquet by claiming that poems were songs without music; the actress encouraged her to read Edmond Rostand's popular plays, *L'Aiglon* and

Cyrano de Bergerac. Edith's home became a refuge where her friends could forget the Occupation.

Yet she was still unsure of herself, Billy thought, because of her background and because she had been insufficiently loved. She flirted with attractive men to prove to herself that she could be seductive. "She was very unstable; she could be remarkably kind or really unbearable." Edith's friendship with Cocteau was the exception to this unsteadiness, Billy believed. Their love was platonic, yet profound: "A real passion united these two beings." The madame studied their mutual absorption whenever Cocteau came to dinner. Afterward, as he read his poems aloud, Edith's face softened: "She became the good little girl who was keen to learn and understand." If she asked him to explain obscure words or images, "he did so patiently, translating the thoughts behind the words, making clear the sense of the images." Often, as Edith recited his poems, she became radiant: "She was as beautiful then as when she sang."

Cocteau considered Piaf a genius in her own right. He hoped to cast her in a film opposite Jean Marais—in his view, she had more charisma than any professional actress—and wrote her another dramatic monologue, *Le Fantôme de Marseille.* The singer's purity of spirit was apparent as soon as she came onstage, Cocteau observed: "She transcends herself, her songs, the music, and the words. . . . It's no longer Madame Edith Piaf who sings: it's the rain falling, the wind sighing, the moon spreading her mantle of light."

Friends saw that they thrived in each other's company. Their affinity was based on deep trust and affection, but also on a shared obliviousness to possessions or money, which both acquired and spent almost absentmindedly. When the poet celebrated his birthday at his tiny Palais Royal apartment, he asked only "his closest intimates"—Jean Marais, Jean Giono, Maurice Rostand, and Edith.

By then, Piaf was singing again, after being forced by the censors to remove "L'Accordéoniste" from her repertoire. For much of the spring of 1943, she did double duty, performing first at the Casino de Paris, then at the prophetically named La Vie en Rose cabaret. That summer, she sang at both the A.B.C. and the Bobino, with different programs for each venue. Although she and Contet were seeing less of each other, she featured his songs along with Emer's "Le Disque usé"—which somehow escaped the censors' notice.

Some critics welcomed these changes while warning her against too much art: "You have skillfully renewed your old repertoire with Henri Contet's reveries," one of them wrote. "From 'Mon Légionnaire' to 'Monsieur Saint-Pierre' it's a straight line but one that leads to the clouds. You've let yourself be captivated by the magic of the words." Others hailed her performance as miraculous. *Paris-Midi*'s reviewer planned to "keep going to see this extraordinary interpreter of all human sorrows, hear her huge voice with its immense accents, look into her eyes, which reflect all the pain in the world and the . . . genius that animates her."

With Piaf's rise to fame, journalists began digging up any gossip they could find about her. In May 1942, when Edith's mother had a gig in Pigalle, *La Semaine* published photos of both women under the headline "Line Marsa Sings with the Same Voice and Gestures as Her Daughter." Having been abandoned by her second husband, the article explained, the older woman sang in the streets "like her daughter" until "La Môme Piaf, now famous, came to her aid." What it did not say was that Edith had been sending her mother a monthly allowance for years. Nor did it mention that Line was a drug addict.

Since 1940, when Line spent some months in a home for destitute old people (when she was forty-five), Edith had been responding to her pleas for funds, as well as hard-to-find items like sugar, jam, chocolate, and cigarettes, with the help of Dédée. Line got in touch in May 1943 to beg for an increase in her allowance. In July, back in jail on drug charges, she had her lawyer ask Edith to pay her legal fees; she also needed clothes for her court appearance in August. Line thanked her *"petite Didou"* for additional support when she was sentenced to six months in prison and signed her note, "Tender feelings from your mother."

For the next year and a half, Line would be in and out of jail. Some evenings she turned up drunk at Edith's stage door. One day, when the police came to Madame Billy's to tell Piaf that her mother was again in prison, the singer flew into a rage, shouting that she didn't give a damn. Billy prepared another package of supplies as Edith, "more upset than indifferent, pretended not to notice." When Line got out of jail, she asked for the right to sing her daughter's songs. Dédée sent her off with sheet music and pocket money, "enough for several doses," Billy noted.

Line continued to disturb her daughter's home life. One night, when Cocteau and their friends were listening to Edith sing, strains of "Mon Légionnaire" performed just as she did echoed from the street—it was Line, stationed beneath her window. A new friend of Edith's, a model named Manouche, recalled that, despite Edith's objections, Cocteau tossed her mother a banknote—which Line pretended to use as toilet paper. "Every morning for two weeks she was out there, crowing until one of us threw her some money to shut her up."

As Line awaited her court appearance in the summer of 1943, interviewers prodded Edith about her new persona. Asked why she no longer sang her prewar songs, she protested, "I'm not a *chanteuse réaliste!*" Although a creator of "popular songs," she disdained the vulgarity of her old repertoire, its streets full of "tough guys in caps and prostitutes." The public no longer wanted to hear about the *milieu,* she said. "Now you must write refrains that touch the hearts of those who hear them, errand boys, workers, salesgirls, men and women who are pure enough to be moved by love stories." The public always embraced such songs: "The heart . . . is still the healthiest part of us."

This artistic manifesto was picked up by a journalist who put her remarks in the context of the Occupation. The French had been deprived of everything, he wrote—most recently, green vegetables— "but they could still dream and shape their dreams as they liked." At such a time, music was a kind of covert resistance, as shown by the recent success of a nostalgic waltz entitled "Ah! le petit vin blanc" that looked back to the joys of working-class life and forward to a German-free future. Asked to elaborate on her dislike for the *réaliste* genre, Piaf replied that it belonged to another time. She wanted to put the past behind her, to let her imagination and those of her listeners rise beyond the constraints of everyday life. (And also, perhaps, to distance herself from the mother who still sang these "vulgar" refrains when at liberty to do so.)

In contrast to her knotted feelings for Line, Edith's affection for her father never wavered. Once she commanded high wages, she added to Louis's monthly stipend the services of a houseman, whom the aging acrobat liked to call his *valet de chambre*. Though marked by a lifetime of acrobatics and *gros rouge*, Louis dressed well in the clothes his daughter bought him and told amusing stories about his exploits: "Groomed and coiffed by Edith, he looked like an ex-pimp," Contet noted. She often visited Louis at his apartment in Belleville, where her reputation as a local who had made good enhanced his reputation. Her father came to see her several times a week, Madame Billy recalled, but never stayed to lunch: "He didn't seem to feel at home."

The aging acrobat surely saw that his daughter had formed a new kind of family, whose members were related through artistic affinities. That Edith was esteemed by Cocteau placed her in an unfamiliar social world. (The poet called her Madame Piaf to show his respect; though Edith often gave intimates nicknames, such as Riri and Dédée, she addressed him as Jean.) What was more, her reserved young secretary was setting a good example. Without seeming to criticize her rambunctious employer, Dédée often told her, "Mademoiselle, that just isn't done. This is what you do in such circumstances," Billy noted. "At first, Edith did whatever she felt like, but in time, one saw that the lessons had hit home"—though her high spirits never left her.

～

Dédée's tutelage had a greater effect on the singer than Madame Billy realized. A number of loosely organized resistance groups had begun to sabotage the Germans by whatever means possible—attacking railways, power lines, and the sinister black automobiles in which the Gestapo patrolled the streets. Workers rioted when forced by the occupiers to leave France to become "volunteers" in German factories; by 1942, the Compulsory Labor Service (Service de Travail Obligatoire, or STO) had produced thousands of *réfractaires*—the term for those who refused to comply with the Führer's plans for occupied populations to support the war effort. Clandestine groups of the refractory, or, as they were soon called, *la Résistance*, operated throughout France at great risk to their lives.

When Dédée joined one of these networks, she hesitated to tell Edith, not wanting to compromise her, but also because she was unsure how Edith would cope with the information. Soon, "with her remarkable intuition, she guessed that I was plotting something," Bigard recalled. "She became a highly effective partner and got us out of difficult situations by making use of her vivacity and notoriety."

Starting in August 1943, Edith turned an invitation to entertain French soldiers imprisoned in Germany into a way to help Dédée carry out a mission. Singers were told that their visits would improve the prisoners' morale; most knew that to accept the offer—the kind one could hardly refuse—meant being seen to compromise with the enemy. Maurice Chevalier, who initially supported the Vichy regime, agreed to perform at the German prison camp where he had been held during the Great War on the understanding that ten prisoners from Menilmontant and Belleville would be freed following his visit. When his actions were misrepresented by the Free French broadcasts from overseas, which condemned him as a traitor, he retired to private life.

Even so, Piaf agreed to tour Germany for seven weeks with Charles Trenet, Fred Adison's band, and Dédée. A few days before their trip, she spoke with a journalist about her plans. She would perform new songs for the soldiers, she said. Asked whether they might not prefer older ones, she said, "I don't think it would be helpful to stir up old memories. . . . What I hope is that when they listen to me they'll think less about the life they left behind and more about the one they'll find again one day"—a coded way of saying "once the war is over."

The newspapers documented the tour with photos of Edith sharing conditions at the stalags—grooming herself alfresco, having her shoes mended by the camp shoemaker, sitting with a group of emaciated men. She was also seen visiting Berlin, where the first person she met was from Belleville, but there was no record of her many photographs with the prisoners, taken as souvenirs of her visit. On her return to Paris in October, Piaf told a reporter that the prisoners were "top-notch," then, as she was hustled away by the press, shouted the stalags' watchword, "*Solidarité.*"

Edith's morale got a boost in January 1944, when she again applied to the SACEM for recognition as a lyricist and this time passed the test.

The set theme, "My song is my life," could have been chosen for her. Confirming her new status, *Paris-Midi* published her lyrics: "*Ma chanson, c'est ma vie, / Et parfois, le bon Dieu / Y met sa fantaisie / A grand coup de ciel bleu.*" ("My song is my life / And sometimes, the Divine / From out of the blue / Makes use of mine.") Though the article does not mention Germany, she was already planning her next trip there. Dédée's Resistance group was preparing false identity cards made with the enlarged faces from her souvenir photos; Edith was to distribute them, along with supplies to help the prisoners escape.

Before leaving, she gave the interview that told her cover story. The singer had received numerous letters from her pals in the stalags, she explained, as well as visits from their mothers and sweethearts, urging her to return. She knew about the Allied bombardments, but what mattered to her were the prisoners. Accompanied by her orchestra, a humorist, a dancer, and an actor named Robert Dalban, Edith and Dédée left for Berlin in February with the fake identity cards concealed in their suitcases.

It was snowing when they arrived. Their hotel lacked both heat and food; it was hard to find much to laugh about. Returning to her room with a bag of apples after going out for food, Edith exclaimed, "It's all I could find in this shitty country!" As Dalban set upon the apples, she produced a roast chicken—the sort of joke she liked to play even in desperate situations. An ominous summons to meet Goebbels, head of Nazi propaganda, turned out well when Piaf's party, including Bigard and Dalban, were received instead by a General Wechter, Goebbels having been called away. The general said that, as the head censor in Paris, he had been at the A.B.C. on the night when Piaf nearly caused a riot by singing "Le Fanion de la légion." "We adored that song," he said; "still, given the public's reaction, we had to remove it from your program." He gave Edith his card and said he would do anything he could to help.

Edith's troupe visited eleven stalags but had to cancel their tour of the smallest, near Nuremberg, when the Allies stepped up bombardments. She compensated for this missed opportunity by singing at another camp, even though no transportation was available. "Edith, the pianist, and I walked through the snow," Bigard recalled. "She couldn't keep going, she was exhausted, we had to make a chair with our arms to carry her." General Wechter himself could not have saved her if he had learned that she was distributing identity cards, maps, and compasses. Sometimes the escaped prisoners caught up with her tour and were passed off as musicians. After officials at one camp became suspicious and told Piaf to leave, she feigned illness to gain time so that those who were to join them would not be caught. "We were too fearful to try this again," Bigard wrote: "the plan had become too dangerous." She added, "[Piaf] was exceptionally brave."

When they returned to Paris on March 5, Edith learned that her father had died two days earlier. He was barely sixty-three. On March 8, she attended the funeral service at the Church of Saint-Jean-Baptiste in Belleville, the occasion for a rapprochement with her half sister, Denise, their brother, Herbert, and her aunts from Falaise, the former acrobats, who represented the family at their brother's last rites.

On March 31, she told Glanzberg, who was in hiding near Toulouse, that she had been unable to write until then because of her father's death. "I loved him very much. . . . It's terrifying to come suddenly face to face with what you cannot change." Things were bad in Paris, worse than people imagined. "I hope this abomination will come to an end soon," she continued. Only the thought of the songs that he was writing for her gave her any pleasure.

Throughout the spring, while performing at benefits for bombing victims and families whose breadwinners were doing forced labor in Germany, Edith continued to mourn her father. "She wasn't up to getting together with the family to talk about our loss," Denise reflected, "but she often went to the cemetery to put a bunch of violets on Papa's grave."

Denise had turned thirteen on the day of Louis Gassion's funeral. When Edith learned that he had been looking forward to Denise's first communion in May, she took Denise to Au Printemps, the department store, to buy her the traditional outfit—a white coat and dress, white shoes, and a gold cross. But on the day itself, too full of grief for her father, she could not bring herself to attend the ceremony.

CHAPTER EIGHT

1944–1946

Throughout the spring of 1944, as Allied bombers hammered the German war machine, French workers were shipped in increasing numbers to toil in German factories. Many of those who went underground to avoid the STO joined the network of Resistance groups operating under threat of discovery by the Gestapo. Despite the widespread sense that the Germans were losing the war, they still had the upper hand in Paris, where it was a struggle to survive each day. Many Parisians sought distraction at the theaters and cabarets. As the Gestapo rounded up Jews in increasing numbers, Parisians began to notice non-Jewish names on the hostage lists, which were bordered in black.

Edith alternated between nightclub engagements and benefits for bombing victims, STO workers, and the families of prisoners in Germany—including Stalag III-D, for whom she served as unofficial godmother. (Her black dress may have seemed doubly appropriate as she continued to grieve for her father.) Late that spring, she moved to an apartment near the Champs-Elysées—a less compromising address than Madame Billy's. With the Allied invasion the topic on everyone's lips, an apartment that could not be linked to collaboration with the Germans made sense. "We said goodbye as friends," Madame Billy wrote. "She wasn't easy to live with, but a star of her order has the right to behave as she likes."

During the first week of June, as the Allies prepared for D-Day, Edith sang nightly at the Moulin de la Galette, in Montmartre. On June 5, the five hundred spectators crowded into the converted mill turned their attention to the tiny singer on the bare stage. Normally boisterous patrons became as silent as if they were in church while she chanted Contet's "Y'a pas de printemps"—whose vision of a future full of springtimes was understood as a reply to the dark present. Piaf surpassed herself with Contet's other new tunes, "Les Deux Rengaines" (the song's two rhythms, one sad, the other gay, alternate like contrary views of life) and "C'est toujours la même histoire," a classic love story. She gave the audience "powerful emotions," a critic wrote, "at once solid and diaphanous. . . . Her heart-wrenching voice, its metallic tones, her reserved yet mobile face and eloquent hands have never been so powerful."

This paean to Piaf's mastery appeared just as news of the Normandy beachheads reached Paris. Her response was not recorded. Perhaps she was too busy to think beyond her next engagement. (Some years later, she would be asked to sing at the launch of the D-Day film *The Longest Day,* as if hers were the voice of France's liberation.)

In July, the director of the Moulin Rouge signed Edith to re-open the cabaret, which had been functioning as a cinema. Though she had already heard of Yves Montand, the young man from Marseille who was to audition for second billing, she did not think much of his repertoire—which was inspired by the pro-American sentiment that swept France with the invasion. On the day of his audition she changed her mind: "His personality was terrific. . . . His hands were eloquent, powerful; his face handsome and tormented, his voice deep and, miraculously, with little trace of the Marseille accent." Montand needed just one thing—songs to replace his "impossible cowboy refrains." His recent success would evaporate unless he found something more profound to say than "yippee-yi-yay."

Edith agreed to hire Montand and find him better material. Within the week, she also became his lover, a situation that replayed while reversing her relations with Asso. At twenty-three, Montand was starting what would become a major career; at twenty-eight, Piaf was already famous. The young man was touched by her loneliness. "I had fallen in love without even knowing it," Montand said much later. "She was fresh, flirtatious, both funny and cruel, passionately devoted to her profession, ambitious, a shopgirl on the town, loyal when she loved, . . . one of those people who made you feel that you were God, that you were irreplaceable." But in her role as mentor, she could also be a tyrant.

Piaf talked Contet into writing music for her new costar—which put the lyricist in the position of unwittingly helping his rival at a time when he and Piaf were still intimate. (She invited Contet to meet Montand, but it took the older man months to understand the basis of their rapport.) One night, when Contet called Edith with the lyrics for "Ma Gosse," which he had written for Chevalier, she convinced him to save it for Montand: its breezy mood suited his persona. Even though this comical situation worked to Montand's advantage, Dédée let Contet know that Edith would drop Yves as soon as Henri decided to leave his wife.

Meanwhile, Edith forced Yves to take their shared profession as seriously as she did. Contet watched her put him through his paces. "Yves never argued with any of Edith's orders," the lyricist noted. "He must have gritted his teeth more than once . . . [and] told himself that the rewards of the exercise were greater than its torments." Contet went along with her plan to boost Montand's career by praising his Moulin Rouge act in *Paris-Midi;* Edith began writing songs that would present her protégé as a man of the people, the counterpart to her image as the street singer who made good. The tall, gangly southerner and the Parisian waif formed an endearing couple. With Piaf, a critic wrote, "Montand, who is beginning to forget cowboys and rolling plains, has found himself a new personality."

On August 15, as news of the Allies' gains in Normandy reached Paris, Yves and Edith toasted their advance with champagne. Within a few days, posters urging Paris to battle went up around the city; Montand joined the actors defending the Comédie-Française; as battles raged outside, the company intoned "La Marseillaise," the French anthem having been banned during the Occupation. On August 25, as the liberation of Paris began, he and Edith watched General Leclerc's tanks roll down the Champs-Elysées. They fell to the pavement when German snipers fired at the crowd, many of whom sported the French tricolor and the white armbands of the Forces Françaises de l'Intérieur (in slang, "*les fifis*"). The next day, Edith kept a *fifi* from hurling grenades at the retreating Germans: "Don't be a fool!" she yelled. "They're leaving."

In September, the euphoric mood of the Liberation was still palpable. At the same time, purge panels were being set up to deal with collaborators. Many journalists, writers, and artists came under scrutiny as pro-German influencers of public opinion; some of the country's best-known performers had been compromised by their participation in German-sponsored events. Even those who called themselves anti-Nazis worried as it became clear that the purge panels offered the opportunity to settle old scores. Mistinguett received a reprimand for singing on the German-controlled Radio Paris. Chevalier barely escaped execution by *Résistance* militants, despite his recent broadcasts of "Fleur de Paris," a song that offered a vision of a united, post-Occupation France. Trenet was blacklisted for ten months, as was Suzy Solidor, despite her claim that her only offense was to have sung the old favorite "Lili Marlene." Arletty served a prison term for "*collaboration horizontale*" with her German lover but was allowed out under guard to finish filming *Les Enfants du paradis*. (She is reported to have said, "My heart is French, but my ass is international.")

There had been few actual collaborators in the entertainment world, but even fewer who actively supported the Resistance. When the purge panel published a list of names of those whose voices were banned from the radio, Edith's was among them because of her trips to Germany. Called to testify before the panel in October, she said that, though she had been forced to take the first trip in order to keep on singing, she had taken the second one to give her earnings to the French prisoners along with the maps and identity cards that helped many of them escape; Andrée Bigard supported her testimony with details. After Piaf also gave the names of the Jewish friends whose shelter she had arranged and financed, the panel voted unanimously, "No sanction and congratulations."

Performers like herself had been forced to comply with the occupiers' demands, she told a reporter from *Ce Soir*. She knew about the rumors, "some of which were not well meaning," surrounding her trips to Germany. Now that the panel had cleared her, she could explain her actions, since she had just learned that 118 prisoners had used their fake cards to escape. "I forced myself to navigate around the pitfalls of the Nazi propaganda machine to keep the trust of the French public," she explained. In the photograph illustrating the article, Edith has a hangdog expression and wears a dark dress buttoned to her chin, as if mourning the losses of the past four years.

Edith had already left Paris when this interview appeared in October. After a series of benefits for war victims, she toured the south of France with Yves. His renditions of Contet's songs—"Battling Joe," an upbeat tune about a boxing hero; "Luna Park," on a workingman's holiday; and the lighthearted "Ma Gosse"—went over well except in Marseille, where the public wanted cowboy refrains. Piaf told him not to lose heart. Under her wing, he learned to identify "the songs you can't drop, and to try out other titles as I went along, fine-tuning the ones that worked, monitoring those that didn't work right away but might one day." The newspapers were full of praise for Piaf but also for her protégé, "this tall handsome guy full of enthusiasm . . . who all by himself makes the stage look very small."

In December, they performed for the American soldiers stationed in Marseille. While Edith paced backstage, Yves delighted the audience by dosing his patter with Yankee slang. He took her to meet his family, Italian immigrants who had settled in one of the "macaroni" neighborhoods of Marseille in the 1920s, when his name—not yet Gallicized—was Ivo Livi. The whole neighborhood greeted the couple; the Livis welcomed them with a festive meal.

Yves's sister Lydia, who would become Edith's intimate, observed the star's response to their clan: "She was a little shaken by our noisy celebration and seemed surprised that we talked so much and so fast. But she was also attracted by our warm family spirit." Edith chided Yves for complaining about the Livis. He was fortunate to have them. Having grown up without one, she had tried to create such a family in her entourage of musicians, songwriters, and staff. The Livis understood that she and Yves were now betrothed, their relationship sealed by the clan's embrace.

If the couple's brief stay in Marseille represented their unofficial engagement, the party Piaf gave on their return to Paris introduced her new partner to the press. A throng of journalists assembled at the Mayfair cabaret on January 15, 1945, where she announced her first star turn in Paris since the Liberation and their debut as a duo. They were to perform at the Etoile, the Empire-style theater on the Avenue Wagram, from February 9 to March 8. Over the next few weeks, they polished the repertoire they had developed on tour in the south.

Three days before the opening, Edith learned that her mother had died of an overdose. She was forty-nine. A newspaper account stated that her corpse was left on the sidewalk by the man with whom she lived, then taken to the morgue. Piaf asked for Contet's help with arrangements for Line's burial in the Thiais Cemetery, Cécelle's resting place, but did not attend the funeral. Though she had sent Line an allowance each month and helped when she was in crisis, Edith claimed to feel little for the mother who reappeared in her life only to exploit her. Once the Gassion tomb that she had purchased at the Père-Lachaise Cemetery was completed, Edith would transfer her father's and daughter's remains there but leave her mother where she was.

Judging by photographs of Yves and Edith at this time, she was deeply in love with her new partner. In the euphoric early stages of their romance, she wrote several songs to refurbish his repertoire and expand his range. "Sophie," a jazzy farewell to love, resembled any number of tunes that others had written for Edith (the eponymous Sophie loses her zest for life when her lover leaves her), but it gave Yves the chance to carry off a torch song. In a different vein, her witty lyrics for "Il fait des . . ." depict a pop-music fan who becomes "*hystérique*" when he hears "*musique*" but turns "*mélancolique*" if it is "*classique.*" She was having fun with the lyrics while giving him the chance to make the audience smile.

It no doubt pleased her to watch Montand perform "Elle a . . . ," another of her tender, teasing songs about a woman like herself. "*Un petit bout de femme pas plus grand que ça,*" it begins ("a little woman no bigger than that"), she was his "bouquet of laughs." Rhyming "*tour-*

ments" and "*moment,*" Piaf implied that love and its torments were both momentary. She would have smiled as her lover crooned her praises: "*Elle a des rires / Pour me séduire,*" a line linking seduction to laughter. By then she was sufficiently comfortable in her dual role as lyricist and lover to let his uncertainty emerge in the refrain: "*Elle a . . . / Des tas de choses / Des choses en rose / Rien que pour moi. . . . Enfin . . . je le crois.*" ("She has . . . / All sorts of things / All of them rosy / Only for me. . . . / At least . . . I hope so.")

For the time being, Montand was on top of the world. At twenty-three, he shared the billing at the Etoile Theater, whose elegant arcades and pink marble staircase must have made him feel that he had arrived. (L'Etoile, once a venue for light opera, featured concerts by well-known stars rather than variety shows.) As the first act, he was such a hit that Piaf had to work harder than usual to win back the audience, for whom her new songs by Contet—especially the one entitled "Mariage"—seemed too subtle.

"Don't try to rise above yourself," the critic Serge Weber scolded in an open letter to Piaf on February 15. People loved her because she was "simple and natural," he claimed: they wanted songs to match, "with words that everyone understands." (Weber's gibe at Contet's poetics came at a time when French musical life was marked by an intense desire to affirm the prewar values that had been suppressed under the Occupation.) Though other critics who taxed Piaf with being too intellectual also blamed Contet's lyrics, *L'Aurore* disagreed: his songs suited her new persona. Ignoring the criticism, she would sing his lyrics (including some of her biggest hits, "Padam . . . padam" and "Bravo pour le clown") for the rest of her life.

In March, Piaf and Montand performed at the Casino Montparnasse, where the predominantly working-class audiences applauded his repertoire so enthusiastically that rumors began to circulate about the protégé's surpassing his mentor. When Piaf went on tour, Montand was not included, but she changed her mind at the last minute. The songs she wrote for him found favor in Marseille, especially "La Grande Cité," a trenchant critique of workingmen's lives in a city "*Là où les hommes turbinent / Toute une vie sans s'arrêter*" ("Where men slave away / All their lives without end"). Piaf's pensive lyric, in the view of a local critic, was full of a "*tristesse souriante*" ("a smiling sadness"). But it was Montand's new confidence that impressed viewers. "No longer a supporting act for Piaf's program," the critic continued, he had become "the equal, by the end of the first act, of what she is in the second."

Piaf confessed to Contet and others that she often felt anxious about coming onstage after her costar. "When I toured with Yves," she told one of them, "he scored triumph after triumph, and night after night I stoically bore my cross." Even though Edith's recording sessions for Polydor that spring may have reassured her, Yves cut his own first record for a rival firm. Show-business wags remarked on the aptness of his stage name: *montant,* its homonym, means "rising"—a fitting pun on his rapid rise to fame.

Despite her worries, Edith kept writing songs that would become her own triumphs. One day, when she was sitting with her friend Marianne Michel at a café on the Champs-Elysées, the young woman complained that she had nothing new to sing. Edith began scribbling words on the paper tablecloth, a tune that she had been thinking of for some time: "*Quand il me prend dans ses bras, / Qu'il me parle tout bas / Je vois les choses en rose.*" Her friend thought about the "*choses en rose*" (an echo from Piaf's recent song for Montand, "Elle a . . .") and suggested instead "*la vie en rose.*" Suddenly Edith had the title, lyrics, and music of the composition that would be translated into scores of languages as her theme song. But meanwhile she made a gift of it to Marianne; Piaf would not record "La Vie en rose" until two years later.

In July, she and Montand performed at Chez Carrère, a chic nightspot with white walls, chairs, curtains, and piano where they were to sing as if they had dropped in at a private club. At Piaf's request, Montand was given a role in her new movie, *Etoile sans lumière,* to be directed by her friend Marcel Blistène. The scenario, written for Piaf while Blistène was in hiding during the war, became the occasion for her finest cinematic performance. As Madeleine, the double (or "invisible star") whose incandescent voice replaces that of a silent-film actress in her first talkie, Piaf would sing five new songs; Montand would play her provincial sweetheart. It may have hit home when Madeleine told her fiancé that their nuptials had to be postponed:

"You're still a bit young," she explains. "You have to grow up!" By then Montand's growing reputation had made his offscreen "fiancée" apprehensive.

Still, they found much to enjoy despite the strains in their relationship and the bleakness of postwar Paris—where the power often failed, and staples like milk and meat could be had only at extraordinary prices. The day after Yves's brother and sister watched them perform at L'Etoile, Edith invited her "in-laws" to a restaurant for a banquet, which they washed down with the best wines. The next morning, Lydia found the couple reading a Molière play aloud in bed, Edith having taken on the role of mentor as she learned it from Bourgeat, Asso, and Meurisse. (To interest both the masses and the intellectuals, she said, Yves must read the poet Verlaine and the philosopher Bergson.) The couple celebrated the first postwar Bastille Day at the Place de la Concorde, where Piaf sang in honor of De Gaulle. For the rest of the summer, their unspoken tensions simmered as they completed *Etoile sans lumière,* which ends with Piaf walking alone down a dark Paris street.

Some of their friends ascribed the pair's difficulties to professional rivalry. In the more nuanced view of Montand's biographers, "What triggered their shared distress was that the[ir] program had simply become too much for the average audience. . . . They were not evenly matched. Montand, the revelation of the season, could afford to let himself be kicked around a little by a major star, but Piaf, however fervent an admirer of her protégé, had a reputation to defend."

In September, she upheld her reputation in a solo stint at L'Etoile with the songs composed by Contet and Monnot for *Etoile sans lumière,* including the rousing "Chant du pirate," with Piaf as pirate chief, and "Adieu mon coeur," a torchy farewell to love and to the time when *vagabond* rhymed with *chanson.* The opening-night audience was so enthusiastic that they kept on shouting "Bravo!" A *Paris-Presse* reporter wrote: "She deserves her success. Her voice is unique, sonorous, incisive, tossing off notes like birdsong that reach to the farthest seats in the house." Awed by her dramatic ability, he praised her enactment "of a distress that has more to do with the soul than with the world." When Chevalier came to applaud her, she told the audience how honored she was to sing for him; two weeks later, Montand accompanied her to dinner at Chevalier's apartment.

It may have seemed that Piaf had nothing to fear, but two days before Montand was to follow her as the star attraction at L'Etoile, an adverse critique of her show there appeared in *Spectateur*. Her new songs were too literary, the critic wrote, too remote from her days as La Môme Piaf. She should jettison these pretentious tunes (Contet's) and revive her old repertoire, with its cast of "small-time hoods and whores . . . things that are simple and true." The arty new Piaf was "impossible," he concluded, "too far removed from my poor dear little Môme Piaf, who was once as real as life itself."

The day after Yves's opening night at L'Etoile, Edith left on a tour of the north of France and Belgium. On October 28, *La Dépêche de Paris* hailed him as "the strongest personality to have emerged in *music-hall* since Charles Trenet's now distant beginnings." Perhaps coincidentally, Montand cabled Edith in Brussels to end their affair: "Maybe you're right," the cable read. "I'm too young for you. With all my heart I wish you the happiness you deserve."

The next day Edith wrote to Jacques Bourgeat about the breakup and included Yves's telegram with her letter. It was just as well, she rationalized. His way of breaking off revealed his character, or lack thereof: "A telegram . . . is easier than a letter, a letter takes too long, you dictate a telegram, what thoughtfulness, what a way to think about love." Though her sarcasm barely disguised the blow to her pride, she declared herself better off without him. "I'm desperate to devote myself to my work. . . . My lovers cost me far too much!" But she needed Bourgeat's support: "I hope . . . you can stop seeing me as a strange little phenomenon and know that I am a woman in great pain who feels very much alone."

Piaf was more charitable toward Montand in her memoirs. Recalling his joy in the audience's acclaim at L'Etoile, she said, "I shall always be proud of having played a part in his success." But after this attempt at kindness, she quoted a remark of Chevalier's: "There are those who say . . . 'It's taken you a while to get to the top,' and those who say, 'You got there fast.' Have you noticed that it is the first who are one's real friends? They're my pillars of strength, the ones who know I've had to work hard." In her own voice, she observed that "a sense of *métier*, which has to accompany talent, cannot come from nowhere; it has to be acquired gradually."

Piaf may have believed that Montand had reached the top too fast (and at her expense), but friends observed that their relations followed a familiar pattern. "When Edith managed to get from someone what she hoped to obtain," Danielle Bonel explained, "there wasn't much left for her to do. When she had nothing more to say or to impart, that person no longer interested her." Having played Pygmalion to her lover/protégé/partner, she would watch him continue his climb to fame without her.

Piaf celebrated her thirtieth birthday at the Club des Cinq, the chic Montmartre nightspot where Michel Emer's orchestra was adapting American jazz to French taste. Singing Emer's "Je m'en fous pas mal" each night encouraged her to thumb her nose at life's vicissitudes: "*Y peut m'arriver n'importe quoi / Je m'en fous pas mal.*" ("No matter what happens to me / I don't give a damn.") During her December engagement at the club (which had been launched by friends of the boxer Marcel Cerdan), she also sang at a Christmas Eve gala on the same program as Montand but with top billing. That month, there were more milestones to celebrate. It had been ten years since her discovery by Leplée and her first record. In January 1946, she moved back to the Hôtel Alsina, perhaps to put the Montand affair behind her even as they took care to maintain good relations once he too started singing at the Club des Cinq.

By then Piaf had formed the team that would bolster her professional life. Emer put her in touch with a classically trained musician named Robert Chauvigny, who signed an exclusive contract as her accompanist and would compose the music for many of her songs. When Chauvigny brought the accordionist Marc Bonel as a possible addition to the orchestra, Piaf hesitated because he could not read music, but changed her mind once Bonel learned all of her songs by heart. In November 1945, she had met Louis Barrier, who worked in the Office Parisien du Spectacle (Paris entertainment bureau). With her usual acumen, she saw that he was the kind of person she could rely on and asked him to be her manager. After some hesitation, he agreed. Chauvigny, Bonel, and Barrier would stay with Piaf for the rest of her career, providing the stability and devotion that she required of her entourage.

Although the fractious French parties had recently formed the National Constituent Assembly, the body that would write the Fourth Republic's constitution, the postwar political scene had not yet stabilized. De Gaulle's election as head of government had been unanimous, but he was unhappy with the near majority of old left-wing parties. In January 1946, believing he could not govern, he resigned. Materially, France was hardly better off than under the Occupation; beans and lentils were imported from South America to compensate for dwindling supplies of French grain.

By the time Edith went on tour in January, the franc had plummeted and thousands of Parisians had the flu. She sang first in Besançon, where the management could not pay her, then in Saint Moritz, Switzerland, and other winter resorts. Changing venues daily was tiring, she told Bourgeat, but it was beautiful in the Alps, "mountains of snow and a grand silence." She asked for news of a certain "*chou-fleur*" (Montand) and told Bourgeat to get her records back from "that big mug." The press and the diplomatic corps treated her "like a little queen," she continued. "That's why I no longer have the right to be ignorant; people here take me seriously and I must do the same!" Each book Bourgeat sent gave her joy. Men could be disappointing, but she had found "other satisfactions" in all she had learned since Jacquot first introduced her to the classics. She ended with the hope that her prose showed the benefits of his ongoing tutelage.

A few days later, in Lausanne, Piaf made the discovery that would lead to the next phase of her career. Barrier had booked her at a cabaret run by a prewar acquaintance named Jean Villard who had performed with her at the A.B.C. under his stage name, Gilles. Edith's old friend offered her his recent composition "Les Trois Cloches," which sounded like a modern version of the traditional folk music that had become popular during the Occupation—when the Vichy government promoted an idyllic vision of village culture. Piaf took "Les Trois Cloches" back to Paris, almost certain that she would sing it, but not on her own.

In addition to the widespread enthusiasm for American jazz, which came to seem like a form of resistance under the Nazis (they dismissed it as degenerate), many postwar audiences responded to the revival of songs of the kind they called *folklorique*. While urban youth, especially the defiant Paris crowd known as *les zazous*, flocked to the dark basement jazz clubs on the Left Bank, their counterparts in the provinces appreciated clean-cut choralists like Les Compagnons de la Chanson, eight young singers whose old-fashioned harmonies were helping to restore popular taste for the traditional French repertoire.

Edith met Les Compagnons at a benefit for French railway workers, when she expressed her interest in them despite their "boy-scout-like" style. "They lacked experience," she recalled, "but youth is a charming defect. . . . One didn't have to be a crystal-gazer to see that they had great potential." On her return to Paris, she began thinking of ways to put behind her the image of "the poor little môme." It came to her in April, during an army-sponsored tour of eastern France and Germany with Les Compagnons de la Chanson. Though she was touched by their freshness (the oldest was twenty-six), she told them that they would never achieve success with their current repertoire. But when she offered them "Les Trois Cloches," they turned it down—until she proposed to sing it with them.

In May, Piaf orchestrated the campaign to launch the group in Paris, the first step on what would become an international career. While singing at the Club des Cinq, she rehearsed "Les Trois Cloches" to heighten the play between their crystalline tones and her dark timbre. On May 10, Les Compagnons auditioned for Columbia, which had just recorded Piaf's score from *Etoile sans lumière* (the film was a big success).

The next night, she and the group performed at the Club des Cinq. Jean Cocteau, who at Edith's request was present, was so moved by their performance that he wrote a hymn of praise to "the strange marriage of Madame Edith Piaf and the young crew." In his view, "their twin solitudes combine to make a sonorous whole in which *la France* is so touchingly expressed that it brings tears to our eyes." Singing a cappella, Les Compagnons replaced the orchestra while forming an honor guard around their costar, whose incandescent tones echoed in their harmonies. It was as if the fragile figure in black had gathered these youths to protect her, yet once she began to sing, her intuitive sense of their rapport carried them. Les Compagnons were, Cocteau concluded, "the treeful of music" that gave shelter to France's "nightingale."

By June, Piaf was also finding support in her rapport with the group's leader, Jean-Louis Jaubert. Like Montand, Jaubert was nearly five years younger than she was, but, unlike his predecessor, he was not likely to become her rival. An Alsatian Jew who had survived the war under a false name, he had the gift of making Edith laugh. From Nice, where she had a week's engagement, she told Bourgeat of her hope to resume their "lessons" on her return to Paris and of her happiness with Jaubert. "I'm sure that I really love him," she continued, "and also sure that he won't disappoint me since he has never lied. . . . I'll finally be able to be what I've always wanted to be, a good woman, one in whom a man can place his trust."

Those who knew Piaf well, like Contet, had doubts about her ability to be faithful. In his view, what mattered most for her was *la chanson.* "Words and music are her beloved slaves," he wrote in May. "Miraculously they submit because of her passion. She loves them as much as the earth loves the rain." With great respect and affection, he described the one way in which Piaf was always faithful: "She sleeps with her songs, she warms them, she clasps them to her. . . . They possess her."

CHAPTER NINE

1946–1948

Piaf's affection for Jaubert would wax and wane during the next two years, but her belief in Les Compagnons' ability to revitalize *la chanson française* did not waver. After the deeply demoralizing years of the Occupation, it seemed imperative to renew French cultural life, and, for Edith, to secure her image as the country's "nightingale"— Cocteau having promoted her from sparrow status to divalike stature.

To understand her enthusiasm for Les Compagnons, we must imagine the postwar ambience. It may be difficult for English-speakers who first heard "Les Trois Cloches" as "Jimmy Brown" to picture the tonic effect of its (to our ears) insipid lyrics or to grasp its resonance in 1946, when the song's ringing tones impressed even jaded Parisians. Though Vichy had encouraged chorales as effective propaganda, church choirs, Boy Scouts, and other singing groups had adopted the traditional repertoire on its own merits. Les Compagnons' success in bringing this form to *music-hall* audiences relied on their clean-cut image and transparent harmonies. By conjuring up the ideals of *la France profonde,* where people's lives unfolded to the sound of church bells, Les Compagnons took on the aura of a village choir. "In the troubled post-Liberation period," a historian writes, "these harmonies resonated forcefully, then gradually diminished, like the echo of a world in retreat, soon evoking no more than a nostalgic dream of serenity for numerous city-dwellers."

This nostalgic dream still captivated the French imagination in 1946, when reassuring visions of a more harmonious life were an antidote to the war years. On tour with Les Compagnons in April, Piaf found that she too liked certain folk songs. One night, when the group was performing a particularly sad one entitled "Céline," she surprised them by singing the part of the heroine, whose sweetheart returns from the war to learn of her death, then hears her angelic voice pledge that they will meet again. This inspired moment became part of their program, as did Edith's impromptu drumming when they sang another folk song, "Le Roi fait battre tambour." But although she saw the importance of keeping some traditional songs, she urged them to "modernize," to sing tunes that could become popular, "and, naturally, love songs."

To help them make the transition, Edith gave the group "La Marie," which had been written for her but would have been better suited to the voice of a man reassuring his beloved of their future. Soon lyricists began composing songs for Les Compagnons. The poet Blaise Cendrars gave them "La Complainte de Mandrin," the ballad of a Robin Hood–like brigand; Jacques Bourgeat wrote "Les Vieux Bateaux" for Edith and the group; and Raymond Asso later gave them "Comme un petit coquelicot." Their popularity with Parisian audiences confirmed Piaf's intuition that she and Les Compagnons would go far together. When they added a third baritone, she arranged for a series of joint radio broadcasts entitled *Neuf Garçons et un coeur*—with herself as the choral group's "heart."

For the next two years, Les Compagnons took part in all her major tours, performances, and recording sessions. Piaf included them in benefits for French prisoners of war and for the children of her adopted stalag. They sang with her on May 16 at the vast Palais de Chaillot, where she had the backing of a sixty-piece orchestra and the imprimatur of Cocteau, whose hymn to Piaf's "*génie*" (read by the master of ceremonies) gives a sense of the adulation with which she was now received.

"Madame Edith Piaf is a genius," Cocteau's text began. "There has never been anyone like her; there never will be." The audience was directed to study "this astonishing little person . . . her Bonaparte-like forehead, her eyes like those of a blind person trying to see" as she came onstage. After a moment of hesitation, "a voice rises up from deep within, a voice that inhabits her from head to toe, unfolding like a wave of warm black velvet to submerge us, piercing through us, getting right inside us. The illusion is complete. Edith Piaf, like an invisible nightingale on her branch, herself becomes invisible. There is just her gaze, her pale hands, her waxen forehead catching the light, and the voice that swells, mounts up, and gradually replaces her."

To perform with a star of this magnitude was a huge gift to Les Compagnons. Fred Mella, the lead tenor, was in awe of Piaf's strength and determination but also of her respect for the audience. ("I cannot allow any rudeness toward my public," she told a general who made them late on their army tour.) Edith soon felt completely at home with her youthful entourage. Like them, their "big sister" loved to laugh, Mella recalled. At times they harmonized in the Métro, "to the grand astonishment of the passengers, who couldn't believe their eyes and ears."

"She thought of herself as the tenth *compagnon*," Jean-Louis Jaubert said. "With us she was a big kid misbehaving with her pals," who were not above pinching her bottom as she went onstage. Though Jaubert was her favorite, she played tricks on him as well. But once they began rehearsing, "she gave herself completely," he added, "even though she was a star." Edith made Les Compagnons work as hard as she did, rehearsing harmonies and intonations until they were perfect.

In Paris, they often performed at the Club des Cinq—by 1946, the place to hear *le swing*. One walked through a courtyard and down a few steps to the large basement room where Michel Emer's orchestra might be playing "In the Mood" or the latest tune by Benny Goodman. Patrons returned to their tables by ten, when the deep-burgundy curtains parted and Piaf came onstage. One evening, Montand showed up to watch her sing with Les Compagnons. Another night Marcel Cerdan came with his friend Jo Longman, who asked Edith to join them after the show. Cerdan, dazzled by her presence, said how much he liked her voice. When she ordered tomato juice, he followed suit—as if his table had become hers. Some months later, the day before he impressed New York boxing fans by defeating Georgie Abrams at Madison Square Garden, Edith cabled, "Know that all of Paris is with you. And that little Piaf sends you a piece of her heart."

Piaf's feelings for Jaubert had already begun to waver, but not because of Cerdan. She flew to Athens on August 31 for a three-week solo stint at the oddly named Miami Club. "It began very badly," she recalled. "I arrived in time for the elections. People were quite nervous, and when the Greeks get nervous, they do it in a big way." The country's focus on the plebiscite, which would end the recent civil war by bringing back the monarchy, made it hard for audiences to respond until a journalist dubbed Piaf *"la chanteuse de poche."* Though the French-speaking Athenians warmed to the "pocket-sized singer" once the election was over, Edith told Bourgeat that she disliked "the heat, the climate, how people think, their greasy cuisine and dirty corridors. I have neither your wisdom nor that of Plato or Socrates." She would feel better with Jacquot there, though he too might be dismayed by the contrast between ancient Greece and the modern state.

Edith found that Athens did have something to offer when she met a handsome actor named Dimitris ("Takis") Horn, who showed her the Acropolis by moonlight and taught her to say "I love you" in Greek— a phrase she remembered as *"sarapo."* She became enamored of Takis on the spot. His proposal of marriage moved her, despite the fact that he already had a wife, whom he promised to divorce. Just before boarding the plane to Paris, Edith gave him the Saint Thérèse medal she had worn since childhood as a keepsake. The writer Edmonde Charles-Roux, her seatmate on the plane, did her best to comfort Edith—who sobbed all the way home, certain that she had lost the love of her life.

"I love you as I have never loved anyone, Takis," she wrote Horn on September 20. "I think that I could really make you happy and that I understand you very well. I know I could give up everything for you." Takis was to reply care of Dédée Bigard, who would give Edith his letters. Soon she was besieging him with telegrams. It is not known whether they met again. Within a few years, Horn was enjoying a successful career in the movies, including some in which he sang the sort of love songs that delighted Edith.

Despite her emotional distress, Edith joined Les Compagnons as planned on a tour of the provinces that autumn. (One wonders what she told Jaubert about Athens.) The singers polished their repertoire before enthusiastic audiences in provincial capitals, then returned to Paris for a six-week engagement at L'Etoile. At first all went well. Edith gave an opening-night reception to introduce Les Compagnons to a select group of friends—Jean-Louis Barrault, Madeleine Renaud, Marcel Carné, René Clair, and Maurice Chevalier. Ticket sales exceeded all previous records; the press reported her plans to keep broadcasting with Les Compagnons and noted the star's bond with her public: "If a song is good and you put your heart into it," she told a journalist, audiences would not think about their problems. "That's our mission as singers," she explained, "to make people forget for three hours that they even exist."

That autumn, Piaf showed her dedication by multiplying broadcasts and engagements. On several occasions she lost her voice. Friends stepped in to replace her, including Montand, whose name was still linked with hers in the press. After an article about their affair appeared in *Cinévogue*, Bourgeat told Edith that the journal had contacted him but that even if he had known the reasons for their breakup he would not have divulged them. *Le Journal du dimanche* promoted the idea of Piaf as a present-day Messalina with nine lovers—an image at odds with her new song "Si tu partais," a lushly orchestrated ballad inspired by her feelings for Takis Horn that begins, *"Notre bonheur est merveilleux / Notre amour fait plaisir à Dieu"* ("Our happiness is marvelous / Our love is pleasing to God"). But the popular press—perhaps in response to her defiant recent hit "Je m'en fous pas mal" ("I don't give a damn")—continued to sensationalize her love life.

This negative publicity, as well as her regrets about Horn, may have influenced Piaf's desire to spend more time abroad. Pro-American feeling was at its height in the postwar years. Like many French entertainers, she wanted to sing in the United States, where Chevalier had been warmly received (and richly remunerated) before the war. About this time, Barrier made contact with Clifford Fischer, an impresario from New York who came to see Piaf perform at L'Etoile. Although Fischer was unsure how New Yorkers, who were accustomed to lighter fare, would respond to her sober style, he drew up a contract and told her to learn English. Les Compagnons could not believe their luck when Edith announced that they were going to New York. After they gave her a fur coat for Christmas, she teased that, since there were nine of them, each had given her what amounted to half a sleeve.

Toward the end of 1946, Edith met two young performers, Pierre Roche and Charles Aznavour, who had won a following in Paris with their adaptations of swing and bebop. Like Piaf's family, Aznavour's were entertainers; he too had begun by singing in the street. When the young Armenian came to her apartment one night, she tested him by asking in slang if he could waltz. He said he could, both forward and backward, and after rolling up the rug, he demonstrated his skill with Edith. Assured that he was the real thing, she asked him and Roche to join her on a tour of Switzerland in March 1947. They would come on before Les Compagnons, and Aznavour would introduce Piaf in the second act.

From the start, she treated the young singer like a brother. One night in Geneva, when the take was minimal, she declared, "We're street kids, we can cope, but the others have to eat"; they burst out laughing at the idea of the well-brought-up Compagnons passing the hat. Fred Mella got on well with Aznavour and Roche, but Jean-Louis Jaubert worried about the duo's propensity for living it up, which meant encouraging Edith to misbehave. (Aznavour stocked their train compartment with beer hidden under the seats and in the luggage rack.) After leaving the tour in April, Charles realized that he cared for Edith. "I wasn't in love," he wrote. "I was dependent. In a few days I saw . . . it was the same for her: 'I'd never have thought I'd miss you so much,' she wrote, signing the cable, 'your little sister from the streets, Edith.' "

Although she normally banned traveling companions from her entourage, Edith agreed that wives could accompany Les Compagnons on their Scandinavian tour that spring. What she did not know was that one of the group, Guy Bourguignon, had fallen in love with a sixteen-year-old named Ginou Richer. The stress of keeping his sweetheart hidden in their hotel room shattered Bourguignon's concentration. When the group learned the reason for his distracted air, they told Edith—who ordered Ginou to leave but changed her mind when the girl volunteered to do her hair. Ginou soon became her accomplice. Years later, writing about their friendship, she emphasized Edith's joie de vivre—"her sense of humor, her mischievous ways, her love of jokes and nonsense"—and her own role as the singer's "playmate."

Egged on by Edith, the group enjoyed themselves at every opportunity. In May, it was warm enough for picnics in the forest. They brought more beer than sandwiches, Ginou recalled; she and Edith danced the cancan while the men played drinking games they had invented in Edith's honor. After weeks of sampling the varieties of smoked fish on the menu, Edith invited everyone to her room for pasta, prepared in the bathroom. Her only disappointment came in Stockholm, when most of the audience did not come back for her star turn, after the intermission. The manager explained that in Sweden stars appeared before the second half, which featured lesser acts. Piaf then changed the order of performance to suit the Swedes, who came in great numbers. On their last night, when the orchestra played "La Marseillaise" and a member of the audience gave her a heart-shaped bouquet of blue, white, and red flowers, she burst into tears. "When you've been singing in your own language in a foreign country and you are honored this way, with no warning," she recalled, "it touches you very deeply."

Edith returned to Paris in June to finalize plans for their engagement at the Playhouse Theater in New York. After a round of appearances at resorts, she sang for a month at L'Etoile with Aznavour's duo and Les Compagnons, who joined her for recording sessions and one of the first French television broadcasts. It would have been a shock to receive a negative review of her Etoile recital. The critic asked whether the audience's "fervor" was justified, since in his view her voice did not have "the same ardor" as in the past; moreover, the staging was too polished to evoke a response, a state of affairs he attributed to her preparations for New York. Rather than adapt to the American love of glamour, "she should go back to being what she was, a girl from the poor districts," he advised. (Les Compagnons, he wrote, were "perfection.")

Piaf was perhaps too busy to notice this criticism in the month before her departure, when she also began filming a movie entitled (like her radio broadcasts) *Neuf Garçons et un coeur*. Counting on Piaf's fame, the director Georges Freedland devised a fairy-tale script that let his one set do double duty—as the sordid Pigalle club where her character seeks work for her singers, and the paradise to which they are transported in a dream. Although the film was a musical (including "Sophie," which she took back from Montand, "Les Trois Cloches," and "La Vie en rose"), characters did not burst into song for no reason, Freedland explained. In his view, Piaf was a fine actress: "She didn't just sing her songs, she interpreted them, played with them, lived them." Moreover, she revealed her sense of humor in the scenes that allowed her to be "droll." He added, "Piaf was very funny. . . . She never played the 'star' or put herself first."

On October 9, the day after they finished shooting, she, Les Compagnons, Marc Bonel, Loulou Barrier, and the rest of her entourage boarded the *Queen Elizabeth* for New York. "I don't do things by half-measures," Piaf observed. "I was saying goodbye to old Europe for a time. . . . The theater managers knew that I was going away, that it would be some time before they would see me again."

Even before they docked in Manhattan, Piaf was besieged by journalists. "Smile, Edith," the photographers said, to her dismay until she got used to the American habit of using first names—their way of showing affection, she decided. It was harder to get used to their way of saying her name: to French ears it sounded like "Eedees." (To Americans, "Edith" pronounced in French resembled "Ay-deet.") Unsure how to introduce the little French star to its readers, the *New York Times* called her a torch singer who "during the war won a large following among our GIs." She was an odd kind of chanteuse, another *Times* reporter wrote: "no sequins, no slinkiness, no sophistication for Mlle. Piaf," nor would her appearance have matched "a Hollywood casting director's notion of good looks."

While Les Compagnons marveled at the scale of life in prosperous New York—the skyscrapers, street carts purveying hot dogs at all hours, the Camel cigarette man blowing smoke rings over Times Square—Edith studied the American character. New Yorkers were always in a hurry, she decided, yet they were punctual, "a quality that I find commendable because I do not possess it myself." What was more, they kept their promises. They were also "practical" and "easily pleased," and had a touch of "just-a-boy-at-heart naïveté" that she found endearing. Soon after their arrival, a small plane flew over Manhattan with a streamer that read "Maurice Chevalier is coming back," the United States having finally granted him a visa after his exoneration at home. If Chevalier was the typical Frenchman abroad, Piaf might become his female counterpart—provided she could express herself in English as he did, with a touch of Belleville *gouaille* and a "charming" French accent.

Edith set about learning English with the help of a tutor named Miss Davidson, one of the punctual Americans she admired in principle but whose 11 a.m. arrivals quickly lost their charm. In between lessons she studied a manual called *L'Anglais sans peine* (*English Without Tears*), which explained that the English "th" was pronounced as if one were lisping. But Miss Davidson's knowledge of Belleville slang soon outshone Edith's command of English. Still, she had "La Vie en rose" and other songs translated for New York audiences and set about learning them word by word. "What a marvelous country, and such kind people," she wrote Bourgeat. "My nerves are on edge. I really want to touch their hearts, because I'm quite fond of them."

Opening night, October 30, was a success, in large part because of the luminaries who came to the Playhouse in numbers—among them Lena Horne, Greta Garbo, Noël Coward, Gene Kelly, John Garfield, and Marlene Dietrich, who would become one of Edith's closest friends. These veterans of show business enjoyed the old-fashioned variety show (hetero- and homosexual dance teams, unicycle riders, and two male gymnasts billed as "Poetry in Motion") that preceded Les Compagnons, the highlight of the first act. After the intermission, they applauded warmly for each of Piaf's eight numbers, including "Le Disque usé," "Si tu partais," and "La Vie en rose"—introduced by a master of ceremonies who gave awkward translations of the lyrics. (Her slangy classic "Je m'en fous pas mal" became "I Shouldn't Care," but listeners responded nonetheless to its insouciance.)

One member of the audience remained unmoved by Piaf's entire program. The prominent critic George Jean Nathan began by allowing that four dollars was a lot to pay for a show "of the kind encountered in the past in one or another of the little music halls on the Paris

Left Bank, admission to which was a few francs, or in some cases, merely the appearance of having enough sous in one's pocket to pay for a beer." Nathan's review went downhill rapidly. Calling those who applauded Les Compagnons a claque, he reserved his barbs for the "small, chunky woman with tousled reddish hair, heavily mascara'd eyes, and a mouth made up to look like a quart bottle of [mercurochrome]." After noting her "forlorn appearance," he disparaged her voice, "which, whatever the nature of the song, cultivates the pitch and tone of gulpy despair." In his view, her repertoire was "the standard boulevard one: the song about *l'amour*, the song about the married woman retracing the joys and sorrows of her tragic life . . . the other one about the forsaken prostitute, and so on." Nathan ended by dismissing those who liked Piaf because she was French: "In a colder and more critical land . . . her appeal misses something."

She could have not found much comfort in the lukewarm *New York Times* review: "She is a genuine artist in a particular tradition," the critic allowed, "making no concessions to a heedless metropolis abroad." The audiences' lack of response to her in the weeks that followed made Edith feel that she might as well go home. New Yorkers did not respond to her storytelling: they simply wanted to dance. Years later, she understood that by 1947 most Americans preferred musicals to vaudeville-style revues, or favored bubbly tunes like "Zip-a-Dee-Doo-Dah." Except for the GIs who had seen her in France, they had little knowledge of songs that lacked a happy ending. Audiences had expected her to sing "syrupy melodies where *amour* rhymes with *toujours* and . . . *tendresse* with *ivresse* or *caresse*," Piaf recalled. What she did not say in her memoir was that Les Compagnons had stolen the show. If her *réalisme*, which came across as world-weariness, puzzled Manhattanites, the group's boyish energy suited their wish for an upbeat evening.

Her memoirs also fail to mention her disenchantment with Jaubert. Despite her threats to dissolve their partnership unless he married her, he refused to do so, because she was a Catholic. A misalliance would break his mother's heart. "I've had enough," she wrote Bourgeat on November 4. "I deserve better." She had already found Jaubert's successor—Marcel Cerdan, who was in New York for a few days before his return to France. Once in Paris, the boxer would call on Bourgeat at Piaf's request. "I hope you will love him as I do," she continued. "He loves me sincerely, without any thought of gain. I hope you will show him how to improve himself as he really wants to. . . . Before each match he makes the sign of the cross." Cerdan, a man of the people, respected her but did not need her, she wrote: "I need him, he makes me feel safe." Because Cerdan was married, she told Bourgeat to keep their affair a secret.

Edith's professionalism kept her from breaking her contract despite New Yorkers' failure to embrace her. Their lackluster response did not change until the composer Virgil Thomson wrote in the *Herald Tribune* that her performances demonstrated "the art of the *chansonnière* . . . at its most classical." Showing his compatriots how to take this foreign import, he noted her stationary stance and sparing gestures, the purity of her diction, and her "tremendous" power of projection. "She is a great artist because she gives you a clear vision of the scene or subject she is depicting, with a minimum injection of personality. Such a concentration at once of professional authority and of personal modesty is both delightful and no end impressive."

A few days later, a *New Yorker* "Talk of the Town" piece extolled Piaf's charms. Having heard the singer in Paris, a staff writer wanted to see if she had "brightened up her repertory . . . on the theory that Americans demand optimism." Asked about "those wonderful sad songs she used to sing," Piaf said that though their heroes all died at the end, she was not a pessimist: "there is always a little corner of blue sky . . . somewhere." Her song entitled "Mariage" was different in that it began "in the cell of a woman who has *already* murdered her husband. She reviews her life, she hears the wedding bells, she sees herself in the arms of this man whom she has killed, an innocent young bride." Though Piaf had not herself married or killed anyone, in her view love always turned out badly. "But," she added, "I'm always optimistic." At the Playhouse, the writer was delighted to hear some of her gloomier hits—"Mon Légionnaire" ("that old honey about the woman who falls in love with a Foreign Legion soldier . . . and he gets killed"), "L'Accordéoniste" ("an accordionist goes off to the war and gets killed"), and "Escale" (a woman's "one big night" with a sailor who "gets drowned"). The article concludes, "I haven't had such a good time in years."

Together Virgil Thomson's review and the tongue-in-cheek *New Yorker* piece provoked a turnaround in public opinion that kept Piaf from going home. She told Les Compagnons to perform in Miami without her over the holidays when they received an offer, and gave all of them presents to show that there were no hard feelings. After their departure, she went back to work with Miss Davidson, in the hope of introducing her songs by herself. At the end of November, Clifford Fischer negotiated an eight-week solo engagement for her at the Versailles Club at the handsome fee of three thousand dollars per week, starting in the new year.

Edith hesitated at first because of the club's name: it brought back memories of the night she and her friends spent in the Versailles jail after their misadventure with the innkeeper who let them dine on credit. Once she agreed to appear there, she realized that the Versailles was one of Manhattan's most intimate yet sophisticated clubs. The room filled each night with celebrities, people from the *Social Register,* and, as Piaf learned to say, VIPs. Less boisterously commercial than the Stork Club, the Versailles appealed to New York's cognoscenti— those who thought the rococo décor worth the price they paid to sip champagne and listen to the chanteuse they had read about in *The New Yorker.*

Each night, the talkative crowd went silent when Piaf stepped onto a raised platform. "She had us mesmerized," a member of the audience recalled. "You thought about the sadness of her songs; even the boys got misty-eyed. The language didn't matter a bit. You felt that she'd had a hard-knock life, that she'd seen everything and turned it into this hypnotic music." At the end of the show, people climbed on the tables to applaud in hopes of hearing "La Vie en rose" all over again.

The European-born critic Nerin Gun found Piaf's English "quaint but understandable." He thought so highly of her performance that he quoted the reaction of the VIP politician at the next table. "Until now," the man said, "the French stars we have seen have been sophisticated images of Gay Paree, ready to sell their sex appeal. Edith Piaf is different. She is a great artist whose voice hits you in the gut, but at the same time she's a wan little thing who looks hungry, as if she suffered as a child and is still somewhat afraid. She represents the new European generation that so much deserves our help." We do not know what Piaf thought of being a justification for the Marshall Plan, but she quoted Gun at length in her memoirs.

Just the same, illness and depression plagued her at times during the cold New York winter. At 4 a.m. one night she sounded delirious when she phoned Marc Bonel and Loulou Barrier to ask for help. "She said that she was dying," Bonel recalled. "No one loved her, she had no father, no child, no friends except for Loulou and me." She did not recognize them when they arrived but, calmed by their presence, fell asleep. Piaf was working too hard, Bonel thought, with English lessons, piano lessons, rehearsals all day, performances at night, "and no love since Jean-Louis left." He understood for the first time that there was another Piaf: "a woman thrown off-balance by success and money. Though she's made her way with her talent, she's a sad little bird, a poor kid deprived of tenderness."

Les Compagnons returned from Miami in time to replace Edith at the Versailles when she again fell ill. Having decided that he could go against his mother's wishes after all, Jaubert asked her to marry him. It was too late. Yet she would go on working with the group, she told Bourgeat, though she found their attitude disappointing now that they were a success. Still, they were right to sing without her, because "we both have to make our names here on our own." She would stay with them until she had turned them into stars. Meanwhile, she was having a fling with John Garfield. She had worshipped the actor since she first saw him on the screen, she told Bourgeat, but, though his virility was impressive, he too was married. Their affair ended after a few weeks, when Garfield introduced her to his wife. "You have no idea how much I crave a calmer, gentler life," she wrote. "I'm not meant to have heaps of lovers. At the end of each affair I'm more disgusted than ever. I'd like one true, wholesome love."

Though Edith wished that Bourgeat could come to New York to help her through this time, she found solace in her growing rapport with Marlene Dietrich, the "fairy godmother" to whom she turned for advice. The actress was touched by Edith's lack of self-confidence.

"She was for ever calling herself ugly and insecure," Dietrich recalled, "yet such was her charisma that she could have had any man she wanted." Piaf's memoirs are dithyrambic on the subject of the tall, self-disciplined actress: "When she saw me downcast, worried, near breaking point, she made it her mission to help me; she took care not to leave me alone with my thoughts. Because of her I was able to face my problems. . . . I owe her a profound debt of gratitude." In the future, she would always wear Marlene's gift, a gold cross set with emeralds, around her neck.

Men like Garfield, Piaf came to see, were attracted to her fame. Years later, she wrote, "Men treated me like some territory which had to be conquered, even though deep inside I still felt pure. . . . I have never kept the man of my life in my arms for very long. Sometimes it is over nothing—a word out of place, or some unimportant lie and my lover vanishes. Then I pray that a miracle will lead me into other arms." During the icy winter of 1948, she closed each performance at the Versailles with "La Vie en rose," the audience's favorite and her private prayer for a miracle. As far as the French were concerned, the little chanteuse had conquered New York: "Edith Piaf has won the Americans' hearts," *Ce Soir* told its readers. "She will have a career there for many years now that Broadway has adopted her."

CHAPTER TEN

1948–1949

On February 27, 1948, as Piaf's engagement at the Versailles was coming to an end, Cerdan returned to New York to prepare for his March 12 match with Lavern Roach, boxing's "Rookie of the Year" in 1947. The contest between the young ex-marine and the "Moroccan Bombardier" was something of a mismatch, given Cerdan's greater experience—except that the American had the local boxing world's support. If Roach prevailed, Cerdan believed, he would lose his chance at the world middleweight championship, the crown he coveted.

Marcel spent as much time as he could with Edith despite his managers' attempts to keep him in training, which required celibacy. More cautious than usual about their affair—it was too new and mattered too deeply—she did not mention it again to Bourgeat, saying only that she missed her old friend and looked forward to seeing him after her return on March 17. She would explain everything once she was in Paris.

It would have been difficult to tell all at this point. Piaf still had strong ties to Les Compagnons, who had just come back from an engagement in Boston. They planned to sail to France together on the day of Cerdan's bout until Piaf announced that she intended to take the plane a few days later with Jaubert (who would unwittingly serve as her cover). After seeing off the group, Jaubert accompanied Piaf to Madison Square Garden. Cerdan had asked her to stay to bring him luck, she told the French journalist who noted her presence there. (A photo shows her in an uncharacteristically frilly hat with a bow tied under her chin.) Having "conquered the American public," he wrote, Piaf was now "giving her whole voice to encourage Marcel."

Cerdan would not have needed extra support except that the referee, a certain Donovan, was said to favor his opponent. Edith watched from her ringside seat as Marcel kept knocking Roach down while Donovan waited however long it took for the younger man to stand up again. After Donovan allowed Roach thirty-two seconds on the canvas, an unheard-of respite, the crowd called out in the Frenchman's favor. Even Donovan had to admit that the match was over when Cerdan gave Roach a decisive blow in the eighth round.

A *Paris-Presse* journalist asked Edith what she thought of the evening. "I've felt all sorts of emotions," she said, "but this goes far beyond them. It's fantastic to see one of our guys, all alone in the ring among thousands of 'Ricains' [Americans], defending our prestige." She had taken no interest in boxing before; in fact, she hated it. But now that she knew Marcel, she had changed her mind. "It's not the same, it's beautiful when he does it." Having surprised herself by yelling, "Go on, Marcel, kill him!," she knew what it meant to have "heart trouble."

Although Edith's heart trouble was not apparent when she and Marcel came down the gangway from the plane at Orly, it would have been impossible to miss their happiness. Both are radiant in the many photographs taken that day to welcome France's champions. Just as telling— for those in the know—was Jaubert's position several steps behind them. When Les Compagnons asked about Edith at their reunion the next day, he said wryly, "With Marcel, it's not a contest of equals."

One can imagine Edith's joy at having found her equal—to her mind, the perfect match. Having been in the maternal role for years, as she nurtured the younger men who claimed her affections, she now felt cherished by someone who would protect her as she had protected others. Marcel would look after her despite the obstacles on their path, his marriage and their place in the public eye as France's best-known celebrities. Meanwhile, they would present themselves as friends— compatriots whose desire to conquer the United States had brought them together.

Cerdan's blend of gentleness and strength made Edith go weak at the knees. "I worshipped him like a god," she wrote. "I would have done anything for him!" Like many strong men, he had a softness that showed in his generosity to those who were weaker than himself. At the same time, his self-confidence allowed him to accept her love tokens, the gold watch, tailored suits, and nubbly sweaters she kept knitting and tucking into his suitcase to bring him luck. Marcel's purity of spirit, seemingly untainted by success, made her feel utterly safe in his presence.

What was more, they had an intuitive understanding of each other's professions. Both had come from nothing and made their way to the top while retaining an innate modesty. (Perhaps remembering Aïcha's flea circus, Piaf laughed out loud when Cerdan told her about his pig farm.) Both knew what it meant to stand before the volatile public. Just as Edith took possession of the stage to establish communion with her audience, so Marcel occupied the ring like the celebrant of some ancient rite. Being the cynosure of all eyes allowed both to know the mixed state of trance and solitude often felt by those who perform in public.

Cerdan fell for Piaf's charm, her talent, and her conviction that what mattered more than anything was passionate love. He deeply admired the little singer. "Just look at her," he often said. "How can such a big voice belong to such a tiny woman?" He confessed to a friend that she had shown him what love was; he was besotted, she "had gotten under his skin." Cerdan asked only that their liaison be kept secret to spare Marinette, his wife. Accepting his conditions, Edith said that she had no intention of breaking up their marriage; the few journalists in the know honored the boxer's request.

Soon after their return to Paris, Edith rented an apartment where they could live together discreetly. Its location—in the sixteenth arrondissement, near the Auteuil Church—may have recalled the days when, accompanied by Momone, she sang for the residents of this bourgeois quartier. What mattered most, she told her old friend (Momone having been reinstated in her good graces at this propitious moment), was to provide privacy for Marcel—to hide him from the journalists who dogged his footsteps while he prepared for his next fight.

Cerdan rose early to run in the Bois de Boulogne, then trained all day with his sparring partners. Barely managing to stay awake at night while Piaf rehearsed with Monnot, he lost himself in his favorite reading matter, children's books and comics about heroes like Buffalo Bill, Joe Palooka, and Tom Mix. When they went out for the evening, the boxer lay down on the backseat of Edith's car to avoid being seen, an obligation that vexed him but made Edith laugh. Meanwhile, she performed throughout the spring with Les Compagnons, who were still her official partners: as a group, they were much in demand following the successful run of their film, *Neuf Garçons et un coeur*.

One day Edith invited Bourgeat to meet Marcel, in the hope that her mentor would introduce him to the classics as he had done for her. Whereas her engagement with Plato had given her a taste for readings on the spiritual life, Marcel preferred lighter things, like A. J. Cronin's best-seller *The Keys of the Kingdom*—the story of a priest who lives in imitation of Jesus, his hero. The book became a talisman for the boxer; he carried it everywhere. Yet, though it opened his eyes to higher things, he let Edith go alone to the nearby church when she wanted to pray. In time Bourgeat would be able to educate Cerdan, she thought, but it was better to start "with things that aren't too complicated," and to acquaint him with what Jacquot called her own "evolution."

Edith had already come a long way. Inspired by having found the love that she craved, she entered into a period of creativity that resulted in new songs for herself and her singing partners. "Les Yeux de ma mère" ("My Mother's Eyes"), in the voice of a man who travels the world asking himself why he must fight "guys with thick skins," became her gift to Les Compagnons. With Monnot she co-wrote several songs that alluded to her happiness—"Un Homme comme un autre," about the ordinary man who "resembles" her songs, and "Tu n'as pas besoin de mes rêves," an address to the man (surely the same one) whom she loves just as he is, without recourse to her dreams.

During Piaf's spring engagement at the A.B.C., she took part in two events that, given her origins, would have seemed unlikely. Since 1947, De Gaulle's partisans had been organizing a force capable of combating what they saw as the red menace. The RPF (Rassemblement du Peuple Français) was not a political party, De Gaulle said, but a movement that would prevent a takeover by the French communists, who claimed that they, not the Gaullists, were the heirs of the resistance. While the left held its traditional May Day parade in Paris, Piaf performed at a massive RPF festival in the suburbs. Whether she too saw De Gaulle as the one figure capable of uniting France is not known.

Two weeks later, the future Queen Elizabeth of England asked to hear Piaf sing on a state visit to France. Deeply moved to find herself in the royal presence, Edith could only stammer that she was exhausted from having just done two matinees. The princess told her that she had been marvelous just the same and that her father, King George VI, wanted copies of her new records. But Piaf kept on babbling about her matinees: "When I went outside, I told myself, dear Edith, you must have struck her as the queen of dummies."

The next week, she followed Cerdan's defense of his middleweight crown against the challenger, Cyrille Delannoit, in Brussels. What should have been an easy victory became a disaster when the referee proclaimed Delannoit the winner, and Cerdan collapsed on the canvas, his dream of retiring undefeated in shreds. When he told Edith that his career was finished, she said that he must not disappoint all those who loved him and saw him as their hero—advice that she gave herself when feeling low.

Soon after Cerdan agreed to a rematch, the scandal sheet *France Dimanche* ran a front-page article with the headline in extra bold: PIAF A PORTÉ MALHEUR À CERDAN ("Piaf brought Cerdan bad luck"). "Since his return from America," it read, "Cerdan has seen Edith Piaf every day. She goes to all his bouts, he goes each night to hear her sing. . . . She tells him about music, literature, and poetry—all new to him since he has become a man of the world." To someone as superstitious as Edith, it was unbearable to be considered a bad influence. "Oh, the bastards," she is said to have exclaimed. Their idyll was no longer their own affair. At the same time, Edmonde Charles-Roux recalled, the average person saw in them "the perfect couple, two people of modest background and immense talent who represented France to the world as the hero and heroine of popular imagination."

For the next year, Piaf planned engagements in order to spend as much time as possible with Cerdan while also trying to evade the mounting public interest in their liaison. During the summer of 1948, between engagements in France, Belgium, and the Netherlands, she recorded several songs written by friends whose lyrics allude to her romance with the man she called the love of her life. "Les Amants de Paris," composed for her by Léo Ferré, let her ponder her role as a singer of love songs: "*Les amants de Paris couchent sur ma chanson. / A Paris, les amants s'aiment à leur façon.*" ("In Paris lovers go to bed with my songs. / In Paris couples make love as they wish.") Ferré's waltz ends with a request for more such melodies, so that Parisians can keep on making love: "*Donnez-moi des chansons / Pour qu'on s'aime à Paris.*"

About this time, Charles Aznavour brought Piaf "Il pleut," a moody evocation of Paris in the rain, along with a more upbeat song entitled "C'est un gars" about "the guy" who entered her life. Its heroine, who sounds like a waif from Edith's *réaliste* period, does not care that she is down at the heel. "A guy has come into my life," she croons in the rising lines of the refrain, an "angel" who says what no one said before, that she is pretty. Recalling the past, she muses: "*Je vivais depuis mon enfance / Dans les rues noires de l'ignorance. / Soudain, tout s'est illuminé. / Mon coeur se mit à chanter.*" ("I've lived since childhood / In the dark streets of ignorance. / Suddenly all became light. / My heart began to sing.") But the optimism of the final couplet may have seemed like wishful thinking: the "guy" asks the woman to spend her life with him, and she replies simply, "*Oui!*"

Despite the difficulty of organizing time with Cerdan, who was again in training, Edith remained in high spirits. In July, the fledgling television station Télé-Paris broadcast her concert of songs by Raymond Asso—who, with his new wife, joined her for the occasion—and a second program, with Roche and Aznavour. She slipped away to Brussels for Cerdan's rematch with Delannoit, but stayed in her hotel room at the request of Lucien Roupp, his manager—for whom her presence in the boxer's life was, as the headline said, a misfortune. (This time Cerdan won the match.)

In August, she arranged a week's vacation at his training camp in Normandy. Ginou Richer, who accompanied her to the boxer's hideout, recalled Edith's efforts to adapt to his schedule. She rose early, drank a glass of carrot juice, and took walks or bicycle rides. After his training sessions, they strolled in the fields of flowers surrounding their hideaway, played Monopoly (she let him win), and discussed the writers on Edith's handpicked reading list—including Steinbeck (Cerdan liked *In Dubious Battle*) and Gide (of whom he asked innocently, "Do you think he might be gay?"). They made a secret pilgrimage to Lisieux to kneel at Saint Thérèse's shrine; Edith asked the saint to take Marcel under her protection and bought the statue of her benefactress that would sit on her bedside table for the rest of her life.

Three days later, the boxer flew to New York to train for his match with Tony Zale, the world middleweight champion known as the Man of Steel. Roupp managed to keep Piaf from traveling with the fighter, but, despite her upcoming engagement at the Versailles, she flew to New York with Ginou and Momone, her old friend having rejoined her entourage. Even greater precaution was required, Roupp insisted when Edith and Momone showed up at Cerdan's camp at Loch Sheldrake, in the Catskills. The boxer was a favorite at the small resort; on a visit there with the mayor of New York, the head of the French Municipal Council hailed Cerdan as the "best propaganda for France, the sort of man France needs." Since Americans were known for their puritanism and the press was everywhere, Roupp had their chauffeur present Edith as his sister when she and Momone moved into the cabin next to Marcel's. They spent their days playing gin rummy and knitting. Marcel visited each night but slept in his own cabin. "Easy on the sex," Roupp told him. "It slows you down."

After a week of this regimen, which excluded wine as well as sex, Piaf joined Les Compagnons on tour in Canada. She would return with enough money to buy a farm where Bourgeat could spend the rest of his days, she told him. Meanwhile, she had found happiness. "The only thing that troubles me is that Marcel isn't free," she continued. "One must be content with what one has, and you know very well that I would never try to destroy a part of my life. I came into his too late, so I'm the one who has to make sacrifices." She wondered how much longer they could hide their love. "Perhaps as God sees that my goal is simply to make [Marcel] happy, He will help me as He has done till now? Dear Jacquot, sometimes I want to cry out in joy, other times my heart aches. . . . When I see him everything will be fine again and I'll steal a little more happiness."

Piaf felt that she had stolen more than her share in September, when she and Cerdan were acclaimed by the "Ricains" while managing to live undisturbed at her Park Avenue apartment. Their excitement mounted in the days before his match. The *New York Times* announced, "Voici M'sieur Cerdan, seeking a K-nock-oot"—a sympathetic piece mentioning his popularity with the thousands of GIs who had seen him defeat their compatriots during the war "with such finesse that at the end they cheered him." Just the same, though boxing fans were curious about the "Frenchie," the odds were eight to five on the Man of Steel.

On September 21, following a pre-fight steak dinner, Cerdan lit a candle to ask for the Virgin Mary's protection, and Edith prayed to Saint Thérèse to look after "*le petit.*" While the boxer and his manager drove to the huge Roosevelt Stadium in Jersey City, Ginou implemented the plan that she and Edith had concocted. In anticipation of Cerdan's victory, Ginou was to scatter the petals of seven dozen roses from the elevator door to Edith's bed; if he lost, she would get rid of them.

Edith's group claimed their seats just before the start of the fight. That night the photographers were more interested in the skating star turned actress Sonja Henie than in the singer or her companions—Loulou Barrier, Ginou, Momone, Marc Bonel, and, nearby, the French comedian Fernandel. Edith stood up when the band played "La Marseillaise." The boxers touched gloves; Cerdan crossed himself, and the match began.

Zale, who had recently wrested his crown from Rocky Graziano, came on strong, and Cerdan fought back vigorously. Keeping to the strategy he had devised with Roupp, the Frenchman battered the American with right and left hooks. He performed with a stunning blend of precision and grace, but Zale never stopped punching back. The spectators yelled, "Come on, Tony, kill the frog!" With each blow, Edith groaned as if she felt it herself, wringing Ginou's arm as Marcel's stamina seemed to desert him, then pounding the hat of the man in front of her. Cerdan erupted into a vicious two-fisted attack that baffled his opponent until the twelfth round, when Cerdan finished him off with a right uppercut. The crowd roared their approval of his artistry, and Edith burst into tears. "You won, Marcel!" she shouted. "You're the world champion!"

The spectators were streaming into the ring to congratulate the Frenchman when Ginou raced to Manhattan, to put up Marc Bonel's homemade signs: "*Honneur à Marcel Cerdan,*" "*Vive notre champion du monde.*" At 2 a.m., the lovers returned from their post-fight celebration at a French restaurant. Cerdan kept replaying the match until fatigue overcame him an hour later.

The next night, it was Edith's time in the spotlight. Her opening at the Versailles had been sold out for weeks. Marcel, awkward in the tuxedo she insisted he wear, kept her company in her dressing room before taking his place in reserved seats with Charles Trenet, Sonja Henie, and the former French boxing champion Georges Carpentier. Edith opened with "C'était une histoire d'amour," a bittersweet Contet song about romances that begin joyously but come to a sad end. Then she surprised the audience by singing five songs in English. Her command of the language had improved so much in a year that she was able to summarize her French repertoire—including "L'Accordéoniste" and "Le Fanion de la légion," which electrified the crowd. When she obliged those who called out for old favorites like "Elle fréquentait la rue Pigalle," some enthusiastic young women climbed on the tables. "Marcel had never felt so close to her," his biographers write. "Yesterday it was his turn, today it was hers."

The only impediment to their happiness was Roupp's insistence that the boxer return to Paris for the celebrations that awaited him. He put off his departure for another week to be with Edith. Their mutual absorption was obvious. She beamed when New Yorkers called out, "Hello champ!" but preferred to stroll around Manhattan with him without being recognized. "Like Marcel she wore her heart on her sleeve," a friend observed. "They would stop to talk to the bums: Marcel gave them change but Edith went overboard, handing out twenty-dollar bills. . . . What was touching about their rapport was their shared admiration."

One night they drove to Coney Island after Edith's gig at the Versailles—"the happiest moment of my life," she recalled. He lifted her onto the merry-go-round before buying tickets for the kids who recognized him as "the champ." Holding hands, they rode the roller coaster "like a couple of children. . . . He shouted with delight. I screamed with terror." People gathered round them, shouting, "It's Cerdan! It's Piaf!" The crowd called out for "La Vie en rose." Edith started to sing; the merry-go-round went silent. "When the people applauded for me," she continued, "Marcel seemed stunned. He said, 'What you do, Edith, is better than what I do. You bring them happiness and love.' . . . It was the finest compliment a man could pay me, one I did not think I deserved."

When Marcel flew back to Paris, Edith turned to Bourgeat. "I love him so much that when he isn't near me I don't want to go on living," she wrote. "Never in my life have I loved like this." Marcel cabled on arrival in Casablanca, but she feared that he was forgetting her. Though her engagement at the Versailles was a great success, "there are times when I feel like giving it all up. . . . Could you tell me where one can find happiness?" After getting a letter from the boxer, Edith wrote that she was "literally obsessed." Even if she was unable to sleep, people seemed friendlier, and Momone became "the nicest girl in the world" when seen with the eyes of love. "I don't know anyone kinder . . . than [Marcel]," she continued. "God set him on my path to make him happy. He gave me this mission and you can be sure that I will accomplish it."

In November, she kept busy with piano lessons, English lessons, and two performances a day. Now that Marcel had promised to return to New York, she was no longer having "dark thoughts." Trying to be optimistic even though the political situation looked unstable (because of the communist takeover in Eastern Europe?), she told Bourgeat, "This century is exciting; you know, it must not have been so easy in the days of the Romans or of Napoleon!" The Americans were about to elect a president. "Their kindness to me keeps growing and I realize that each day is a great step forward!" Shortly before Marcel was to arrive, she already felt his presence: "I'm going to have him all to myself and I can assure you that I'll take advantage! . . . How I'd have loved him to be my husband!"

A few days later, after Cerdan's return to New York, a crisis erupted that threatened the couple's happiness. Momone's long-standing jealousy of Edith, fueled by alcohol, got the better of her. She threatened to inform both the police and the press of their liaison, and to adduce proof with copies of their letters. When Marcel tried to reason with Momone, she became hysterical and fled. The boxer brought her back to the apartment, where they kept her until Barrier could put her on a plane to France. "I had to send Momone away," Edith told Bourgeat. "She was drinking again and nearly caused a scandal. . . . She's more to be pitied than anything else. I don't hold it against her, but as far as I'm concerned, that's that."

The couple flew to Orly on December 18, at the end of Piaf's three-month run at the Versailles. A photographer for *Ici Paris* who was hoping for a scoop became angry when she spotted him and deliberately turned her back. After he told his editor that she had told Marcel to punch him, word of the incident reached the Paris press. Noting that Piaf and Cerdan had again returned to Paris together, the *Parisien libéré* noted coyly, "Edith is known to like tough guys but she does not wish to say anything more."

⚊

Piaf returned to work almost immediately in the new year. After singing for a radio program called *C'est ça la France* (*That's France*), she began rehearsals for two performances at the Salle Pleyel in January, which were quickly sold out. On the first night, as the red velvet curtains parted, the crowd went silent. "We never tired of . . . being seduced," a spectator wrote. "The singer's infinite artistic resources [kept] the audience holding their breath all night long." Her art was "extremely sober," he continued: "Each of her gestures, which are few, slow, and measured, conveys intense meaning; after the last note of a song, her performance ends with the enactment of deep emotion." If some still missed the "môme" of her prewar years, the street kid was now a princess who bestowed her love on her adoring audience.

Edith continued to believe that Momone was, above all, to be pitied, even when her old friend filed charges against her and Cerdan two days before her next concert. Calling herself Piaf's secretary, Momone claimed to have been subjected to "violence and illegal detention at their hands," according to a *New York Times* article that called Piaf one of Cerdan's "most ardent fans." Knowing that Roupp disapproved of their liaison, Momone tried in vain to enlist his support. Edith explained to the magistrate that she, not Marcel, had struck her friend when Momone became drunk and disorderly. When Momone got what she wanted, a generous settlement, she withdrew her suit and apologized. Edith forgave her because of their years together, and despite Marcel's doubts about her intentions.

Piaf gave the press her version of the affair in an attempt at damage control. She was sending Momone away for a rest: "She's like a sister," she said, "but I don't know what evil spirit gets into her sometimes." As for the singer's relations with Cerdan, they were "sincere and fraternal." Knowing each other abroad had brought them together in a shared struggle to succeed, "which inspired in each of us a friendly affection." Was this so difficult to understand? she asked with the artfulness usually reserved for performances. Piaf ended the interview by quoting the medium who had called her a positive force in the boxer's life: "Marcel is a little superstitious. He thinks I bring him good luck. You have to take all that into account."

The boxing world took note of Piaf's increased influence when Cerdan told *France Dimanche* that she had not, as their reporter claimed, brought him bad luck and, some days later, announced that Jo Longman would replace Roupp as his manager. Tongues wagged about her power over the champion. Roupp recalled Cerdan saying that he wanted his sons to have what he had missed: "I've been made to see that I lack culture, that it isn't only fists that count in life. I read all sorts of books that I barely understand; I listen to music that makes me yawn. I'm a peasant and don't want my sons to be like me. . . . I'm not to hang out with my old pals any more; they don't have anything in their heads. I need to see people who are educated, well behaved. I must forget the old gang, and that hurts."

Edith could not accept that others might not share her passion for self-improvement. Marcel's soul was "superior to the circumstances of his birth," she told a friend. He loved all that she was able to give him in this realm; his "inferiority complex was disappearing little by little."

Tino Rossi recalled an evening at Piaf's apartment when she urged a reluctant Cerdan to show the guests what she had taught him: "Cerdan got up, thought for a moment, then, to our great surprise, like a good schoolboy, recited a long sequence of Racine's *Britannicus*." When they applauded his rendition of this French classic, Edith said admiringly, "He learns well, doesn't he!" Her love blinded her to the cost of learning on demand and at the expense of one's former associates.

For the next nine months, Edith was happy and productive. During this time she wrote a number of songs, including "Hymne à l'amour"—the hymn to love that conveys her adoration of Cerdan. To the music of Marguerite Monnot, whose soulfulness complemented her own, she set a lyric that is as brave as it is poignant: "*Le ciel bleu sur nous peut s'effondrer / Et la terre peut bien s'écrouler. / Peu m'importe si tu m'aimes. / Je me fous du monde entier.*" ("The blue sky can tumble down / And the earth can fall apart. / It won't matter, if you love me. / I just don't give a damn.") The woman lists all that she would do for her lover: go to the ends of the earth, unhook the moon from the sky, renounce her country, even dye her hair blond—a humorous note in an otherwise heartrending lyric.

By the end, the song's resemblance to a hymn is striking: "*Si un jour la vie t'arrache à moi, / Si tu meurs, que tu sois loin de moi, / Peu m'importe, si tu m'aimes / Car moi je mourrai aussi. / Nous aurons pour nous l'éternité.*" ("If one day life takes you from me, / If you die when far away from me, / If you love me, it won't matter, / We'll have all eternity.") In the final line, "*Dieu réunit ceux qui s'aiment*" ("God reunites those who love each other"), Piaf's earthly and spiritual faiths match up like hands in prayer. Her credo—love conquers all—had never been stronger.

Edith and Marcel were often apart in 1949 because of professional commitments. She flew to Egypt for a series of concerts at the end of February, including four at the Ewart Memorial Hall in Cairo—where the Egyptian diva Oum Kalthoum often performed. The French-speaking elite filled the hall: "Words are too poor to express the range

of emotions that this grand little woman, this admirable tragedienne . . . made us experience," one of them wrote. When she took a
day off to visit the Pyramids with her entourage, Marc Bonel filmed
her astride the camel that she renamed Mistinguett because of the
resemblance she saw between her mount's teeth and those of the
French entertainer. Piaf sang next in Beirut, at that time an outpost of
French culture known as "the pearl of the Orient."

Between engagements, she flew to London in March to bring Cerdan luck at his next match, with Dick Turpin—who collapsed under
his assault in the seventh round. In April, while Edith was singing at
the A.B.C. with Les Compagnons, Marcel spent time in Casablanca
with his family, a separation that made her miserable until she began
paying for Ginou to fly there to deliver her letters and return with his
replies.

In her spare time, Edith shopped for Marcel. She chose piles of shirts
made to order, ties, scarves, and sweaters, often in the hue she preferred for him, pale blue—perhaps reasoning that, if he could not be
with her, his wardrobe could. His scent filled their bed, she told him in
one of the letters that Ginou took to Morocco that spring; he replied
that he missed the touch of her skin. In May, Edith searched for housing that would offer greater privacy than her Auteuil apartment,
finally settling on a house in nearby Boulogne, where the press was
unlikely to find them.

A well-paid three-week stint at the Paris Copacabana kept Piaf from
accompanying Cerdan to Detroit in June to bring him luck at his match
with the redoubtable Jake La Motta. Her heart was with him, she
wrote: "I'll be in your gloves, your breath, everywhere. I'd like to bite
La Motta's ass, that bastard. He mustn't touch you or he'll answer to
me. *Au revoir, mon petit,* my boy, my life, my love." When Cerdan
damaged his left shoulder early in the fight and lost his crown to La
Motta, it seemed that Edith's medium had been right about Marcel's
needing her. Blaming herself for not being by his side, she made
arrangements to travel with him in secret for the rematch in September.

Meanwhile, according to the contract Barrier had devised to maxi-
mize her time with Cerdan, Piaf toured other colonial capitals in
preparation for her summer engagements in French watering spots. In

July, she sang to huge crowds in Oran, Algiers, and Casablanca, often accompanied by the boxer, who also joined her for a week on the French Riviera. The day after their return to Paris in August, Piaf slipped past the press at Le Havre to board Cerdan's ship to New York: he would train for the rematch with La Motta while she rehearsed for her engagement at the Versailles. This bout was "God's way of letting me be close to you always," Edith wrote, since each time they were apart something bad seemed to happen.

In New York, their schedules allowed the couple stretches of time with each other. Edith spent several days incognito at Loch Sheldrake; Marcel came to stay at her apartment on Lexington Avenue, accompanying her on daily walks to Central Park to see the squirrels. She planned to sing "Hymne à l'amour" for the first time in public on September 15, opening night at the Versailles: it was about Marcel and herself, she told her entourage. The crowded nightclub audience, full of such luminaries as Cary Grant, Gary Cooper, Rex Harrison, Barbara Stanwyck, and Claudette Colbert, greeted her as the queen of song. "Edith Piaf made her debut before the most select group ever assembled, and she is better than ever," one critic wrote. "She's the star of the year," another observed, "even greater than Sarah Bernhardt." Betting on Piaf's growing American fame, Columbia issued *Chansons parisiennes*, two albums of her best-known songs, with covers featuring maps of Paris and dancing policemen.

A change of plans brought Cerdan to Manhattan sooner than expected when the match scheduled for September 28 was postponed until December 2 because of La Motta's damaged right shoulder. At first Edith was overjoyed: the postponement meant that she and Marcel could have two more months together. But, despite her supplications, the boxer insisted on going to see his family in Casablanca. "I'm terribly disappointed," Edith told Bourgeat. "I thought that Marcel loved me more than anything and I see that I'm only his mistress. . . . This time was a gift from heaven and he let it go." Since they would never have the chance to be together "without causing any harm," she announced her intention to drop out of his life by organizing increasingly longer separations, even though they caused her great pain. "I thought he suffered when we were apart," she continued, "but the day he was to leave, he was singing at the top of his voice in the shower!"

When Jacquot told her to think of Cerdan's wife, Edith displaced her anger at the boxer onto her mentor: "Does that woman deserve to be happy? She isn't capable of bringing up her children, he's the one who takes them to the doctor when they're ill." Jacquot was wrong to judge Edith on conventional grounds: "If all women did their duty as I do, they wouldn't have many regrets. Because if one day those kids get a good education, it will be thanks to me, not her." He was more concerned with his prose than with the heart's truths, she scolded: "Don't tell me about the poor unhappy children . . . !" Still, she loved her old friend and hoped to get a letter "written from your heart, not taken from the books in your library."

After a training match outside Paris, Marcel phoned to say that he would soon sail for New York. Edith begged him to take a plane, which would give them more time together; he promised to come as soon as possible. After their conversation, the boxer gave a statement to the press: "I have to beat La Motta, I will beat La Motta. I'll be perfect on December 2. You can be sure I'll come back to France with the middleweight crown placed securely on my head." Just before boarding an Air France night flight on October 27, he told the millions of fans glued to their radios, "I'm so eager to get back to New York and Madison Square Garden that if I could have left sooner I'd have done so." He promised to fight like a tiger.

CHAPTER ELEVEN

1949–1952

Loulou Barrier and Marc Bonel drove to La Guardia on October 28 to welcome Cerdan. They were to bring the boxer to Edith's apartment to greet her when she awoke after a night at the Versailles. On the way to the airport, they heard an ominous report about his plane's disappearance; at La Guardia, they learned that it had crashed in the Azores. Everyone on board had died.

All New York knew of the disaster by early afternoon, when Edith, still in her dressing gown, emerged from her bedroom to find her friends pacing nervously. Thinking that they were playing a joke, that Marcel was behind the door, she asked gaily, "Why are you hiding?" Barrier took her in his arms. "Edith, you must be brave," he said. "There are no survivors." As she began screaming, the men rushed to secure the windows. Edith sobbed all afternoon, unable to accept what she knew to be true.

When Barrier alerted the Versailles to cancel her appearance, the manager came to her apartment with the vegetable broth he brought her each night before she went onstage. She drank it, turned to him, and said that she would sing after all. Her entourage tried in vain to protect her from the journalists besieging the apartment. Once she realized that the whole town knew of the disaster, she spoke briefly with a photographer who asked her about her plans. "Oh, Marcel!" she exclaimed, and burst into tears.

On the way to the Versailles, she stopped at a nearby church to light a candle in the hope that he was alive. The club was tense, sympathizers having rushed to book all available seats. When Piaf came onstage, Bonel and Chauvigny had tears in their eyes. She embraced them and told the audience, "Tonight I'm singing for Marcel Cerdan." She managed to get through her repertoire until "Hymne à l'amour." Feeling faint, she clutched the curtain, then collapsed before she could sing the final line, "God reunites those who love each other."

⟜

"I can think of only one thing, to join him," Piaf told Bourgeat three days later. "I have nothing left to live for. Singing? I sang for him. My repertoire was full of love, and you can be sure that I'll sing my story each night. What's more, each song reminds me of his gestures, things he said, everything reminds me of him. It was the first time I was really happy. I lived for him, he was my reason for being, for my car, my clothes, the springtime, they were all for him." Along with intense grief, she was also suffering from acute arthritic pain in her joints. The first of a series of attacks that would plague her for the rest of her life, it was a condition brought on, her entourage thought, by the shock to her system after the death of Cerdan.

Some weeks later, she told another friend, "I try in vain to understand but I can't. The pain gets worse each day. I would never have imagined I'd wish for death as a deliverance, a joy. I was someone who loved life and now I hate it." On November 10, after Cerdan's remains were identified by his watchband (a gift from Piaf), a state funeral was held in France, where his disappearance was a national tragedy. Piaf wrote to the actor Robert Dalban—who, like her, believed that the living could contact the spirit world: "You can take me where I'll be shown that he is still alive. . . . If I don't get that chance, I'm done for."

Since Edith's early readings in Greek thought with Bourgeat, she had continued to read philosophical texts on the nature of the soul, which led her to more esoteric theories. Another friend recalled: "I would have expected her to like detective stories, but no, she read Plato. . . . We talked about things like the immortality of the soul." If one accepted this doctrine, it was only a step to think that twin souls would meet in heaven, a hope that she deemed essential to go on living.

At her request, Piaf's intimates flew to be with her while she completed her run at the Versailles. Dédée Bigard came to New York soon after Cerdan's death and resumed work as Edith's secretary. A few weeks later, despite his poor health, Bourgeat arrived to console his Piafou; he introduced her to the doctrine of reincarnation as propounded by the secret society known as the Rosicrucians. Though the revelation of these mystical truths was comforting, Edith derived more immediate solace once Momone also joined her and saw the advantage in giving Edith what she desired—a way to contact the Beyond.

A small pedestal table purchased in New York became the means of communication during the séances conducted by Momone and her co-conspirators over the next two years. Berteaut later justified her actions by saying that this piece of furniture had been necessary to keep Piaf alive. Others close to the singer saw the séances as Momone's chance to obtain large sums of money by playing on Edith's need to feel that she was in touch with Marcel, whose ghostly voice dictated the names of those on whom she should bestow a variety of gifts. Marc Bonel, who refused to take part in the séances, found that he was out of favor; Emer, Contet, Aznavour, and all those who told Piaf that she was being manipulated were in disgrace. It is possible that the singer knew more than she let on about the table-turning, but she wanted desperately to believe that she had not lost contact with Marcel.

Piaf's professional life nonetheless continued as if she were in control. Not only would it damage her career if she left the Versailles before the end of her contract, but she had no wish to return to France. "I'll wait a few months," she told a friend. "I'm afraid to see Paris again without him." On December 19, when she turned thirty-four, it would have been hard not to recall their trip to Paris the year before to celebrate the day together.

About that time, Piaf wrote the lyrics for a slow blues in memory of Cerdan, which she performed like an offering to the crowds at the Versailles. Until the end of her run, on January 31, 1950, she appeared each night in her black dress, went through her repertoire, then stood with her head in her hands to sing the blues that told her story, as if mourning in public. "Mon amour, je te retrouverai dans l'éternité" ("My love, we'll meet again in heaven") became the audiences' favorite but was never recorded.

Years later, Piaf recovered some of the serenity that had deserted her when Cerdan died. Near the end of her life, she wrote, "I know that death is only the start of something else. Our soul regains its freedom." But at the time, unable to regain her equilibrium, she kept on performing through sheer force of will. Piaf later wrote that she made the decision to live for her public: "Our lives do not belong to us. Courage makes us keep on till the end. In any case, since then Marcel has never left me." But her intimates agreed that she was never the same.

Some believed that Piaf worshipped the boxer for the rest of her life because he left it when their love was at its height. "If it had gone on another year," Berteaut conjectured, "she might have dismissed him, like all the others." Although Danielle Bonel rarely agreed with Berteaut, she too thought that it was Cerdan's untimely death that kept Piaf from forgetting him. In this view, his leaving her before she could tire of him allowed their story to take on mythic proportions. An early Piaf biographer wrote: "Had he lived, he probably would not have 'lasted' longer than the others. We must demystify this story from the start and see it as a dream, the perfect image of Piaf's life, a bright, naïve cliché from her dark legend."

Although tempting, it is beside the point to speculate about their relationship had Cerdan survived. Piaf's view of earthly love as akin to the divine is disconcerting to those who do not sympathize with her spirituality. But, whatever one thinks of her mystical bent, it is more fruitful to grasp what the loss of Cerdan meant to the singer's imagination than to "demystify" her response—to see how it shaped the rest of her career and her rapport with the audiences who shared her grief. To this end, we may recall the Freudian notion of sublimation—the coping mechanism by which erotic energy is transformed into achievements like artistic expression. From this perspective, Piaf's actions after Cerdan's death may be seen as ways of refocusing her energy, comforted by the knowledge that, in their own way, her compatriots mourned the death of their hero along with her.

Piaf's fans embraced her on her return to Paris. On March 13, she sang on national television. On March 14, 16, and 18, she performed to sold-out houses at the Salle Pleyel. The opening-night audience, which included Paulette Godard and Maurice Chevalier, was overwhelmed. "She brought to life all of suffering humanity," a critic wrote. "Each time she comes back to us from America, we are astonished by her repertoire and captivated all over again." Her entire show—lights, staging, orchestrations—was "perfection," he continued, but it was her particular "genius" that made audiences feel that, though she had just returned "from the land of the dollar," her songs exhibited the same humility she had always possessed. Audiences were gripped with emotion each time she sang "Hymne à l'amour," from then on backed by a chorus of angelic voices: the song would come to have almost mythic status. "She's no longer just a woman," a teary-eyed spectator exclaimed, "she's a god."

Critics and fans alike turned to religious imagery to express what they felt. "Piaf is a fallen angel, a creature of heights and depths," another critic rhapsodized. "Her story is simple: she begins with love and ends with death." It was agreed that Cerdan's name was not to be mentioned, but readers understood the reference, just as they grasped the critic's allusion to the singer as Mary Magdalene. Over the years, each time listeners heard "Hymne à l'amour," it became more deeply identified with Piaf as celebrant of the cult of eternal love.

By the end of March, when the newly consecrated diva left for two weeks at the Variétés Theater in Marseille, she had already begun gathering round her the entourage that seemed to offer her practical and emotional support. The large Boulogne residence bought for Cerdan in 1949 (where renovation was still ongoing) became the space in which she reinvented her "family." Edith moved into the ground-floor rooms intended for the concierge, where she would remain even when the work was complete. Dédée Bigard worked in an office on the same floor; Aznavour, who occupied one of the maids' rooms, joined Piaf's staff as chauffeur, lighting man, and, within a short time, songwriter; other show-business friends moved in and formed a court around their hostess. Despite their reservations, members of her household had to accept Momone and her daughter, Edith, along with the séances to evoke Cerdan's spirit.

On arrival in Marseille in March, Piaf met a man she took to be a kindred spirit—Tony Frank, the manager of the Variétés, who told her that he was having trouble keeping the theater afloat. They became lovers. She hoped that his idea of love accorded with hers: "I need to feel that those I love really need me," she wrote after returning to Paris. "When a man, a real man, becomes a little boy with the woman he loves, it's the most beautiful gift." Love was everything; it was her god, she wrote (reversing the usual formulation): "*L'amour c'est tout puisque c'est Dieu.*"

Edith's conviction of love's divinity was already being tested in her Boulogne household. Soon after her return from New York, she contacted Marinette Cerdan, who invited her to Morocco even though she knew of Edith's affair with Marcel. Their entente as co-mourners resulted in the Cerdan family's moving to Boulogne. Edith took responsibility for their welfare (including benefits like a mink coat for Marinette) out of her desire to give the boxer's sons the life he had wanted for them and also to show the world that his widow embraced the woman who had been her rival. Only conventional minds found their rapport hard to understand, she wrote: "Marinette and I had been changed by [the same] man."

By the beginning of May, with Momone suffering the consequences of an overactive love life and Cerdan's son Paul needing an operation, Edith wondered if she had taken on too much. "I don't know if I'm an artist or everyone's mother," she told Tony Frank. She was praying for a solution to his financial woes; meanwhile, he should read Marcel's favorite, *The Keys of the Kingdom*. Love was "more precious than money," she continued; he had "a real fortune" in his daughter. Edith trusted her lover enough to tell him about Cécelle's death, a subject she rarely mentioned.

Momone's unexpected pregnancy meant that there would soon be five children in the house, she told him a few days later. She would have to turn the living room into a dormitory; meanwhile, she, Momone, and Marinette were all knitting. The star wished that she could drop everything and spend time with Tony, especially now that Momone was quarreling with Dédée—who would soon leave Edith, after ten years in her service. Submerged in "this bitch of a life," Edith wrote, she found solace at church: "It's the only place where I can draw new strength."

Her current run at the A.B.C. and her new records lifted her spirits somewhat, especially "Hymne à l'amour." In the first recording of the song she had written for Cerdan, the orchestration and choruses create a mystical sound that builds to the coda, where, on an almost Wagnerian note, Piaf exalts love's ability to outlast death. "Playing with a very effective use of rubato and the alternation between vocal power and restraint," a critic writes, "Edith Piaf's interpretation is highly expressive, in complete accord with the ecstatic intensity of the words."

Piaf's mood often darkened when she returned to Boulogne, where she spent most of her time with Momone. "When she knows that I'm sad, she is all the more so," she told Tony Frank. "I see the reflection of my pain in her eyes. It's amazing, don't you think, a friendship like this brings one comfort and makes up for a lot?" But she also yearned for the warmth of Tony's "*beaux yeux*," a phrase that recurs in her letters and may have inspired her to compose "C'est d'la faute à tes yeux"— the confession of a woman who tells her dead lover that she killed him "because of your eyes."

With Momone as her mirror, the singer's moods were reflected back in ways that worked to her old friend's advantage. Having regained her ascendancy, Momone found that she could share Edith's largesse with the Cerdans, who returned to Morocco some months later with suitcases full of presents. In this context, Tony Frank's reluctance to exploit his liaison with Piaf seems admirable—though he may also have found her idea of *l'amour* too exalted. "We live in a time when money and business are more important than feelings," she told him. Being deeply in love meant that "nothing matters except the beloved," she wrote when he started backing away from their relationship.

Only one man had loved her as she wished, Edith wrote on May 26. "I will never again encounter such a wonderful thing," she continued, because men were so "*petit.*" Because of their spiritual smallness, they could not compare with this "grand" member of their sex (there was no need to name him), who had done everything he could to please her: "When I put him to the test, he was upright and willing." She would gladly see Tony if he chose to awaken from his slumbers, but in the meantime, it was goodbye.

—

Piaf again turned her mind to the business affairs that, in her view, assumed too much importance, and all that spring rehearsed the new songs composed for her by her old favorites, Monnot, Emer, Contet, Glanzberg, and, soon, Aznavour. Between engagements, in June, she recorded six new songs, including Glanzberg's somewhat predictable waltz "Il fait bon t'aimer" ("It's good loving you"), which may have evoked Marcel as she crooned seductively, *"Auprès de toi je n'ai plus peur / Je me sens trop bien à l'abri / T'as fermé la porte au malheur / Il n'entrera plus, t'es plus fort que lui."* ("Close to you I'm not afraid / I feel so safe / You closed the door on unhappiness / You're so strong it can't come in.")

On a different note, Piaf's lively rendition of Emer's "La Fête continue" evoked her youth in a counterpoint blending fairground noises with tales of *le petit peuple*—a *"gosse"* with sick parents, lovers planning suicide because they cannot marry, mourners who (like Edith) resort to séances to reach loved ones. Her subtle changes in coloration enhanced the contrast between these individual lives and the festive crowd's oblivion: *"La fête bat son plein, musique et manèges / . . . /Chansons, balançoires, la fête continue."* ("The fair's in full swing, music, merry-go-rounds / . . . /Songs, seesaws, the fair carries on.") Listeners resonated as Piaf sang of life's way of going on despite loss; Emer's melody was named the best song in the *réaliste* tradition at the Concours de la Chanson Française.

About this time, when Edith was also recording songs in English for her first American album, she met the man who would help her to carry on. During her June engagement at the Baccarat club, a brawny American with a pockmarked face presented himself as her new translator, having already done an English version of "Hymne à l'amour." After studying music in Vienna, Eddie Constantine had pursued a lackluster career in the United States. In France, playing on the vogue for American culture and his resemblance to a gangster, he had opened shows for Lucienne Boyer and Suzy Solidor. But it was Constantine's nearly incomprehensible French that caught Piaf's attention. As he struggled to make an impression on the star, she burst out laughing. Constantine sized up the opportunity. He was separated from his wife, he said, who was living in the States with their daughter. Piaf told her entourage that, given this state of affairs, she would not be wrecking a marriage, though some thought that the Constantines had an understanding that left the brash "Ricain" free to pursue his career as he saw fit.

Just the same, Edith's entourage was glad when Constantine moved into the Boulogne house and received her regulation gifts for lovers—a gold watch, cuff links, alligator shoes, and a blue suit tailored for his impressive physique. "Edith always needed someone to love," Aznavour wrote. "We knew that a page had been turned in the story of the household; a new one was being written even though Marcel was not forgotten." When Piaf recorded "Hymne à l'amour" in English that summer, it seemed like an endorsement of her song's translator.

Constantine and Aznavour worked out a division of labor, with the former in the role of Monsieur Piaf (the household's name for her latest beau) and the latter her right-hand man. They accepted her *idées fixes,* such as seeing her favorite films (*Wuthering Heights, The Third Man*) every night for a week, eating only when and what she wanted, or dropping everything to listen to Beethoven's symphonies. In July and August, while they toured resort towns together, she tried to teach Constantine to speak French and worked on his performance style. Although he was no Montand, she took him to New York for her three-month engagement at the Versailles that fall, partly to shield herself from memories of life there with Cerdan, partly to show that she was recovering from his loss with the aid of her "Ricain."

"Edith Piaf's summer tour will end with her marriage to her partner, Eddie Constantine," *L'Aurore* announced. Their engagement was all but official, the paper claimed, except for the fact that Constantine was still married. Meanwhile, the two singers were "the best of friends"—their close rapport made clear in the accompanying photo of the couple. Piaf persuaded Aznavour to write for Constantine, jazzy melodies to exploit his nonchalant manner and establish his image as a tenderhearted tough guy. Looking back on this time, Constantine let on that it had been impossible to resist Edith once she made up her mind: "When she turned on the charm, it was over. She could have made a tall building fall down with just one look."

After Piaf, Constantine, Aznavour, and the rest of her entourage arrived in New York on September 7, she took them all by taxi to a Brooklyn cinema where *The Third Man* was playing. Reigning over her court like a despot, she handed out punishments (such as no more movies) to those who disobeyed orders or, like Aznavour, fell asleep when Orson Welles came on the screen. In public, she showed the professionalism she always brought to performances, but she told Constantine that in the midst of a classic like "L'Accordéoniste," she sometimes thought about finances.

After several episodes of nearly fainting onstage, Piaf saw a doctor, who explained that she was dangerously anemic. "I should have dealt with this a long time ago," she wrote Bourgeat. On the doctor's orders, she was taking a powerful new drug, and for an uplift, immersing herself in Homer's *Iliad:* "It's . . . tremendous for my morale." She would need all her strength on the impending anniversary of Marcel's death: "Eddie is wonderful to me," she added, but did not say that she often scolded him for lapses in taste and minor disagreements.

By the end of October, after managing to get through the memorial mass she arranged for Marcel, Edith told Bourgeat that she felt better. She asked for a translation of the *Odyssey* and thanked him for the poem he had recently composed for her. "Like a Mary Magdalene . . . who appeared by the Seine," it began, the singer bore on her frail person "all the sorrows of humanity." His vision of Piaf as a vessel for the divine concludes in praise of her effect on her audience: "When you appear, a pale supplicant / To sing the refrains that we love / The hearts of those who suffer open up to you."

Though Bourgeat was no Cocteau, he knew how to encourage his Piafou when her spirits were low. By December, she felt well enough to record six more songs in English for Columbia, including the popular "Autumn Leaves," a tame version of "Je m'en fous pas mal" entitled "I Shouldn't Care," and "Don't Cry," a translation of her own "C'est d'la faute à tes yeux." When the future President Eisenhower came to hear her at the Versailles, she performed French folk songs just for him, along with his favorite, "Autumn Leaves." But at home she was often irritable, especially if Constantine mentioned his wife. By the end of 1950, when she turned thirty-five, Edith was relying increasingly on Bourgeat, Homer, and her many prescription drugs.

——

When Piaf and her party arrived at Orly early in 1951, they were met by the playwright Marcel Achard. Achard's plays, peopled by stock figures from the songs he used as titles, had been popular since prewar days, when his modernized versions of commedia dell'arte struck a chord with Paris audiences. Like Piaf, Achard was known as a "*spécialiste de l'amour*." For some time he had been writing a play for her, to suit their shared specialty. Entitled *La Petite Lili*, it took place in Montmartre, where Lili (Piaf's role) worked in a hat shop while her love affairs unfolded in the songs that Piaf had already written for the production. It was to open in March; the only problem was that Achard had not completed the script.

As the driving force behind the show, Piaf had chosen the director, persuaded Monnot to compose the music, and booked the A.B.C., her favorite Montmartre theater. After reading Achard's draft, she took advantage of the delay to demand a role for Constantine. The playwright reluctantly wrote him in as a gangster, to accommodate his accent. "He's a good dancer," the director observed to a radio host three days before opening night. "Good, that way, he doesn't have to say much," the host replied.

La Petite Lili opened on March 10 to an audience in evening dress, a striking contrast to the A.B.C.'s surroundings. The sets evoked familiar Montmartre scenes, from the artisanal hat shop to the hilltop square where Piaf had sung in her pre-môme days. In a wink at the audience, a character remarks that Lili's life is like "those street songs in which love and death hold hands." Piaf was outstanding as an early version of herself, the critics wrote: "[She] is a fine comic actress. . . . Of course the play was written for her, but she also had to like it: it's clear that she does." What was more, Constantine's physique suited his part. The musical was a triumph for Piaf, another wrote: "She proved that she is one of our most sensitive and moving actresses." Her own songs were applauded, especially "Du matin jusqu'au soir," which conjugates the verb *aimer* in each of its tenses, and "Demain il fera jour," with its promise of new dawns.

Ten days after the opening, the star was rushed to a private clinic for the first of a series of urgent hospitalizations. She recovered from the intestinal problems that would continue to plague her, in time to return to the A.B.C. in April, and to record the songs from *Lili*—already a popular success thanks to Achard's nods to Piaf's, and Montmartre's, legends. "Demain, il fera jour" became a hit as soon as its inspirational lyrics were heard on the airwaves: "*C'est quand tout est perdu / Que tout commence.*" ("It's when everything seems lost / That it all begins again.") Piaf sang each night for the next three months, interspersing performances at the A.B.C. with more recordings, gala events, and visits to the theater to watch her understudy play Lili. Just when it seemed that she was successfully conjugating the verb *aimer* in her private life, Constantine announced that he was bringing his wife and daughter to live with him. Edith went into a rage. It was her role to dismiss lovers, not to be left by them.

Years later, after Constantine had established himself as a singer and the star of French films noirs, he admitted that Piaf had helped his career. But he said little about their rapport and did not mention his presence at the séances in which the spirit of Cerdan voiced his approval of Constantine as his successor. The American had taken part in the table-turning "to console her," one of Piaf's friends said, "manipulating the table in secret as much to please her as to win her confidence." Others were less forgiving. He cared only about his success, one of his songwriters said: "Edith never knew about his role at the séances. We did what we could to keep it that way; it was best for everyone."

When *La Petite Lili* closed in July, Piaf went on tour with Aznavour and a vivacious young woman named Micheline Dax, whose talents included comedy and whistling. "Edith liked to laugh almost as much as she liked to sing," Dax recalled. Although the star let on that she had thought of entering a convent after Cerdan's death, "I could always make her laugh," Dax added: "There was a complicity between us that outlasted the cast of characters that went in and out of her life." Along with Chauvigny, Barrier, and the rest of Piaf's musical family, she also brought on tour a man named Roland Avelys, who performed in a mask as the Nameless Singer. A fixture at her Boulogne house, Avelys became Piaf's court jester and, like Momone, found ways to fleece his patron. Piaf pretended not to notice when money disappeared. "She wanted him and the others to be happy," Dax said. "She didn't mind being robbed as long as those who were doing it amused her."

Their summer tour was magical, especially evenings in the Roman amphitheaters in towns like Arles. "Edith outdid herself in such places," Dax wrote, "her unique timbre reaching to the starry sky." The singer crossed herself before each recital, but once she was onstage, "the crowd, in one voice, acclaimed her with fervent, interminable ovations until at last she smiled, reassured by the love the audience, already won over and grateful for all she would give them, gave to her. The longer she sang the more they came under her spell. . . . At the end a hymn of gratitude rose up like incense from the crowd, who were overwhelmed by feelings of happiness. One heard not only 'Bravo,' but 'Merci, Edith.' " At such times the star was truly happy and fulfilled in the exchange of love.

That summer, a new Monsieur Piaf also came under her spell—a bicycle champion named André Pousse, who would become a well-known actor and artistic director of the Moulin Rouge. Since the inauguration of the Tour de France in 1903, the French had idolized cyclists as national heroes, much like boxers. Pousse had been famous in Paris since the 1940s, when he won the grueling six-day cycling events at the Vélodrome d'Hiver.

To show her love, Piaf gave the cyclist gifts just like those that Constantine had received and promised to forgo alcohol—a vow she was unable to keep, in part because of the two automobile accidents that she was involved in that year. On July 21, Aznavour lost control of their car on the way to Deauville, where she sang the next night with her arm in a sling. Three weeks later, when Pousse missed a turn, she suffered a badly broken arm and fractured ribs. Rushed to Paris for surgery, she stayed in the hospital till the end of August, then went home with her left arm immobilized and a craving for the morphine that had been prescribed to manage her distress.

Looked after by her Boulogne "family," she regained her strength over the next few months but found it impossible to do without morphine, then as now a palliative for intense pain. "It was essential for my body," Piaf wrote years later. "I was addicted." Over the next year, until she underwent a cure, members of her entourage procured the drug for her. "I was earning millions; the drug dealers knew this and took advantage. I saw strange, disturbing people come into my apartment. I knew that they were robbing me, that they were exploiting my weakness, but I couldn't put up any resistance." Intimates like Dax, Monnot, and Barrier came to see her daily and did what they could to protect her, often to no avail.

By autumn, Piaf was able to do a star turn in a film called *Paris chante toujours* (she sang "Hymne à l'amour"). She also recorded six new songs, including three by Aznavour that showed her emotional range and his understanding of it: the lilting "Plus bleu que le bleu de tes yeux" (with its insider's allusion to her love of blue eyes), a satiric send-up of traditional bourgeois Sundays called "Je hais les dimanches," and a torrid tale of obsessive love, "Jézebel." Another new song written to order for her, "Padam . . . padam," by Contet and Glanzberg, mimed the singer's possession by the melody that would continue to haunt her: it became one of Piaf's greatest successes.

In November, a journalist praised her performance of "Padam" at her next stint at the A.B.C.: "Edith has found an extraordinary gesture which is not the sign of the cross. She hits herself hard on the forehead and chest; the audience shudders." The star seemed to be telling her own story: "*Ecoutez le chahut qu'il me fait / Padam . . . padam . . . padam . . . / Comme si tout mon passé défilait / Padam . . . padam . . . padam . . . / Faut garder du chagrin pour après / J'en ai tout un solfège sur cet air qui bat / Qui bat comme un coeur de bois.*" ("Listen to it shake me / As if my whole life was marching by / I'll give in to sorrow later / Note by note I parse this air that pounds / That pounds like a hardened heart.")

That winter, as Piaf sang of being possessed by music, the cast of characters in Boulogne went through changes. Marc and Danielle

Bonel legalized their union; Danielle began to manage Edith's chaotic household. After some violent fights, the singer broke with Pousse. His colleague Louis ("Toto") Gérardin, who held major French cycling trophies, replaced Pousse in her affections, despite his status as a married man. Momone left suddenly, taking with her Edith's souvenirs of Cerdan—personal papers, clothes, jewelry, and other gifts that she had given him and, since his death, preserved like relics. Devastated by her friend's treachery—Momone presented some of Cerdan's effects to her own lover and sold the rest—Edith declared that she could never forgive her.

The day before her birthday, the star had another shock. At Alice Gérardin's urging, the police came to Boulogne in search of the Gérardins' missing possessions, including Toto's trophies and eighteen kilos of gold bars. Although Edith was cleared of any misdeed, the scandal landed her back in the pages of *Détective,* as if fifteen years of consummate professionalism since the Leplée affair counted for nothing. For the popular press she was a husband-stealer, "the George Sand of the twentieth century." Like the novelist known for her love affairs, Piaf was said to be strangely seductive: "From her frail person emanates a magnetism that envelops, subjugates, conquers, ravishes." Her troubles with men, the journalist implied, were the lot of the "extraordinary woman."

Even though the press thought that Edith's relations with Toto had ended with the return of the gold bars, she kept hoping that they might be regularized. Her *"ange bleu"* (his eyes were the shade of blue she loved) had shown her that she was a passionate woman. During a separation she wrote, "No-one has ever made love to me as much as you do. . . . How I'll miss your body, your beautiful thighs and soft skin, your adorable ass." She would do whatever he wished, she wrote some weeks later: "Think of Joan of Arc, who would have believed that a simple woman would do such great things. She did it for the love of God, I'll do it for you." In another letter she fantasized about "lying between your beautiful thighs with my head on Popol . . . letting my dreams come true." Hoping they might have a child, she again vowed to stop drinking. But their rendezvous had to be discreet since his wife's detectives were still on the job: "The more difficult our love is," she said, speaking as much to herself as to Toto, "the more beautiful it will be!"

Meanwhile, Edith dedicated each performance of her hit song "Plus bleu que le bleu de tes yeux" to her "blue angel." (An avid movie fan, she may have associated Gérardin with Dietrich's role as the temptress in *The Blue Angel*—an intriguing gender reversal.) Some time later, with greater sympathy than the journalist who wrote that Piaf's tangled love life was the lot of the "extraordinary" woman, her friend René Rouzaud observed, "This exceptional being had the right to an exceptional life without our standing in judgment. And if the tradition of French *chanson* was enriched by her love affairs, we should only be grateful."

CHAPTER TWELVE

1952–1956

Hoping to put the past behind her, Edith sold her house in Boulogne and moved to an interim rental in the seventeeth arrondissement. The highest-paid French entertainer in her category, she still often spent more than she earned and for this reason multiplied professional engagements. In the spring of 1952, she was so busy that there were few opportunities to join Toto at the out-of-the-way hotels they frequented to elude the press. While touring the south of France with Aznavour, Avelys, and a group called Les Garçons de la Rue, Edith no doubt spent time with Tony Frank in Marseille during her ten-day stint at the Théâtre des Variétés. But soon after her return to Paris, she told a reporter that it was the only place for her. The city that she had celebrated in song after song claimed her heart, "especially now," she said with a smile, that she had met a man for whom she might give up her career. His predecessor, she added, had been "a mistake." What she did not say was that, although her rapport with this new man seemed promising, she was hedging her bets by continuing her liaison with her previous lover, albeit in private.

Edith's run of romantic mistakes let her see that she had gone from one lover to another to anesthetize herself after the death of Cerdan. Over the next months, while dallying with Gérardin, she came to appreciate the man whose presence in her life would bring stability—the singer Jacques Pills, known in the United States as "Monsieur Charm." They had been acquainted since prewar days, when Pills, né René Ducos, was part of the duo Pills and Tabet. He had recently been divorced from Lucienne Boyer; five years earlier in New York Piaf had remet Cerdan in their company. They belonged to the same world.

Shortly after Piaf's move to her new apartment, Pills and his young pianist, Gilbert Bécaud, called to offer her their latest song, "Je t'ai dans la peau" ("I've Got You Under My Skin"). The frank sensuality of the lyrics ("*J'ai froid, j'ai chaud / Je sens la fièvre sur ma peau*" ["I'm hot, I'm cold / I feel the fever on my skin"]) appealed to her, as did the older of the two men (Pills was forty-six). "Jacques came back the next day and each day after that," Piaf said discreetly: "We had to rehearse the song, work on it, perfect it!"

By June, the singers were preparing their joint appearance at the Drap d'Or club, Piaf's way of announcing that they were an item. On the eleventh, Edouard Herriot, the head of the French National Assembly, awarded her the Grand Prix du Disque for "Padam . . . padam" at a ceremony attended by the writer Colette, perhaps at the urging of their mutual friend, Cocteau. Piaf and Pills took a brief vacation at the home of a Mr. Frank (Tony?) in Marseille, where they announced their engagement before going on tour for the summer. In September, Piaf rented the nine-room apartment on the Boulevard Lannes, opposite the Bois de Boulogne, where she would live like a Gypsy for the rest of her life—as far from Belleville as one could go and still be in Paris.

The singers flew to New York in early September, in time for Pills's debut at a club aptly named La Vie en Rose and Piaf's fifth engagement at the Versailles. Two weeks later, she informed Gérardin of her wedding plans: she planned to be faithful to Pills, whom she loved sincerely. Marlene Dietrich helped Edith choose the blue gown and bonnet that she wore on September 20 to the Saint Vincent de Paul Church in New York, where the union was blessed by the priest who had comforted her after the death of Cerdan. Despite the press's attempts to cover the event, only Les Compagnons (then in New York), the French consul, and Piaf's entourage were allowed into the church. With Marlene as maid of honor, Edith walked down the aisle to Schubert's "Ave Maria." Loulou Barrier gave her away; Danielle Bonel tucked a white mink bolero over her shoulders as they set off to Le Pavillon, where the guests—Ginou Richer, Dietrich, Aznavour, Barrier, Chauvigny, the manager of the Versailles, and the Bonels—toasted the newlyweds.

That night at the Versailles the couple sang the teasing duet that Piaf had composed for them, "Et ça gueule, ça, madame"—whose lyrics reflected their amorous byplay. The next night, they appeared on Ed Sullivan's television show *The Toast of the Town;* two weeks later, *Life* ran a two-page article entitled "Mlle. Heartbreak: Singer Edith Piaf Finds 'La Vie' Can Be 'Rosy,' " with a full-page montage of Edith singing. "I'm truly happy," Edith told Bourgeat. "The better I know Jacques the more I appreciate him. You so much hoped to see me be calm. Now I am." Pills's reputation meant that, unlike previous partners, he would not become a rival. "I don't think she was deeply in love with Pills," a friend said, "but she was very fond of him. He was charming, handsome, a good companion. She could trust him. It was . . . more of an *amitié amoureuse* than a great passion." At this point, an amorous friendship offered the balance she needed.

Amused by their easygoing rapport, the couple called each other *mémère* and *pépère* (Mom and Pop). But, although Pills was no prude, he soon found that his wife needed more than the quantities of good wine they drank together. Addicted to morphine for chronic pain, cortisone (the new drug prescribed for her arthritis), and sleeping pills, she required greater care than Pills may have imagined at the start of their courtship. By November, Edith had lost her high spirits. "In America," she told Bourgeat, "you are tired as soon as you wake up." Still, while performing at the Versailles, she also found the energy for a UNESCO benefit, another Ed Sullivan show, and, with Pills, two broadcasts for the French radio. Looking ahead to their December engagement in Hollywood, she promised to keep to her diet in order to be svelte.

Before leaving to tour the Western United States, the couple flew to Montreal to perform together and see Edith's sister, Denise, who had lived there since her marriage. The young woman was shocked by the changes in Edith brought on by cortisone: "Her face was puffy, she had gained a lot of weight. . . . Her hands were not yet deformed but her feet hurt terribly." But she was relaxed enough to cajole Pills into promising her a mink coat as well as one for Denise. Her sister amused her by taking credit for her success, since Edith had begun singing in the streets after Denise's birth changed the dynamics in their household. "I never thought of that," the star replied. "I'm famous because of you."

Once they reached Los Angeles, it was clear that Piaf was far from famous there. Despite her appearance at a Hollywood gala for John Huston's *Moulin Rouge* and the publicity for her stint at the chic Mocambo Club, her New York success had had little impact. In January 1953, she and Pills appeared for a week at the Curran Theater in San Francisco, where Judy Garland, to whom Americans often likened her, had recently performed. On their return to Los Angeles, the couple met Joan Crawford, Spencer Tracy, and Humphrey Bogart, and Edith befriended Lena Horne, who had come to her opening night at the Playhouse in 1947. Edith admired Lena as a highly professional performer who, like herself, had had her share of adversity. (Horne and Lennie Hayton, the white musician who become her second husband, had fled to Paris in 1947 to escape the widespread hostility toward interracial marriages.) After a two-week gig in Las Vegas, where they applauded Horne's glamorous show at the brand-new Sands Hotel, Piaf and Pills flew to Miami Beach. "You'll weep, sob, thrill, you'll stand up and cheer," her Riviera Lounge poster promised. But even though the local critics deemed her show a "smash hit," she missed Paris, her friends, and their way of life.

Edith planned to come home in March, she told Cocteau. "What a joy it was to read and reread your letter. I know how many people love you, but if you could only know how much I love you in spite of the rare times that we see each other. I have a funny feeling each time I see you that I want to protect you against the world's meanness, then I realize each time that it's you who make me feel better and give me the strength to deal with this hard world. Don't you think it's marvelous to love someone without needing him, to love him just for himself? Well, that's the way I love you."

In March, Piaf and Pills moved into the Boulevard Lannes apartment, which had remained empty during their six months in America. "It was too big for Edith," Jacques's sister Simone recalled. "She felt lost." When Simone came to live there after their return, she found little furniture but many signed editions of French classics, including the works of Cocteau. Edith preferred the bedroom, the kitchen, and the salon, where aspirant composers waited by the Bechstein piano until she was ready to receive them. (She preferred to pick out tunes on its companion, an electric piano called an Ondoline.) "From the start," Simone said, "I was seduced by Edith's intelligence, her desire to keep learning, her enormous talent."

Simone soon learned to do everything Edith's way. When she writhed in arthritic pain, her sister-in-law called the doctor for more cortisone. When she had insomnia, Simone sat with her while she told the story of her life. Each day, at 1 p.m., she stroked Edith's wrist to awaken her, then handed her a cup of black coffee and *France-Soir*, with the latest installment of Edith's favorite comic strip, the tale of a wrongly incarcerated man who finds marital bliss following his release. After bathing, Edith doused herself with Arpège, made phone calls, took up the sweater she was always knitting, or jotted ideas for songs in the lined notebooks meant for schoolchildren that she favored. Later in the day, Simone watched show-business people file into the salon in hopes of winning Piaf's esteem: "Some were good, some less so, some were dishonest, but all were intelligent. Edith couldn't stand dummies!"

In the evening, friends often called to find her serving only white wine, her response to her husband's efforts to limit her drinking: "Naturally, everyone had to eat and drink the same things," her sister-in-law recalled. Meals consisted of the same dish for weeks at a time, such as chicken with *sauce suprême* (mushrooms, shallots, white wine, and cream). If a melody came to the star, she ran from the table to the Ondoline or summoned Chauvigny for his opinion—even at 3 a.m. Simone observed, "No one dared to tell her no."

Rehearsals started at midnight. Her entourage watched while Piaf worked with Chauvigny, who doubled as her pianist, on the fine points of performance—timbre, articulation, gestures—and gave notes for the accompaniment or made changes in the lyrics. After a restorative meal at 3 a.m., Edith entertained the group with the tunes of her youth, American melodies (often those interpreted by Lena Horne or Billie

Holiday), and, to their surprise, Fauré songs, all in her private repertoire. Rehearsals ended at dawn, when the singer went to bed.

Piaf earned large sums of money in these years, but most of it went
"into the stomachs and pockets of her friends," her sister-in-law
recalled. "Anyone could help himself from the refrigerator at any time,
but it was the army of so-called friends who borrowed from her without paying her back that ruined her." Piaf also paid the salaries of the
Bonels, Chauvigny, several musicians, and the domestic staff, which
consisted of her cook, Chang; two or three maids; and other person-
nel. (Chang went home with the champagne and other luxury goods
after his employer's parties.) When Barrier noticed her picking up the
restaurant tab for twenty people, some of them unknown to her until
that night, Piaf protested, "It's my money." She had long seen to the
needs of old friends like Camille Ribon, but many acquaintances now
took advantage of both her generosity and her drinking.

Taking herself in hand, Piaf underwent a series of "cures" at a clinic
specializing in aversion therapy. The night before the cure began, she
downed bottles of wine like a child defying the grown-ups. The next
day, the clinic staff had her drink whatever she liked and, a few hours
later, administered drugs to induce vomiting, a treatment that made
her detest alcohol but required weeks of recuperation. "We took her
there three times," Simone wrote. "She struggled and finally overcame this temptation"—in Edith's view, with divine help.

God was a presence in her daily life, her sister-in-law observed. But
though she "brought God into everything, Cerdan had become an
obsession." The household accompanied her to masses held in his
memory at the Auteuil Church. Edith gave Marinette and her sons
expensive gifts and had them stay for months at a time in her apartment. Simone had little to say about her brother's adjustment to Edith's
obsessions. For the most part, he humored her. "I was happy with
Jacques," Piaf recalled. "He'd understood that I couldn't bear to be
caged, that as soon as I felt shut in I would smash everything and run
away; he didn't try to keep me from living and thinking. . . . I often
made him unhappy without meaning to. But he was as solid as a rock."

Pills's equanimity served him well as Piaf's consort. The day after their wedding, he watched from the *Toast of the Town* studio wings as she sang Aznavour's torrid "Jézebel" and the haunting "Padam" ("This melody . . . seems to mock me for my past sins," she lisped in English.) Ed Sullivan joked that Piaf's spouse could now collect her salary and asked "Monsieur Peals" to take a bow. On November 16, as a regular on the Sullivan show, Piaf performed "La Vie en rose" in French and English against a backdrop of roses, then "L'Accordéoniste," running her hands up and down her torso. (Sullivan did not censor her gestures, as he had Elvis Presley's that fall, presumably because the audience did not know that she was singing about a hooker.) Between 1952 and 1959, she would appear on eight *Toast of the Town* programs, each time smiling up at the tall, ungainly Sullivan when he called her a "*petite* little French star" and patted her on the head.

Americans never learned to spell Pills's name, but he was acclaimed as Piaf's partner when they returned to Paris. In April 1953, they sang separately and together for a month at the Marigny Theater while also rehearsing Cocteau's *Le Bel Indifférent,* planned to follow their engagement at this elegant venue. After poking fun at their audiences ("good citizens glad to go slumming for a night by hearing the most famous muse of the streets"), *Paris-Presse* noted that Piaf owed her fame to "the art with which she extracts from daily life all the particles of poetry it contains." In the slums, the critic wrote, she had discovered "dreams of all sorts—of perfection, pity and compassion for human suffering, a generalized tenderness . . . pure romanticism barely camouflaged." As for Pills, this "charming" singer brought the audience back to earth with "a marked personal triumph."

Despite the success of her heartbreaking new song, "Bravo pour le clown," some reviewers were less than enthusiastic about the Piaf-Pills partnership. Their joint appearance was "conjugated and conjugal," *France-Soir* ironized, as if this coupling of professional and private lives meant that the singer known for her unconventional ways had joined the bourgeoisie. The public remained unaware that in order to perform each night, Piaf had recourse to the morphine prescribed for her chronic pain. When the revival of *Le Bel Indifférent* ended, on May 28, she went back to the rehab clinic; three weeks later, after a successful treatment, she left, determined to find a new focus.

Since many believed that a *chanteuse réaliste* should not forget her origins, the singer took this view into account when choosing projects. The two films in which she acted that summer seemed tailor-made for her. For a cameo appearance that winked at the "conjugal" side of her life in *Boum sur Paris*, a musical starring Pills, the couple performed the tune that had brought them together, "Je t'ai dans la peau," along with Piaf's "Pour qu'elle soit jolie, ma chanson," a witty "dispute" about music that dramatized their relations. For *Si Versailles m'était conté*, a reconstruction of court life at Versailles, Piaf, in peasant garb, sang the revolutionary anthem "Ça ira." (She nearly fell off the ladder from which she called for the death of the nobility.) Leading an insurrectionary mob, even a pretend one, inspired her to add "Ça ira" to her concert repertoire, but after performing the song in costume, Piaf dropped it when she saw that she could not change fast enough for her modern songs. When the film came out, audiences applauded her as France's *pasionaria*, ignoring the debate surrounding its tremendous cost and its vilification of the monarchy.

Pills may have wondered whether his wife's revolutionary ardor would manifest itself during the holiday they planned in the conservative Landes region of southwestern France in September. Rather than return to New York and the Versailles, they were to spend three months at his family home—playing Ping-Pong, taking walks, and writing the occasional song. Villagers watched the couple ride tandem down the region's long, flat roads and cheered at their benefit for the local school, an idea of Edith's. While Jacques and Simone held their breath, the star behaved "like a real lady" at a reception in her honor: "She answered all the questions put to her by the local dignitaries, who seemed surprised, even disappointed, to find that she was a normal woman with good manners." For their livers' sake they drank only mineral water, Pills told a journalist who had arrived to find them playing Monopoly. They returned to Paris a few days after a pilgrimage to Lourdes, with holy medals for the household.

In December, better able to cope with the stresses of her career, Piaf spent her time preparing radio and television broadcasts and at the Pathé-Marconi recording studios. Of her new songs she particularly liked "Heureuse," by René Rouzaud and Marguerite Monnot. Its view of true love as the shared experience of the best and the worst in life—

"*Le meilleur et le pire, nous le partageons / C'est ce qu'on appelle s'aimer pour de bon*"—described her situation: rather than an ode to sensuality like "Je t'ai dans la peau," it evoked the desire for lasting love. At Christmas, Pills welcomed the Cerdans as part of their extended family, which included Jacqueline Boyer, the daughter of his first marriage. The couple's public and private lives seemed in balance. Though there was still something undomesticated about the star, she had created a home.

The year 1954 brought several occasions for looking backward. In January, Pathé-Marconi gave a reception to celebrate Piaf's millionth record since her first recording session—at that time an unusual accomplishment, even for a singer of her renown. On the same occasion, Pills gave his wife a belated anniversary gift—bronze molds of her expressive hands, the bearers of the signature gestures with which she illustrated her songs. "Last time I asked for your hand," he teased. "Today you're getting two of them." It was no doubt touching to receive sturdy duplicates of parts of herself that suffered arthritic pain yet fluttered like birds at each performance.

After touring the south of France later that month, the couple prepared for their spring season. In February, Piaf recorded a new song by Rouzaud and Monnot, "La Goualante du pauvre Jean." "It was easy to write for Edith," Rouzaud said. "She inspired you, and it was stimulating to work with Marguerite Monnot's music." His *goualante*, or "lament," an updated medieval form, would be known worldwide as "The Poor People of Paris"—the homonyms of "Jean," the poor man of the title, and *gens* (people) conveyed its universality. What was more, the song's slangy lyrics suited Piaf's persona, and its refrain— "*Sans amour on n'est rien du tout*" ("Without love you're nothing")— conveyed her personal and artistic beliefs.

By this time, the singer's long-standing collaboration with "Guite" had resulted in twenty-seven songs composed together, and scores of tunes with lyrics by others since they had met through Asso. Like Piaf, Monnot had married. At the height of her career, she too was attempting to adjust to domesticity, though her husband, the singer Paul Péri, was as temperamental as Jacques Pills was calm. Monnot's way of blending poetic feeling with popular form had enhanced the construction of Piaf's persona. "Thank you for helping me to be Edith Piaf," the singer told Monnot on a 1955 television show celebrating the composer's life.

In 1954, the two women wrote "Les Amants de Venise," on the mind's ability to turn dross into gold, or a slum into Venice, and "Tous mes rêves passés," an address to their former selves: *"J'ai dépensé toutes mes illusions / Suis revenue riche de souvenirs."* ("I've spent all my illusions / I've come back rich with memories.") Though successful veterans of a music business that had rarely welcomed women, each was at heart the *fleur bleue* of "Tous mes rêves passés"—a dreamy young girl in search of love.

Conjugating marriage and careers proved to be more complicated than it had seemed when Pills and Piaf remet in 1952. After her third stay in the clinic, the couple rehearsed for separate engagements in March, Pills at the Moulin Rouge and Piaf at the Alhambra. It was difficult to appear on the same program, they told a journalist who asked why they were not performing together. Still, each sang on the other's television special: Piaf's, on April 3, brought together people from all phases of her professional life, including Bourgeat, her former secretary Suzanne Flon, Emer, and Contet. As Contet came onstage, Edith said, "Now we'll have fun!" Bourgeat's reading of his poem on Piaf as the Magdalene made a somber note in an otherwise joyful evening.

Piaf recorded "Ça ira" before leaving with Pills to tour France with Achille Zavatta's Super Circus, an extravaganza combining circus acts with big-name stars. The year before, Tino Rossi had earned a small fortune as the featured entertainer. This year, Pills would end the first half of the program, and Piaf—"the most famous female singer in the world," according to the poster—would close the show. Zavatta no doubt knew that her family had been circus people. Piaf's memories of touring with her father may have made her look with favor on the engagement, but the chance to earn a handsome salary would have been hard to refuse in any case. One can imagine her camaraderie with Zavatta, who clowned, did acrobatics, trained wild animals, and played the trumpet, drums, and saxophone; he was also a freethinker who belonged to the Masons. What Edith may not have envisioned was the grueling nature of their tour, eighty cities in nearly as many days.

On May 23, to the delight of those who remembered her as a child, the Super Circus performed in Bernay. The Bernay cinema ran *Boum sur Paris* in Edith's honor. The local paper boasted, "After applauding Edith Piaf, Jacques Pills, and the orchestra, you'll want to hear them all over again." Edith barely had time to see her relatives in Bernay and Falaise before touring the rest of Normandy and all the towns along the Atlantic coast. By July, her health had deteriorated. A local doctor who treated the star for a pulmonary infection and probably gave her morphine ironized, "She's fortunate to have been vaccinated by a phonograph needle, which lets her touch people's hearts when she has another kind of injection."

Edith left the tour in July to return to the clinic. After her treatment, Pills took her to his family home, where she spent most of the next six weeks in bed. Her illness, diagnosed as peritonitis, required surgery and another period of convalescence. By late October, she was able to go onstage but had to intersperse concerts with less demanding engagements, including brief television appearances. With Gilbert Bécaud she wrote "Légende," a ghostly tale of ill-fated love (the narrator speaks from beyond the grave). Introduced by her long spoken prelude, it was a departure in Piaf's effort to reach the audience, like another new song in a different vein, the anti-war "Miséricorde." Both would be recorded with lush orchestration and dramatic background choirs, a popular (though intrusive) device at that time.

In December, Piaf participated in Jean Renoir's first film in France in fifteen years, *French Cancan*—a tribute to the fin de siècle Montmartre that gave rise to the *chanson réaliste* as well as to the cancan, the art forms that had recently been depicted in John Huston's *Moulin Rouge*. A Frenchman from a great artistic family, Renoir meant to celebrate popular culture more authentically than Hollywood had done. To this end, he asked Piaf to play her precursor Eugénie Buffet in a reprise of Buffet's "Sérénade au pavé," a serenade to the streetwalker figure that clung to Piaf's image. This time the star wore not peasant garb but the long skirts and bonnet of the 1890s. She received top billing and a salary of seven hundred thousand francs for a cameo lasting three minutes.

On December 19, Edith's thirty-ninth birthday, she may have reflected that 1954 had consisted of poignant returns to the past punctuated by bouts with illness and rehabilitation. In the new year, she took a holiday with Emer, Barrier, and the lyricist Jean Dréjac, whose songs of prewar life, particularly the nostalgic "Ah! Le petit vin blanc," had made his name after the Liberation. Now, having recorded Dréjac's latest hit, "Sous le ciel de Paris," Piaf wanted him to write for her. Their collaboration produced one of the songs she would record in 1955, "Le Chemin des forains." Dréjac's ode to the *forains* (traveling artistes of the sort that Piaf had been as a child), set to a brassy score that included the ringmaster's cracking whip, expressed the poetry of lives lived beyond social conventions: "*Ils ont troué la nuit / D'un éclair de paillettes d'argent / Ils vont tuer l'ennui / . . . / Et Dieu seul peut savoir où ils seront demain / Les forains / Qui s'en vont dans la nuit.*" ("They pierce the black night / With spangled silver / They'll banish ennui / . . . / Only God knows where they'll be tomorrow / The travelers / Take off in the night.")

Before she herself took off across the Atlantic, Piaf recorded another song with a bittersweet view of the traveling life, with lyrics by Claude Delécluse and Michèle Senlis, set to music by Monnot. "*C'est à Hambourg, à Santiago / A Whitechapel, à Bornéo / . . . / A Rotterdam ou à Frisco,*" it began, a geography of ports where men have one-night stands with women who solicit them in every language— "Hello boy! You come with me? / *Amigo! Te quiero mucho!*" Another of Piaf's best-known tunes, "C'est à Hambourg" restaged the tale of the goodhearted whore multiplied by all the towns conjured in its credo: "*J'ai l'coeur trop grand pour un seul gars / J'ai l'coeur trop grand et c'est pour ça / Qu'j'écris l'amour sur toute la terre.*" ("My heart's too big for just one guy / My heart's too big and that is why / I send my love all round the world.") The cliché kept returning to claim her, as if the image of the woman whose heart embraced multitudes was how her audiences, and the singer herself, wanted to see her.

~

Piaf, Pills, Barrier, and Roland Avelys flew to New York on March 1, 1955, entrained to Chicago, then took the California Zephyr across the plains and through the mountains to San Francisco. While the rest of her party admired the scenery, Edith spent her time in the sleeper, attended by the train's hostesses, the "Zephyrettes." The Bonels joined them at the Clift Hotel. On trips to inspect local attractions, Edith remained indifferent to the redwoods: "Nothing special," she said, taking up her knitting, "just a lot of wood."

Her new show, *Edith Piaf and Her Continental Revue,* featured a mime named Mimmo, dancers, acrobats, and "Jacques Peals" (in America it was unthinkable to use his medicinal-sounding name). After San Francisco, where she was hailed as "France's greatest gift to the theater since Sarah Bernhardt," they took the revue to Los Angeles and Chicago. Each night Piaf sang twelve songs, including "If You Love Me" and "Merry-Go-Round" ("Hymne à l'amour" and "Je n'en connais pas la fin"), "La Vie en rose" in English and French, and "C'est à Hambourg," "Je t'ai dans la peau," and "La Goualante du pauvre Jean," an audience favorite. The critics raved when her songs came out on Angel Records' Blue Label. "Piaf is France," one wrote. "She makes one believe what Jefferson . . . once said: 'Every man has two countries, his own and France.' "

"I was so exhausted when I left Paris," Edith told Bourgeat, "that I've been taking it easy in America." Pills would soon leave the troupe to star in a musical in London; she would remain in the States. Meanwhile, she asked her mentor for more information about the aims and philosophy of the Rosicrucians: "This matters a lot to me, but let's keep it *entre nous.*" What she kept for herself was the presence of the new man in her life—Jean Dréjac, who would later join this esoteric order. The lyricist had come to Chicago to be with her but was staying at a hotel under an assumed name. Even if Pills did not yet know that he had a rival for Edith's affections, his decision to leave her show at the end of May suggests that their duo was unraveling.

The troupe felt relief on arrival in Montreal, where Pills could appear with his name spelled properly. Piaf was "a deeply expressive soul. In her eyes one sees the light from within," a local critic rhapsodized. Of the others, he singled out Mimmo ("another Chaplin") and Pills (a performer "with class"). After an engagement in Quebec City, Pills and Avelys flew back to Paris, the latter in disgrace for having behaved as unscrupulously as Momone. Her court jester, Piaf hinted to Bourgeat, might resort to blackmail; for this reason, Jacquot should not speak to him. "One needs a heart of steel in this life," she continued. Yet she felt fortunate, having met "a good man . . . the kind I never expected to meet again."

Although she omitted Dréjac's name in letters to Bourgeat, the lyricist's influence is clear when one reads between the lines. About this time, having also received a detailed account of the Rosicrucians' beliefs from Bourgeat, Edith applied to join the order. She wished to do so, she wrote, "because I am passionately interested in the quest for truth and would feel closer to God while trying to deepen my comprehension of his marvelous mysteries."

With Dréjac as her companion (to allay suspicions, he was introduced as her doctor), Piaf displayed "a joie de vivre that has nothing to do with vanity or success," a journalist noted; her smile was that of "a rebellious adolescent." The lyricist went with her to Hollywood in July, when she again appeared at the Mocambo, despite her repertoire's mildly incongruous note among the club's cockatoos, macaws, and Latin ambience. She planned to prolong her stay in the United States to earn enough for a country house in France, a project that became feasible when the director of the Riviera Casino in Las Vegas paid her *not* to honor her contract there after learning at the last minute that she did not correspond to his idea of a glamorous chanteuse.

Piaf spent the rest of the summer with Dréjac at an oceanside villa in Malibu, playing cards, entertaining French guests and stars like Marlon Brando (it is said that they had a fling), and using up her earnings from Las Vegas. "When I come back I want to dedicate myself to helping others," she told Bourgeat. Certain that God had destined her for something more than singing, she was searching for what that might be. Jacquot would understand, since he and she were "the last of the romantics."

In September, Dréjac accompanied Piaf to New York for her sixth engagement at the Versailles, where Judy Garland, Charlie Chaplin, Marilyn Monroe, and other stars came to applaud her. Dréjac and Edith shared an apartment with their "chaperones," the Bonels. "It was a time of simple happiness," Danielle recalled. Dréjac's humor amused Piaf, especially when he tested pasta by tossing it at the ceiling: the strands that stuck were done, he said, but had to be taken down to be eaten. During this time, he also adapted two American hits for her. "Suddenly There's a Valley" became the Rosicrucian-inflected "Soudain une vallée": *"Vous avez parcouru le monde / Vous croyiez n'avoir rien trouvé / Et soudain, une vallée / S'offre à vous pour la paix profonde."* ("You thought the world a waste / As you traveled all around / Suddenly a valley / Opens to peace that is profound.") Dréjac also wrote a French version of a tune that could hardly be said to promote serenity—"Black Denim Trousers and Motorcycle Boots," by Elvis Presley's composers, Mike Stoller and Jerry Leiber. As "L'Homme à la moto," the song, with its wild tempo and driven hero, made a striking addition to Piaf's repertoire.

About this time, Chevalier, with whom Piaf discussed her plans for a country house, became concerned for her equilibrium: "She's a moving bundle of complexes mixing courage, talent, and frailty with a nervous energy that inundates her little body and shows in her anxious eyes." In December, Dréjac sailed to France to look after his mother just before the return of Pills, who was booked to sing with Piaf during the holidays. She too felt like leaving, she told Bourgeat: "I'll come home around April and stay in France for a long time. I've had enough of exile!"

Nineteen fifty-six began with rehearsals for Piaf's January 4 concert at Carnegie Hall, an exceptional event at this shrine to classical music. Though she performed two of Dréjac's songs, his lilting "Sous le ciel de Paris" and the rocking "L'Homme à la moto" (while gripping imaginary handlebars), the singer's black dress established "a stark mood," in the view of the *New York Times,* which dubbed her "the high priestess of agony." The *Times* critic seemed surprised when the huge audience nonetheless responded "with an enthusiasm which proved that heartbreak makes the whole world kin." Almost in spite of himself, he praised the congruence of her persona, repertoire, and gestures—which were "of such naturalness and rightness that the performer's whole body is merged into the essence of the song." Won over by the end, after twenty-two songs in both languages, he allowed that watching the star, "You are no longer in Carnegie Hall but in a bistro on a side street on the Left Bank."

The next day, Edith flew to Havana, where she was booked for two weeks at the Sans Souci, a bucolic club outside of town that drew gamblers, Hemingway admirers, and fans who came to hear such performers as Sarah Vaughan, Tony Bennett, and Dorothy Dandridge. Dréjac's reappearance in Havana caught her by surprise. They quarreled, she accused him of being possessive. "Edith had already noticed someone else," Danielle Bonel recalled. "The page had been turned." Edith then took up with Dréjac's replacement, the guitarist Jacques Liébrard—a member of her orchestra since 1953. Her intimates explained these affairs as necessary to her art: "She always needed someone to love in her own way," Barrier observed. "It wasn't just sexual desire or because she loved to be in love, as some have said." Being far from Paris made it easier to forget that both she and Liébrard had spouses, though his union, with a woman twenty years his senior, had never been formalized.

Edith wrote Bourgeat from Mexico, where she was booked for February, that she hesitated to tell him of certain things—such as her transfer of affections from Dréjac to Liébrard. "I'm caught in a struggle with my conscience," she explained. "All I know is that each time it's more difficult to find happiness. Maybe I ask too much of life." But now she had a lover "with so much class that I feel overcome with admiration. That's what I've always lacked, being able to admire the man I love (except, of course, Marcel)."

In her struggles with her conscience, Edith did not forget her husband. From Mexico she counseled Pills about his next recital. He should send her copies of his songs, "so I can listen to your new repertoire." Meanwhile, she told him to limit his movements and simplify his gestures: "The more sober they are, the more true they'll be." Above all, he should be himself—a recipe that always worked to her advantage. She hoped that her "little man" would take her advice: "I so much want you to be wonderful." "I love Mexico more and more," she added: "It's a magnificent country!" Enthralled by the rhythms of Latin music and adored by her audiences, Piaf performed at three clubs in the capital, the Capri, the Patio, and the Tenampa, where she was adopted by the mariachis with whom she sang "La Vie en rose" in Spanish and a brooding ballad with an antithetical moral, "La vida no vale nada" ("Life is worth nothing").

Life seemed more than worthwhile when the star arrived in Rio de

Janeiro at the end of March for a two-week engagement at the Copaca-bana Palace. "I found a marvelous country," she told a French radio host. "It was the first time I said to myself, 'I could live here.'" Each night her fans covered the stage with flowers; for them she sang "La Vie en rose" in Portuguese. But on May 6, after two more weeks of concerts in São Paulo, Piaf flew back to Paris via Rio, Recife, Dakar, and Lisbon, thus ending her fourteen months in exile.

CHAPTER THIRTEEN

1956–1959

I n exile, Edith had absorbed the New World's rhythms while focus-
ing on her art, the privilege of the foreigner to whom local con-
cerns do not have the same resonance as matters at home. Despite
(or because of) her many love affairs, she turned inward in hopes of
finding what the Rosicrucians called the goal of the spiritual path—the
serenity that belies the turmoil of daily life. But on her return to Paris
in 1956, she felt the need to reconnect with her compatriots, her fans of
long standing and the younger generations, whose taste for American-
style music she kept in mind when recording "L'Homme à la moto"
(which to this day is reprised by French singers looking for lively
material). Piaf hoped to become their contemporary not as "Mlle.
Heartbreak" (*Life*'s name for her) but as the queen of song, or, in
Cocteau's phrase, France's nightingale. Her attempts for the next few
years to balance these claims kept her on a merry-go-round whose
pace threatened her equilibrium even as it generated themes so close to
her life that her songwriters seemed to be translating its rhythms into
musical form with their recurrent metaphors (especially the dizzying
ones, like the merry-go-round).

❧

As if their marriage were about to resume, Pills greeted his wife at
Orly with a bouquet of flowers. Their long-deferred reunion took
place amid the embraces of Edith's close friends Marguerite Monnot
and her husband, the music publisher Raoul Breton and his wife, and
Cerdan's sons. Since the increase of anti-French hostility in Morocco,
the Cerdan family had been living in Edith's apartment, looked after

by her majordomo, the new cook, Suzanne, and Suzanne's daughter Christiane, the *femme de chambre*. Piaf moved back to the Boulevard Lannes with Pills that night, and a week later appeared with him on television to perform "Et ça gueule, ça, madame," the song she had written when they were first a duo.

Within a few days, she began rehearsals for her next engagement, at the Olympia, to start at the end of May. "I was scared, much more so than for Carnegie Hall," Piaf told a reporter. In the fourteen months she had been gone, much had changed: "There were new songs, new stars. How was I to find my way?" Only the thought of all that she had overcome in the past allowed her to go on.

The star need not have worried. Her Olympia audiences, only too glad to embrace the môme from Belleville who had conquered America, welcomed her with a standing ovation. The singer's voice resonated through the large, dark theater, a spectator recalled: "It was galvanizing; the high notes seemed to come from her guts rather than her mouth. . . . By her seventh or eighth song I was in a trance."

Piaf's new songs, several of which she had tried out in the United States, invoked popular myths. "L'Homme à la moto" struck a markedly "American" note with its driving tale of the motorcyclist who meets his death despite the pleas of his sweetheart. "Les Amants d'un jour" also ended badly—with the lovers' suicide—yet its alternation of major and minor keys juxtaposed a vision of absolute love recalled by Piaf's persona, the woman who watches the ill-fated lovers from her place at the bar of a tawdry hotel: "*Moi, j'essuie les verres / Au fond du café / J'ai bien trop à faire / Pour pouvoir rêver / Mais dans ce décor / Banal à pleurer / Il me semble encore / Les voir arriver.*" ("Me, I wipe the glasses / At the back of the café / I've too much to do / To dream my time away / Yet in this sad décor / It's enough to make you cry / I can still see them / When they first passed by.") Piaf also sang her classics, including "L'Hymne à l'amour," which brought down the house. Her comeback was such a success that the management extended it for another month.

In a telling contrast to her triumphant return, Piaf's empty apartment struck a visitor as "the image of a separation." Earlier that year, Pills had told the press that he had had to leave her in the States to fulfill his contract. On June 6, the couple issued a press release announcing their plans to divorce. "We reached this decision together," Piaf told reporters. "We're apart too often because of our engagements." What she did not say was that she had lost interest in Pills and that he could no longer bear the cost of being Monsieur Piaf. Still, their parting was cordial; they would remain friends.

Piaf was right about changes in the music business during her absence. Mistinguett had died earlier that year, having kept her name and her famous legs in the limelight since her debut in 1895. Her death marked the end of an era, that of the entertainers who had dominated Edith's start in show business. By 1956, new trends were apparent in French musical culture, to some extent reinvigorated by North American rhythms but also by the successes of Edith's protégés. Montand was now a popular star, often in movies with his wife, Simone Signoret; Aznavour had found fame as a crooner whose emotional intensity resembled Piaf's; Les Compagnons' upbeat harmonies had made them an international success; Eddie Constantine was enjoying a film career as a private eye. Piaf's mentoring had transmitted to each of them her sense of *métier* but often at a cost to herself that she acknowledged only to close friends like Jacques Bourgeat.

There were also the new *chansonniers* who wrote and performed their own songs, among them Georges Brassens, Léo Ferré, and Jacques Brel. Piaf admired each for his way of extending the tradition. Brassens's bawdy poems on the lives of working people and his carnal singing style gave what was called the *nouvelle chanson* an idiom that spoke to the young, as did her friend Ferré's subversive lyrics about gutter denizens, which were sometimes banned from the radio on charges of obscenity. Piaf also thought highly of Brel's dark cadences, his way of turning each song into a brief drama that moved audiences at all levels of society while remaining intensely lyrical, an approach that owed much to her own.

Since the late 1940s, the jazz clubs in the Latin Quarter and Saint-Germain had shifted nightlife from Pigalle to the Left Bank, until an enterprising cabaret director reopened Cocteau's old nightspot on the Right Bank, Le Boeuf sur le Toit. Unable to afford a star like Piaf, he had invented one, the sultry, saucy Juliette Gréco, whose on- and offstage nonchalance intrigued well-heeled audiences. Since then, Gréco, the muse of Jean-Paul Sartre's circle in Saint-Germain-des-Prés, had come to epitomize the mood of postwar youth.

Some even said that Gréco was "the new Piaf." Like Piaf, the young woman performed in black, but instead of a dress, she wore the "existentialist" uniform, a turtleneck sweater and pants. A few years before, Piaf had flown into a rage on learning that Gréco was singing Aznavour's "Je hais les dimanches" ("I Hate Sundays"), even though she had rejected it when he first brought it to her. Piaf began performing the song "to show that existentialist how to sing." After recording her own version of Dréjac's "Sous le ciel de Paris" once Gréco had popularized it, Piaf announced that she would not share "her" composers with the singer; Gréco let on that though she admired some of Piaf's songs, she did not like her as a person.

In this context, Piaf feared that, like Chevalier, she had become a kind of national monument. She need not have worried, even if her lyrics-of-the-people tradition was one "in which the slightest exaggeration makes you look ridiculous," as the *Figaro littéraire*'s music critic observed after seeing her at the Olympia. In the past, Fréhel and Yvonne George had hit just the right note, he continued, but few apart from Piaf could carry on the tradition. The public always knew if a singer was faking it, but "no such fears with Piaf. . . . She wins us over with the first refrain."

To the amazement of Edith's intimates, her onstage mastery still hit them right in the heart. Micheline Dax, who had toured with her for years, watched the star from the first row at the Olympia: glued to her seat, she had to mop her tears with her handkerchief by the end of the show. "She had that effect even on those closest to her," Marc Bonel said. "She was like a medium, she had the whole hall in her hands. . . . You have Chaplin, Sarah Bernhardt, Fernandel: she was of that order."

Piaf's celebrity was such that she became a regular guest on television programs in honor of others, like Gilbert Bécaud. For her international audiences she recorded four more songs in English, including "Heaven Have Mercy" ("Miséricorde") and "I Shouldn't Care" ("Je m'en fous pas mal"), before leaving on a summer tour with the Cerdans and Jacques Liébrard, her guitarist and lover. Piaf's onstage reunions with Pills in Le Lavandou and Biarritz, booked before they decided to divorce, took place amicably, but a painful scene disrupted her stay in Saint-Raphaël, when Liébrard's "wife" threw herself at Piaf and called her a thief of other women's husbands. Despite this confrontation, which fed the gutter press's increasingly sensational accounts of her love life, she and Liébrard resumed their affair after flying to New York in September for Piaf's seventh engagement at the Versailles.

Ed Sullivan welcomed her back to his show a few weeks later. That night, she sang "La Goualante du pauvre Jean" and "L'Homme à la moto," demonstrating her ease in these strikingly different traditions, and responding easily to Sullivan's humor (when she translated the first song as "The Poor People of Paris," he asked her to sing to "the poor people of New York"). Each night at the Versailles, she smashed one of the crystal goblets that she used as stage props in "Les Amants d'un jour" to turn the nightclub into the shabby hotel of the song— until the management asked her to stop because of the cost. Booked in the States for the next six months, she hoped to return to Paris in April 1957 for a rest, "something I've never had," she told Bourgeat. She had a surprise that revealed how much he had helped her: "I'm a millionaire. . . . You so much hoped I could start saving, well, I've begun. Do I astound you? I think I owe this to the being who is so close to me and surrounds me with such unconditional love."

Edith often reread Bourgeat's account of Rosicrucianism, a source of solace that she kept among her private papers. That autumn of 1956, she was initiated into the order under the guidance of Marc Bonel, who had joined in 1954. "It helped her to relax," Bonel said. Being a member did not require much discipline, he added: "It's enough to read the monographs . . . in the proper sequence to face life's problems serenely." No doubt at Piaf's urging, her intimates, including Liébrard, followed her example.

In mid-November, Piaf and her entourage began the extended tour that would crisscross North America that winter, starting in Quebec, and in the following spring take her back to South America. After Quebec, they flew to Dallas for two weeks, then to Los Angeles for a return engagement at the Mocambo (one wonders if she found time to see Brando). Already on the verge of collapse by the end of the year, she managed to record "My Own Merry-Go-Round" ("Mon Manège à moi") and "If You Love Me" ("Hymne à l'amour") at Capitol Records' Los Angeles studios for an album that would include all of her songs in English.

By the start of 1957, Piaf's fatigue was so great that she felt "a sort of confusion . . . a total lack of balance," she told Bourgeat—a condition that she hoped to overcome by working twice as hard, so that she could afford to take a long rest. Though grateful for Liébrard's support, she missed her mentor: "The older I get, the more I understand how rare friendship is; if only you knew how precious yours is to me."

After concerts in Washington and Philadelphia, she was booked for her second Carnegie Hall recital on January 13. Despite her poor health (sinusitis, bronchitis, a high fever), she refused to heed the doctor who told her to cancel: "I didn't bring you here for that," she raged. "Your job is to give me an injection so I can last two hours onstage." With the support of Bonel, Liébrard, and the forty local musicians and singers, she lasted an hour and forty minutes, giving the audience some of her best songs in English: "Lovers for a Day," "Heaven Have Mercy," "Happy," "The Highway"; she sang "La Vie en rose" in both languages and the rest of her repertoire in French. Piaf's recital, a matter of national pride, was relayed to France, including her remark to the broadcaster after the final curtain, "I had the worst stage fright of my entire life!"

The star followed her Carnegie Hall triumph with engagements in Montreal, Chicago, and Havana, then flew back to New York in February for a month at the Empire Room. On her nights off, she took in Broadway musicals and listened to her favorites, Judy Garland and Billie Holiday. Unable to overcome her exhaustion, she asked Bourgeat to send her books on spirituality as a cure for her "disequilibrium," the unbalanced state maintained with tranquilizers, mood elevators, and drugs for pain that helped her keep the grueling pace she had set herself. In particular, she wanted Allan Kardec's works on the science of Spiritism (his coinage) to supplement her Rosicrucian readings.

Piaf told Bourgeat that she meant to "study spiritual science seriously this time, without being blinded by grief or surrounded by exploitative bastards," in a letter scolding him when she did not find the books she had requested on her return to a brief rest in New York. That spring, she maintained an even more dizzying pace, flying to Buenos Aires and Rio de Janeiro in May for extended engagements. In São Paulo, on learning that her divorce from Pills had become final, she told Bourgeat how much she missed "Paname" (Paris).

The books on Spiritism finally caught up with her in San Francisco, where she sang two shows a night at the Fairmont Hotel in June. It is unlikely that she had time for study, but she did take a day off to travel south, past the region's apricot orchards, to San Jose, to visit the Egyptianate Rosicrucian Temple with Liébrard and the Bonels. That day, they were all welcomed as brothers and sisters of the AMORC (Ancient and Mystical Order Rosae Crucis). Marc Bonel reflected, "She was seeking a philosophy designed to avoid harm and give protection, a peaceful way to love."

About this time, Piaf found another unexpected source of renewal, in a melody that accompanied her throughout her travels that year. This mesmerizing thirties tune, which she first heard in Argentina, proved to be Angel Cabral's "Que nadie sepa mi sufrir," a *vals criollo*, or Peruvian waltz, with a fast, light tempo that belied its lyrics on the pain of love. In August, after a return engagement in Hollywood, she flew back to Paris with Bourgeat's books and Cabral's score, spirituality and music being complementary paths to the "profound peace" she sought even when embarking on new adventures.

"After Jacques [Pills], my long pursuit of love began again," Piaf said a few years later. "But it was as if I had been playing blind man's buff," she reflected, perhaps remembering the sense of helplessness she had known as a child. But if she wore a blindfold where love was concerned, she was clairvoyant when it came to music. After Monnot heard Cabral's waltz and said that she wished *she* had composed it, Piaf acquired the rights. That autumn, during the long-awaited rest she had promised herself, the star had time to absorb the musical genres encountered on her travels—American blues and jazz, Mexican mariachis, Latin love songs. But it was the Peruvian waltz that stayed with her, inspiring her vision of an updated repertoire for the changed musical scene in France. One day, the lyricist Michel Rivgauche brought her his adaptation of the American folk song "Allentown Jail" (called "Les Prisons du roi"), which she adopted on the spot. As he was leaving, she gave him Cabral's score and asked him for lyrics to suit the tempo, the alternations of strong and weak beats that give the waltz its intoxicating sway.

Rivgauche returned with lyrics that suited both the melody and Piaf's persona, that of the woman who finds love only to see it vanish before her eyes. His poem imagines a couple brought together in the crush of a Paris street crowd—as on a simmering Quatorze Juillet. The woman first evokes the euphoric atmosphere: "*Je revois la ville en fête et en délire / Suffoquant sous le soleil et sous la joie / Et j'entends dans la musique les cris, les rires / Qui éclatent et rebondissent autour de moi.*" ("I see the delirious city at play / Choked with joy and with the sun / In the music I hear cries and laughter / That explode all round me and rebound.")

Piaf recorded this mesmerizing song, "La Foule," along with "Les Prisons du roi," in preparation for her return to the Olympia in the new year, following a brief tour of French leading cities. Meanwhile, she engaged a singer named Félix Marten as her *vedette américaine*, the last act on the first half of the program, even though she did not think much of his repertoire. In November, she told *France Dimanche* that Jacques Liébrard was the love of her life, but soon, on learning that he had slept with her secretary, banished the guitarist from the Boulevard Lannes and from her company. She was already looking to Marten as his replacement.

In December, Piaf joined the cast of Marcel Blistène's new film, *Les Amants de demain*. Playing an unhappy woman who finds peace in prison with the man she loves after killing her brutish husband, she performed four songs, including the saccharine title number and the poignant lullaby "Les Neiges de Finlande," whose lyrics affirmed her love of fairy tales. Piaf allowed that, though she liked making movies, she preferred the *music-hall*—because there, "you're in charge of everything, you make all your own decisions."

In the new year, she began making choices for her engagement at the Olympia. Repeating the same process as with Montand and other protégés, she worked closely with Marten, a tall, good-looking man with a cynical air, to bring out his tender side by teaching him love songs, a genre he had never attempted. Piaf's wish to be in charge came out in force during rehearsals. Marten must move his arms naturally, she shouted; he must *feel* the ballad written for him by Rivgauche, a declaration of love that began: "*Je veux te dire: je t'aime, je t'aime, mon amour.*" Despite Marten's reluctance, understandable given that he was married and the song was addressed to Edith, he rose to the occasion on opening night, February 6, 1958, and earned good reviews.

But it was not Marten that the star-studded crowd (including Juliette Gréco) came to see. When Piaf appeared onstage, *Le Monde*'s critic wrote, "an ear-splitting sound, a long salvo of applause, literally glued her to the microphone. . . . Whatever people say, whatever she does, Edith Piaf generates a flood of enthusiasm. Is it art, science, genius? Anything one could write about her is eclipsed by this perpetual miracle." Her opening number, "Mon Manège à moi," treating love as a merry-go-round, suited her, the critic added, but it was "La Foule" that revealed her genius.

Decades later, we can imagine this moment, the culmination of her mature style, with the aid of contemporary film clips and reviews. Standing under the spotlight with her eyes half closed, Piaf mimed the throng's ebb and flow with her arms. Only her face, her heart-shaped neckline, and those fluttering, swaying hands were visible. Her eyes opened; she sang the packed phrases of the first stanza in a trance but with impeccable diction and phrasing. Onstage yet out in the street, she seemed to lose her bearings until the last line of the opening bars, when the crowd thrusts her into the arms of a stranger.

With each line we hear the throng's cries in her husky tones; with each throb of her vibrato we feel the couple borne along by forces greater than themselves. Like the newfound lovers, the spectators become "one body" ("*un seul corps*"). All of us—singer, musicians, audience—are caught in the rapturous waltz ("*folle farandole*") filling the hall as she sings of her bliss: "*Nos deux corps enlacés s'envolent / Et retombent tous deux, / Epanouis, enivrés, et heureux.*" ("Our bodies entwined soar / And together alight, / Intoxicated, radiant, happy.") Living fully within the music, she reveals her listeners to themselves.

Like many of Piaf's songs, "La Foule" stages love's appearances and disappearances, but it does so more theatrically than most. In the next refrain, the throng wrenches the couple apart; Piaf sweeps the air impotently with her arm and, clenching her fists, curses the crowd that gave her this gift, then snatched it away: "*Et je crispe mes poings / Maudissant la foule qui me vole / L'homme qu'elle m'avait donné / Et que je n'ai jamais retrouvé.*" From the start, the song's swaying rhythms foreshadowed the tug of forces beyond her control as well as her dream of happiness. Piaf's concert was, *Le Monde* concluded, "the triumph of art for art's sake, an exceptional, unequaled success before which even the most skeptical must bow."

Edith could not bear to be without a man for long. A new candidate for her affections was at hand in Félix Marten. Still, while drawing him into her circle, she was also having an affair with the art dealer André Schoeller and flirting with the photographer Hugues Vassal. That winter, Edith's private life resembled a French farce, with men stashed in different rooms of her apartment, and accomplices pressed into service to keep them from meeting. Edith enjoyed each man's company, while playing them against one another as if it were just a game.

Marten, although reluctant to give himself completely to Piaf, saw the advantages in a liaison with the star. As his mentor, she intended to to leaven his mocking air with a touch of charm: "He should sing the way Cary Grant acts in movies, with a sort of tender irony," she told the broadcaster who interviewed them together. One can hear her trying to convince herself that Marten had more going for him than was apparent: "I think he has personality. No, I don't think so, I'm sure." Marten stayed until the end of her extended Olympia run but did not play a big part in Piaf's life: "Like so many others," a friend observed, "he passed through like a comet."

André Schoeller, who was also married, had long had a crush on Piaf. This suave young man—he was twenty-nine and she forty-two when they met—became her lover in the winter of 1958. Schoeller, known as "Dédé," introduced Piaf to modern art; it became her passion. Her entourage thought that she lacked much feeling for the Russian abstractionist Lanskoy, but his work appeared in her salon thanks to Schoeller's enthusiasm for the artist. They tried to be discreet about their liaison by going out in public with her entourage, but one night Schoeller hid in an armoire when Marten showed up. Edith was always in good spirits, Schoeller recalled: she drank only Carlsberg beer, and took mood stabilizers but no other drugs. "She was a healthy woman," he insisted in the face of myths about her addictions. What was more, "With her I encountered love in all its splendor, its purity. That's what it was, splendor, she had that in her, you saw it each time she sang. . . . I loved talking to her, sleeping with her, I loved her company. With her you became more than yourself."

If Piaf's romantic nature prevailed in trysts with Schoeller, it was her mischievous side that had won Hugues Vassal's heart the previous year, when *France Dimanche* sent him to photograph her in Dijon. Sizing up the skinny twenty-four-year-old, the star asked him to help her by telling Liébrard to disappear while she dined with Marten and, since he looked as if he would appreciate a meal, invited him to join them. On Vassal's return to Paris, he became part of the group that gathered nightly at the Boulevard Lannes to wait for Edith to appear from her bedroom; meanwhile, they were served dinner by Suzanne and took their places in the salon. "Thanks to this little circle," Vassal wrote, "Edith could finally play the part of the spoiled child, a priceless luxury for a woman whose past had been marked by so much drama." With the group, he watched the parade of men who at various times slept in her bed: "We were there to help, in silence, to give her our support—that was our only merit, one that didn't cost much, since the mere fact that Edith relied on us was recompense enough."

Vassal became the star's favorite photographer—her confidant and co-conspirator in the press's handling of her many crises over the next six years. Their intimacy grew, but it remained platonic: he too was married and greatly in awe of her, yet able to see the benefit she derived from the younger men who made her feel revitalized. Although none of them had all the qualities that she desired, each had

something to offer—provided he took it on her terms, as an unpredictable ride on life's carousel.

The star's Olympia engagement was the event of the 1958 winter season. The hall was full each night; people had to be turned away. When
Bruno Coquatrix, the director, begged Edith to extend for another five
weeks, she agreed—since her love affair with the public mattered
more to her than her private life or her fragile health, which she liked
to play down. After collapsing onstage in April, Piaf told the press that
though doing three shows on Sundays tired her, she could not disappoint "the Sunday crowd." She added, "They deserve more than the
others. All week they dream of Sunday." When Coquatrix again
begged her to extend her run, she agreed to three more weeks. By the
end of the engagement, she had performed 128 times for some two
hundred and forty thousand spectators, and was back on a regimen of
stimulants, barbiturates, and sleeping pills, followed each day by many
cups of black coffee. "She wasn't an addict, but she had pushed her
luck for so long," her manager said. "She needed stimulants to go on,
tranquilizers to go to sleep. She wore herself out that way."

In May, Piaf returned to Sweden with a suitcase full of pills and an
entourage consisting of Loulou Barrier, Ginou Richer, and the star's
new lover, the twenty-five-year-old Jo (later Georges) Moustaki, an
Alexandrine Greek who had moved to Paris as a youth. They had met
that February, when the songwriter came to her apartment with his latest compositions. Moustaki's shy charm made such an impression that
she invited him to stay after her other guests went home; she beguiled
him by playing the jazz songs she had brought back from the United
States. "I was fascinated, I had no idea that a singer from another time
might share my taste in music, which drew us together," Moustaki
recalled. By May, he had replaced the other men in her life. Combining
her familiar roles as mentor, lover, and collaborator, Edith hoped to
find the inspiration that she longed for in a relationship—love being
the prerequisite and open-sesame to her creative renewal.

The star was so taken with her young lover that she paid little attention to upheavals in France. Since April, when the government fell, the warring political parties had been unable to form a coalition. A provisional cabinet was named in May. At the army's urging, De Gaulle announced that he would take charge. In one of those odd coincidences, Piaf fell ill onstage in Stockholm on May 28, the day that the provisional cabinet resigned, and the next day flew to Paris in a chartered plane just as De Gaulle took power. Rather than focus on the crisis, the popular weekly *Noir et Blanc* ran a photo of the singer looking like the Madonna under the headline "Edith Piaf Gravement Malade?" ("Is Edith Piaf Gravely Ill?").

With Moustaki and her entourage, she spent part of June recovering at the country house that she had recently bought near Paris. Moustaki tried to limit her drinking, but Ginou kept her supplied: "It was not exactly a dry period," the younger woman recalled. About this time, Piaf wrote to Schoeller, who was on vacation in the Alps: she was bored, she missed his laughter. What she did not say was that her fatigue was still so great that she was battling depression. When the reporter Jean Noli came to interview her for *France Dimanche,* she declared, "If one day I can't sing, I think I'll shoot myself." The best antidote for depression was music that refreshed her spirit. Moustaki's new songs, "Eden Blues" and "Le Gitan et la fille," were like a tonic, she continued—"full of the sun, faraway islands, passionate love."

By July, Edith felt well enough to go on tour for the summer with her young lover. Snapshots of them on the beach at Cannes show Moustaki serenading her and Piaf laughing. One day, in a restaurant, she proposed ideas for songs that he could write for her: among them, a love affair in London on a gloomy Sunday. He jotted the word *milord* ("my lord") on a paper napkin; Piaf circled it and told him to start from there. He drafted a lyric; she suggested changes and sent the results to Monnot. Some weeks later, the composer came to Edith's country house with two different melodies. The women preferred one, but Moustaki liked the other, which reminded him of music he had heard in bars in Alexandria; Piaf accepted his choice.

Their song, which revived the whore-with-a-heart-of-gold trope, became one of her greatest successes. "'Milord' was typical of its time," Moustaki explained, "with a marked contrast between verse and refrain, major and minor passages, waltz, Charleston, and fox-trot rhythms—like a classical composition with different movements." Piaf had the gift, he said years later, "of knowing how to nourish creativity in others."

Though the young man's sense of popular music was acute, he was not, in Piaf's opinion, ready to perform his own songs. During a joint radio broadcast, she interrupted his rendition of one of them to show how it should be done. "You have to give more of yourself," she said. "When we come back from America . . . you'll be ready, but until then it's better not to think of performing." In time, Moustaki understood that Piaf had been as demanding with him as she was with herself. "She wanted to be the best," he observed, "not from ambition but as her calling, a somewhat mystical sense that she couldn't do things by halves. Onstage you gave everything; when singing you kept nothing for yourself; when writing you didn't stop until you had given your best."

Piaf recorded two of Moustaki's songs a few days before they were to fly to New York, in September, for her second engagement at the Empire Room. Driving to Paris from the country the day before their flight (Moustaki at the wheel, Piaf beside him), they hit a large truck head-on. The star was rushed to the hospital. She had lost consciousness, two tendons in her arm were severed, her lip had to be sutured. The U.S. trip was canceled.

A month later, after her convalescence in the country, they had a second accident at the same spot, with Moustaki again at the wheel. At first Edith seemed to be relatively unharmed—she managed to appear at Aznavour's opening night at the Alhambra, with Moustaki at her side—but she had to spend the autumn recovering from the two accidents. They were a warning from heaven, she believed, and her survival was "a miracle." By the new year, her lip, which was healing slowly, still hurt when she opened her mouth wide. "My life is over," she told *France Dimanche*. "I can't sing any more; I can't bite into the words." But, with her entourage in the wings, she bit into "Milord" at a test recital in Rouen. The standing ovation for Moustaki's song convinced her that she had been right about his talent. After a series of concerts in France, Tunis, and Algiers, she felt ready to fly to the United States on January 6, 1959.

Moustaki had little to do but observe Piaf's New York life there. He had the satisfaction of hearing her sing "The Gypsy and the Lady," an English version of his "Le Gitan et la fille," when Ed Sullivan welcomed her back to his program in January as "the most amazing ninety-seven pounds in show business." This operatic cry, in the voice of a Gypsy who begs his love to let him prove his devotion, may have given the young man pause, especially when she intoned, "No price is too high." Yet Edith was being an angel, Barrier told Bourgeat: "She's made a marvelous comeback, and as a result I now feel quite optimistic about her 1959 U.S. season."

Looking back, Moustaki recalled that onstage the star was transfigured. "She could breathe there, she was at home, she constructed her own world. If she felt ill in the wings, she felt better once she went on. She couldn't not sing. All she cared about was her songs. Nothing else." They composed together as a means of communication, and because she wanted to transmit her art—to stimulate him to write and, when the time came, perform. "She wanted songs that were poems set to music," he recalled. One of these, with Piaf's words and Moustaki's music, was never recorded. Its lyric, "*On est malheureux / Quand on aime vraiement*" ("You're unhappy / When you're really in love"), speaks for itself.

Five days after Piaf's triumphant return to the Empire Room on January 25, they quarreled. Moustaki left for Florida the next day; Edith wrote to André Schoeller, "It's over. . . . It had to end some time, you were right, all too right. Here I am without a man. I think it's the first time this has happened to me." She had not told him about Moustaki until then because of her scruples, "but this time I was wrong!" After finishing the letter, she implored her manager: "*Loulou, trouve-moi quelqu'un de gentil*" ("Loulou, find me somebody nice").

CHAPTER FOURTEEN

1959–1960

Whether or not they knew French, Piaf's audiences at the Empire Room responded viscerally to the chanteuse. "Edith Piaf never lets you down," a critic wrote after her opening. Her voice "hits you right in the heart. It is pulsating, penetrating, like no other I've heard. There were times when Piaf, in all her power, sounded like an organ and a whole orchestra combined." New Yorkers hung on her every word as she sang the rapturous "La Foule," which he called "a sad tale of a girl who lost her lover in a crowd." Like most of her songs, it seemed to come straight out of her life. "As I look back through years of night clubbing," the critic concluded, "I realize there are only a few genuine artists among the performers. . . . Edith Piaf is among the few, if not the only one."

Loulou Barrier must have been relieved when a nice young man of the sort that Edith asked him to find showed up at her stage door soon after Moustaki's departure. Douglas Davis, a fresh-faced Southern portraitist who hoped to start a celebrity series with a likeness of the singer, had studied at the Grande Chaumière art academy in Paris. While there, he had fallen in love with Edith's voice, he said; it was the most beautiful he had ever heard. The star agreed to sit for the young man, whose French was as good as his manners. Each afternoon, as Davis worked on her portrait, he told her tales of life in Atlanta, where he first studied art: one of his commissions had been a painting of Jesus surrounded by children of all races, for a Baptist church.

Edith's entourage wagered that "Dougy" would soon replace Moustaki. At thirty, the artist was just thirteen years younger than Piaf, and though he lacked machismo (they assumed that he was gay), "it was as if homosexuality didn't matter," Danielle Bonel recalled. "Provided the person didn't wear high heels or feather boas, she ignored it." What was more, Edith was charmed by Doug's attentions (he brought her violets). She began appearing in public with him as her new companion.

Within a short time, their romance was interrupted by the deterioration of her health. On February 16, she ran from the stage to the bathroom, spat up blood, and fainted. The doctor who examined her concluded that she had a bleeding ulcer caused by the quantity of medicines she took for her arthritis and other ailments. Two days later, she felt well enough to sing, but again left the Empire Room in midperformance. On February 24, after two blood transfusions, she was taken to Presbyterian Hospital because the ulcer was still hemorrhaging. Her surgeon operated immediately. "She's indomitable," Barrier wrote Bourgeat. "This morning she was teasing the doctors. . . . No fear whatsoever. Last night she chatted until 3 a.m., like a parakeet."

The operation was successful, but the star had to be hospitalized for a month. When she regained consciousness, Edith smiled at Danielle Bonel and said to tell their friends in France not to worry. *Noir et blanc* informed readers that Piaf longed to see Paris again and ran another photo of the star in a Madonna-like mantle, her hands folded in prayer. Maurice Chevalier did his best to cheer her but worried just the same: "Our little giant is going through a dark time," he wrote in his journal after a visit. Moustaki rushed back from Florida to find a stuffed animal named Douglas by Edith's side and its namesake in attendance. Following a second operation, in March, Edith stayed in the hospital for another month. With the loss of revenue from the Empire Room and the cost of her care, her New York stay had become a financial disaster. Yet, with her usual lack of interest in such things, she told a visitor, "The greater one's suffering, the greater one's joy. . . . There's always a bit of blue sky somewhere."

Piaf weighed just under eighty pounds when she left the hospital in April. She would soon resume her career, she told the journalists awaiting her appearance. By May, she found the strength to perform in Washington (to pay her hospital bills) and Montreal (for airplane tickets to France), while also making television appearances. "Edith Piaf's recent serious illness has not left scars on her artistry," the *New York Times* wrote when she sang a rousing "Padam" for the "Springtime in Paris" evening on *The Voice of Firestone*. "Of course it was not nearly enough," the critic continued, "but it did serve to give reassurance that the chanteuse has lost none of [her] dramatic intensity." And, despite her anger at Moustaki, who flew to Paris after telling her that he wanted to be his own man, she performed "Milord" on the May 31 Ed Sullivan show, ending her former lover's composition with vigorous sweeps of her hands and spirited clapping—as if to mark her return to full self-command.

By June, Edith felt well enough to appear at Carnegie Hall as honorary chair of a jazz concert to benefit the Sidney Bechet Cancer Fund following the musician's recent death. The next day, she flew to Atlanta with Doug Davis to meet his parents. "She was very frail, she took pills all day long," Doug's sister Darlene recalled years later, still touched by Edith's endearing ways. On learning that the girl from the Paris slums had always wanted to pick a ripe peach, the family took her to an orchard. "That was her heart's delight," Darlene continued. Entranced by Doug's Southern drawl, which had come back in force, and his devotion—a new experience for her in amorous relations—Edith told Marguerite Monnot, "There was so much love in his eyes . . . one would die for it. It's a pure, ineffable, unreal kind of love."

The press was waiting when the couple stepped off the plane at Orly on June 20. "What have you brought from America?" they asked. Piaf's reply—"An American!"—prompted the usual speculation about her love life, including a gossipy piece entitled "Piaf Likes 'Em Either Very Tall or Very Strong." (At six feet three, Davis topped the list of the very tall.) "This tiny little woman likes to feel protected," the article concluded. In a more serious vein, Piaf explained that with Davis she at last understood "that a man could give me something even before knowing me. . . . When I was in hospital he spent two hours on the subway every day to bring me violets and chocolates. . . . I hope that this is the real thing."

‿

The singer's tenderhearted companion was "exactly the kind of man I need and love," she told Moustaki in a letter intended to demonstrate her forgiveness. Though she no longer loved the composer, he could rely on her friendship: "What I need now is a very calm, orderly life, which in any case would not have suited you," she wrote with a touch of bad faith.

Davis soon learned that, despite Piaf's wish for calm, it was hopeless to think that she would change. Her entourage made bets about how long "*le doux Dougy*" would survive the demands of being her escort on her summer tour. At her first engagement, in Monte Carlo, he watched the theater fill with celebrities (Gary Cooper, Elizabeth Taylor, Eddie Fisher, Aristotle Onassis), who leapt to their feet when Piaf sang "Milord." After the performance, the star "fell literally into the arms of Douglas Davis, the young painter with whom she returned from America," an observer noted. She declared to all, "Without him I'd be dead."

Since Edith needed her escort by her side at all times, the American found it impossible to do portraits of the celebrities he was meeting, or to lead his own life. One night she insisted that he drive her from the Riviera to her country home, despite his fatigue. Davis lost control of the wheel near the end; two of Edith's ribs were broken. For the rest of the tour, she sang with her rib cage bandaged and blamed Davis for the accident. By the time they reached Bordeaux, the American had had enough. They quarreled; he went back to Paris to devote himself to his portraits, ignoring Edith's threats of suicide. "It was unbearable," he later told the press. "She's killing everyone with her impossible way of life."

Edith had to believe that there was another life after this one, she told Jean Noli, the journalist who would help her write her memoirs. Thus far, her own had been "a series of deaths and resurrections. What the doctors never understand is that I always get well because of my moral strength. . . . You only die of illness when you're afraid." Although these Rosicrucian-influenced beliefs may have comforted the star, the lack of a companion that autumn, when her health again declined, made her doubt her certainty. In September, she was taken to the American Hospital to undergo an operation for pancreatitis.

Jacques Pills rushed to see her; Yves Montand telegrammed from New York. Four days later, Edith's intimates cheered when she awoke with a deep-throated laugh: "Her laughter . . . meant that she had come through, she hadn't decided to leave them."

The star spent October going between Paris and her country home with her entourage, who knew that her health depended on her ability to keep performing. Cocteau arrived in a black velvet cape to read her his new poems and tell her that he loved her. Monnot composed a dramatic setting for Edith's equally dramatic lyrics for "C'est l'amour," a proclamation of *"le droit d'aimer"* ("the right to love"), which was conferred by the tears one shed for the beloved. Michel Rivgauche wrote lyrics inspired by Edith's persona, including the aptly titled "Ouragan" ("Hurricane"); Claude Léveillée, a Canadian composer who had joined the household at Piaf's invitation, wrote music to match Rivgauche's dark poems. Robert Chauvigny played piano at all hours; Marc Bonel devised riffs on the accordion and, with Danielle, calmed Edith, while helping to sustain the household's effervescence.

"This is how Edith thought of creativity," Hugues Vassal explained. She asked him to capture their ongoing rehearsals with his camera. "The music and lyrics had to wed her personality. That way she could give herself to a song. She also wanted to bring out the best in us, to push us as far as we could go." Piaf was teaching her collaborators to trust their intuition. "Infallibly she found the movement or the pause that conveyed an emotion. Her gestures were meant to express the soul of a song, to help listeners feel what she felt." During these late-night rehearsals, members of her entourage were often moved to tears, the photographer added. "She sang from her heart. She gave everything she had."

Her intimates sensed that they were nourishing her spirit in these exchanges, but other members of Piaf's court received more than they contributed. Some took advantage of her largesse. Rivgauche recalled the nightly gatherings of "abject beings, people who amused her, pilferers, spongers, those who took her money—a concept that simply didn't matter to her." By then, Edith had replaced Momone with a group of courtiers who were allowed to manipulate her even when she knew they were not acting in her best interest.

What mattered most to the star was to think that she was well enough to resume her career. In November, she undertook a string of engagements that would land her back in the hospital. For the rest of the year, reporters followed Piaf's every move in their zeal to stoke the public's fascination with what was said to be her final tour. Having transcended her status in the press as a man-eater (*"une mangeuse d'hommes"*) to become a national treasure, she would, from this point on, be subjected to endless intrusions into what remained of her private life.

———

Piaf's comeback began on November 20 in Melun, when she introduced two new songs, "Ouragan" and "C'est l'amour." Marlene Dietrich, who had just arrived in France, came to see her sing; her friend's presence seemed like a good omen. Piaf toured the north of France for two weeks without incident until Maubeuge, where she left the stage after forgetting the words to two songs. The doctor who was summoned advised her to cancel. She objected, "If I can't keep singing, . . . I'll never be able to believe in myself." Barrier let her continue, against his better judgment. Despite the tonic effect of the next song, "Milord," her voice failed before she reached the end. The press was told that her malaise had been caused by an overdose of barbiturates; no one let on that she was again relying on a cocktail of different drugs in large doses.

Accounts of what was now called Piaf's "suicide tour" appeared in the popular press, accompanied by photographs of her swollen face. Pierre Desgraupes, the host of a popular television program, came to Dieppe to interview her on December 11 amid rumors of her impending death. He began by asking if she could imagine *not* singing. "No," she replied. It was the only thing that made her happy: without it she would kill herself. She had to keep performing to get well. To the extent of disobeying doctors' orders? Desgraupes asked. "That's all I do," Piaf replied. "I disobey everyone." Changing the subject, the host asked why she could not bear to be alone. Because of ghosts from the past who came to haunt her, she murmured; asked who they were, she declined to give their names.

Two days later, at Dreux, her face was even more swollen, her hands knotted with arthritis, and she could barely talk. Lucien Vaimber, a doctor of chiropractic known for his success with extreme cases, was called in. Although he too advised her to cancel, Piaf insisted on appearing that night. Gripping the microphone for support, she sang eight songs and collapsed. As the star was carried from the theater, many in the audience burst into tears, certain that they would never see her again.

Piaf was again hospitalized in Paris—her treatment a sleep cure and vitamin injections. The staff refused all visitors until December 19, her forty-fourth birthday. She went home on Christmas Eve but returned a week later with severe jaundice, then spent January 1960 in the American Hospital. Although she insisted that she would recover in time for her Olympia engagement that spring, *Paris Match* began publishing illustrated chapters in "the novel of a life"—her own. "The subject of her songs is her life," the editors wrote. "Interpreting the world of suffering and romance, she bears witness to it, like a Victor Hugo heroine."

During the time Edith remained in hospital, the growing malaise over the government's handling of the civil war in Algeria (technically part of France) had assumed crisis proportions. Since 1958, when De Gaulle returned as the head of the Fifth Republic after a group of officers led a coup in Algiers in support of "*Algérie française*" (Algeria under French rule), civil unrest over the conduct of the war had dominated public awareness. Debates over what it meant to be French given the demise of the country's former rule in Indochina and perhaps in North Africa were carried on daily. Cultural events, including songs, were seen in relation to their political implications, or the views of their performers.

In the hospital, Piaf may have been unaware of De Gaulle's January 29 address to the nation in support of his policy—Algerian self-rule following the restoration of order, a plan that would meet with violent resistance. For the next six months, she spent most of her time recuperating in the country with Rivgauche, Léveillée, the Bonels, and the few members of her entourage who had not jumped ship during her suicide tour. Believing in the power of the mind to overcome physical frailty, she exhorted herself in her notebooks: "No more injections!" "Don't let yourself go physically." "See only those who bring you comfort and spiritual enrichment." And, touchingly, "Give up passions that harm you, renounce your desires, try to rediscover yourself." She must reread her Rosicrucian texts for support. Edith's morale strengthened over these months, because she knew that her compatriots looked to her as an example, and because her friends made it their business to help her get well.

During this time, Piaf worked with Rivgauche and Léveillée on the libretto of a "*comédie-ballet*" called *La Voix,* an homage to her by the choreographer Pierre Lacotte—who would become a specialist in the reconstruction of forgotten ballets. Lacotte imagined a play in which Edith would be heard but not seen while presiding over the action like a benevolent spirit: *La Voix* featured dances set to the songs she was to sing celebrating the streets of Paris, the newspaper kiosks, the Métro ("a fantastic basilica"), and the city's opportunities for just strolling around. "There was a pas de deux to be danced by a couple who were watched over by Piaf's character," Rivgauche recalled. Piaf had Léveillée play the music again and again while she mimed the pas de deux with her fingers: "It was ridiculous and touching at the same time. Those two poor deformed fingers trying to represent the man and the woman in all their lightness."

"Non, la vie n'est pas triste" ("No, Life Isn't Sad"), a song she wrote for *La Voix,* may have boosted her own morale. To find happiness, she advised, "*Il suffirait de tendre la main / Tu trouverais combien de copains.*" ("Just hold out your hand / You'll find so many friends.") The joy of collaborating on a new art form lifted her spirits. Though the project was shelved (*La Voix* would be shown on French television after her death), it served the purpose of immersing the star in the ether of artistic creation, her natural habitat.

Another intimate, Claude Figus, also helped Piaf look on the bright side. His position as her new court jester gave him a license to misbehave, an aspect of his character that had first won him notoriety in the homosexual world of Paris nightlife. After penetrating Piaf's circle through his ties to Cocteau's lover Jean Marais and the actor Jean-Claude Brialy, another of her admirers, Figus decided that he too wanted to sing. Edith made him her secretary, despite his aversion to discipline, a decision she would regret when his memoir of life at the Boulevard Lannes was published in *Ici Paris*, a gossip sheet devoted to the lives of the stars.

Although Edith was not yet ready for the Olympia, she recorded several new songs in May. In "Cri du coeur" (lyrics by the poet Jacques Prévert), she is once again a street singer who warbles like a bird: "*C'est la voix d'un oiseau craintif / La voix d'un moineau mort de froid / Sur le pavé d'la rue d'la joie / Et toujours, toujours quand je chante / Cet oiseau chante avec moi.*" ("It's the voice of a timid bird / The voice of a sparrow that died of cold / Where the streetwalkers are bold / And whenever I sing / That sparrow sings with me.")

Despite Piaf's hoarse tone and unsteadiness when she recorded "Ouragan," Rivgauche's torrential hymn to love, the composer told her, "You gave me such joy yesterday. . . . What a triumph! I'm happy and proud to have written [these words] when I hear you sing them." In spite of everything, she still believed in love, she told a visitor. It was "the most beautiful, the greatest, the truest of human emotions," but lovers should be indulgent with each other: "It's too easy to think you're always right."

On June 2, the star woke in the night with acute stomach pain. She was again rushed to the American Hospital, where she went into a coma caused by acute liver damage. "It is hard to say whether Edith Piaf will recover this time," her doctor declared. "It depends on her liver, which has all but failed. . . . Her system can't tolerate the medicines she must have taken for years." After emerging from the coma she remained in hospital until the end of August. Barrier canceled her summer tour and sold her country house to pay her bills. When she could be moved, he took her to his family home to recover; there she succumbed to dysentery and could not leave her bed. In desperation, Danielle Bonel asked Dr. Vaimber to treat her. The chiropractor had Danielle brew a tea of dandelion leaves: this bitter concoction and his gentle realignment of Piaf's spine stopped the dysentery and allowed her to walk again.

By early October, Piaf was well enough to return to Paris but had not yet regained her voice. In the hope that she might sing again, she obeyed Vaimber's orders: to avoid all drugs, follow her diet, and continue their treatments, though chiropractic was not recognized by the medical establishment. Vaimber, one of a few to practice this technique in France, had to be careful; his patient's fame meant that he could not make a mistake. He came to treat her every other day. On his recommendation, she took royal jelly—which would become known in France as the remedy that had "saved" Piaf. Despite her suffering, she insisted that she had no regrets: "If I had to live my life over again, I'd do it just the same."

October 24 marked a turning point in Edith's revival. That day, the lyricist Michel Vaucaire and the composer Charles Dumont came to the Boulevard Lannes. Having refused their efforts in the past, she claimed to dislike Dumont, who had written for Juliette Gréco. That evening, after a session with Vaimber, she canceled her appointments and went to bed. Changing her mind when she heard that the composers were there, she agreed to hear one of their songs.

Dumont sat down at the piano and spoke the lyrics. "*Non, rien de rien,*" he began, "*Non, je ne regrette rien,*" with the accent on the long, repeated "*non.*" The song's defiant opening (which seemed to echo Piaf's aside about having no regrets) caught her attention. After the bold affirmation of the penultimate strophe "*Je repars à zero*" ("I'm starting all over again"), she asked to hear it once more.

That night, which continued until dawn, Dumont played "Non, je ne regrette rien" more than twenty times for Edith's intimates—Monnot, Chauvigny, Suzanne Flon, the Bonels, Figus, the household staff, and Bruno Coquatrix, who was summoned to hear it at 4 a.m. Knowing that he was close to financial ruin, Piaf told Coquatrix to reserve the Olympia for her at the end of the year. She would do her best to save the theater now that she had the song she had been waiting for. Dumont could not believe what had taken place. Piaf's friends called it a miracle, her resuscitation through music.

"My life changed overnight," Dumont recalled. "It was just as Edith said: my song conquered the world." She recorded "Non, je ne

regrette rien" five days later, and with his help began planning her program for the Olympia. It would be the occasion to highlight her sav-
ior's music. Vaucaire wrote lyrics for one of Dumont's old melodies:
renamed "Mon Dieu," it joined her new repertoire, as did "Mon Vieux
Lucien," composed in honor of Dr. Vaimber. With Dumont, Edith
wrote two new songs, "T'es l'homme qu'il me faut" and "La Belle
Histoire d'amour," the latter in memory of Cerdan. Of the thirteen
songs in her program, the majority would be the work of her new
favorite. Piaf told Monnot that she would have to omit most of her
songs to make room for Dumont's, which had brought her back to life.
Guite was deeply hurt, some said heartbroken, to find herself on the
sidelines after nearly twenty-five years of collaboration with Edith.

Piaf spoke again with Pierre Desgraupes, almost a year after their
first interview, when all France had thought that she was dying.
Though it had been a mistake to continue her "suicide tour," she had
needed to go right to the end: "I always go right to the end," she said
with a smile. "I thought I would die but I wasn't afraid. It was almost a
relief, because I thought I couldn't keep singing. Life no longer interested me. . . . There is love, perhaps, but love without singing, that's
no good. Nor is singing without love." Now she felt apprehensive
about facing the public. Once onstage, Desgraupes observed, she was
a different woman. "I don't belong to myself when I sing," Piaf
agreed. "I'm in an altered state." Their interview ended with a stirring
rendition of "Non, je ne regrette rien" for the television audience—for
the occasion, the beloved *toi* of the final line, "*Ça commence avec toi.*"

Piaf's intimates rallied to give her support at this crucial moment.
After Cocteau heard her broadcast, he told his nightingale that she had
inspired him not to despair in a dark time (he was alluding to the news
from Algeria, where French officers had tried to bring down De
Gaulle). The poet was in awe of her bravery—"your strong heart
saves you each time that death wants you . . . Your faithful heart nour-
ishes your voice, enchants the young couples who listen to you hand in
hand and the solitaries like myself who keep singing despite the terrible
news." He told her she must take care of herself, "so you can astonish
us with the great organ sounds that emerge from your fragility."

Decades later, it may be hard to imagine the reverence with which

Piaf's return to the stage was greeted in 1960. To her contemporaries, it was a triumph of the French spirit, embodied in their little sparrow's revival and her resolve to save the Olympia. Coquatrix spoke for many in his open letter of gratitude: "At this sad time, when passion, enthusiasm, and magnificence are rare, how good it is to be present at this triumphant resurrection, above all the triumph of the individual." Rather than praise Piaf's art, he chose "to honor your courage, your faith, your love of God, of life, and of people." In a similar vein, a journalist who interviewed Edith before her opening turned to religious language to explain her role at a time of unrest: she was a modern Mary Magdalene, a penitent whose illness had brought her close to the divine, a believer whose art had made her its vessel. Like a latterday Joan of Arc, she seemed "to be setting out on a long crusade."

On December 30, opening night, thousands of ticket holders (including government ministers and army generals) waited for hours before being ushered into the Olympia. Shortly before Edith was to go on, Danielle helped her into her old Balmain dress and combed her thinning auburn frizz. Barrier and Dumont stood on either side of her to calm her stage fright. Before going on, she danced the samba with Coquatrix, crossed herself, and walked to the microphone while the orchestra played "Hymne à l'amour." For the next fifteen minutes, the audience applauded nonstop. When their cheers ("We love you, Edith," "*Salut, ma belle*") died down, she launched into the waltzing rhythms of "Les Mots d'amour," by Rivgauche and Dumont. By the end of the song, which projects an ecstatic vision of love pouring through a multitude of voices—"*ta voix / Ma voix, ou d'autres voix / C'est la voix de l'amour*"—the crowd was rapt, in a kind of lay communion, with the star as celebrant.

For a change of pace, she sang Dumont's "Les Flons-flons du bal," a lighter tune contrasting the dance hall's "tra-la-las" to love's sorrows. The crowd gasped when Piaf sang "*J'ai bien failli mourir*" ("I almost died"), but at the last lines, on the world's lack of interest in our tears ("*C'est chacun pour soi / C'est tant pis pour moi*"), they applauded her bracing appeal to the *je-m'en-foutisme* ("don't give a damn" spirit) of French culture—its tough-minded refusal of sentimentality. The rest of the program went smoothly, until Piaf stumbled over the words of "Mon Vieux Lucien." Telling the audience that she would start again, the star reverted to her prewar, *titi* accent to suit the tune's *java* lilt and *faubourien* tale of mateship.

Next came the show-stopper, "Non, je ne regrette rien." Piaf's coiled vibrato and alliterative rolled "r"s underscored the opening's triple negatives ("*non, je ne regrette rien*"). At first the accompaniment was restrained to let her voice ring out: "*Je me fous du passé,*" she cried defiantly: "I don't give a damn about the past." Then the orchestra swelled to enhance the final line, "*Ça commence avec toi*": "It all starts with you." The audience applauded wildly. She was singing for all who believed that old *amours* could be transcended and sorrows overcome—that what counted in life was a resilient heart.

Edith left the stage for a glass of water. By the awed looks on her friends' faces, she saw that she had won their hearts just as she had won the audience's. "I think it's working," she said modestly. There would be twenty-two curtain calls. Coquatrix told her that he had never seen anything like what had just happened—four thousand people enraptured in a collective love fest.

Three days later, for Piaf's gala performance, show business celebrities came to pay their respects. Film directors Claude Chabrol and Roger Vadim sat with actors Alain Delon, Jean-Paul Belmondo, Jean-Claude Brialy, and Johnny Hallyday, the teenage pop star known as the French Elvis. The actresses Michèle Morgan, Romy Schneider, and Piaf's old rival Arletty joined them, as did her former lover Félix Marten, who shouted, "Men, on your feet!" when she sang "Milord." At the end of the performance, Louis Armstrong, in the audience that night, was heard to say that Piaf had ripped his heart out; Duke Ellington presented himself at her dressing-room door as a jazz musician who wanted to say bravo.

If there had been any doubt in Edith's mind about her status as national icon, they were dispelled that evening. "I adore her," an awestruck Johnny Hallyday murmured. He would later acknowledge her influence on his generation, the young French singers who absorbed her emotional style even when it seemed at odds with rhythms inspired by American rock, jazz, and blues. Dumont, whose successful career as a songwriter dates from her Olympia triumph, reflected years later, "Edith was the lynch-pin between an earlier time, starting with the *chanson réaliste,* and the new generation of singers in France—the end of the old era and the start of the new." What was more, at that precise moment, she personified the Gallic way of meeting adversity in her belief that there was no reason to regret the past, no reason at all.

CHAPTER FIFTEEN

1961–1962

I n the new year, the main topics of interest among Parisians were Algeria and Edith Piaf. As De Gaulle prepared a referendum on Algerian independence despite widespread opposition, the press was glad to have something positive to report: Piaf's phoenixlike resuscitation. An observer wrote of her Olympia concert, "It wasn't the dying woman of last year, the pitiful, staggering one with a swollen face, but the Edith Piaf of ten years ago." The star could now support those who had given her support in the past, like Bruno Coquatrix: "He was nearly ruined. . . . Edith was all but penniless, her illnesses and friends having used up what she had. Now they're both saved." She was a *"miraculée"* turned miracle-maker, her recovery an example for all.

For the rest of 1961, as violent conflicts between Algerian separatists and their opponents brought the war home and sporadic bombings terrorized Paris, "Non, je ne regrette rien" was played and replayed on the radio, as if Piaf's voice evoked a national consensus. "This powerful emotive force," a historian writes, "was further enhanced by the unlimited popular belief in Piaf's ability to crystallize the deepest wishes of the human heart." To *Le Figaro* she was the voice of France itself: "More than ever, Edith Piaf strikes us as one of those mythical beings toward whom a large class of people, or an entire era, channels its own frenzy."

After three-quarters of the voters in metropolitan France approved De Gaulle's referendum, he began preparing for Algerian independence despite the opposition of that country's colonial population, the *pieds-noirs,* or "black feet," whose hostility to plans for a Muslim-led country would continue to fuel the conflict. In April, a putsch by rebellious army generals marked a turning point. From then on, the OAS (Organisation de l'Armée Secrète) would wage a bloody war against Algerian independence. After the putsch failed, a Foreign Legion unit that had backed the generals left their barracks singing their new anthem, Piaf's "Non, je ne regrette rien."

Meanwhile, the star was news in her adopted country, where her record albums continued to sell widely. The *New York Times* ran a long article on the resurrection of the "Sparrow Kid" by a reporter who had attended one of her Olympia concerts. Piaf's life, he wrote, was "a cliché of the Paris pavements. . . . But whether the story is true to the last agonizing misfortune, Parisians and the French in general take it to be true. The myth is larger than the woman. To Piaf fans, the question of where fact and fancy blur becomes wholly unimportant when she starts to sing." Though "a frail old woman" (she was forty-five), Piaf "belts them out like Joe DiMaggio," an American in the audience declared, provoking a Frenchwoman to reply, "She's not singing to you. . . . She's confessing."

Piaf's unofficial canonization lasted until the press began speculating about her relations with Dumont. To quell insinuations, she stopped singing "T'es l'homme qu'il me faut"—a song co-written with the composer, who was thought to be its addressee. It went: "*J'ai eu beau chercher / Je n'ai rien trouvé / Pas un seul défaut / T'es l'homme, t'es l'homme, t'es l'homme / . . . qu'il me faut.*" ("I looked in vain / Didn't find a thing / Not a single flaw / You're the man, you're the man, you're the man / . . . I need.") *Paris-Presse* wrote, predictably, "There's a new man in Edith Piaf's life. . . . If her Olympia comeback was spectacular, it's because she's in love." Dumont's presence at her side on the television show *Discorama* showed her feelings for him, the writer continued; her glances at him as she sang their songs were proof of her devotion.

Dumont, who was married and had children, was not her type, Edith protested. Besides, she no longer cared for love: she had suffered too much. Her denials did not persuade those who were intent on seeing her as a marriage-wrecker. "We were very close, but I was not Edith's lover," Dumont maintained, yet their intimacy colors the more than twenty songs he composed for her and the ten they wrote together. Her trust in him is apparent in their reprise of her romance with Cerdan, "La Belle Histoire d'amour," which ends, rather predictably, with the lovers' reunion in heaven. Soon Piaf insisted that Dumont become her singing partner. In their contrapuntal performance of "Les Amants," which they co-wrote, he sings to someone very much like Edith, the "*belle*" who knows that their song resonates with the experience of all those who have been in love.

As she had done with Moustaki, Davis, and other men in her life, Edith demanded that Dumont be available at all times. The composer did his best to keep her in good spirits. Exercising his sway, he had her banish Claude Figus, a bad influence since he supplied Edith with drugs. "When I knew her, she never touched alcohol, except for the occasional beer," Dumont said. "She drank enormous amounts of tea and took far too many pills, often doubling or tripling the dosage. She said she needed them to keep on singing. People have said all sorts of things about Edith," he continued. "They don't realize that the scope of her career meant that she couldn't be like the woman next door."

To the dismay of her entourage, Piaf extended her Olympia run through the first week of April. Physically she was a shadow of herself. What was worse, having abandoned Dr. Vaimber's holistic approach, she now relied on cortisone, Dolosal (a pain medication that leads to dependency, like morphine), and Coramine (a central-nervous-system stimulant injected shortly before she went onstage). After performances, Dumont and Barrier carried the star to her dressing room. At home, Danielle undressed her and put her to bed.

When Barrier begged Piaf to end the engagement, she said that she had to keep going for financial reasons: so many people depended on her. Her deterioration was obvious. She was alarmingly thin; her body was swollen, her face puffy, and her skin yellowish orange from the drugs. Although her memory was suffering and she sometimes experienced vertigo onstage, she stayed the course through strength of will and nightly injections of Coramine.

Unable to admit that she was seriously ill, the star made plans to conquer an unfamiliar country, the Soviet Union, to the extent of ordering a new black dress at Lanvin. She recorded nineteen new songs, including five by Dumont, and English versions of "Non, je ne regrette rien" ("No Regrets") and "Mon Dieu" ("My God") in advance of her U.S. engagements. In the meantime, after a week's rest at Barrier's country house, she insisted on making her spring tour of Brussels and provincial towns in France, accompanied by her exhausted entourage. "If you want to die slowly, go ahead, but at least try to sleep," her doctor told her the night before their departure. "I'm afraid of sleep," she replied. "It's almost like death. I hate it."

On tour, the star was no better. Each night, Dumont carried her from the hotel to her Mercedes (purchased the year before), then from the car to her dressing room, where an injection gave her the strength to go on. In Brussels, she performed even though she had lost her voice, whispering some songs and reciting others until she could sing part of "Non, je ne regrette rien." After each show, her entourage stayed up with her until the effect of the stimulants wore off. The rest of the time, she slept or sat unmoving in her chair.

In May, after recording "Les Amants," Piaf again fell ill. She was taken to the American Hospital for the removal of intestinal adhesions—a routine operation, the press was told—but one that had to be repeated two weeks later, because of complications. Still convalescing from recent surgeries (she had undergone eight in the last two and a half years), Piaf announced that she was preparing several new songs with Dumont for her autumn season. What she did not say was that the composer, who was close to a nervous breakdown, had taken a stand. Unless Edith returned to the clinic where she had been treated for drug dependency, he would no longer work with her. After three weeks there during the summer, she spent the rest of the year convalescing at home and at Barrier's country house. Her run of bad health had begun the year before, she believed, when someone took the cross that Dietrich had given her—which she kissed each night before going onstage.

It may have surprised Piaf to learn that Warner Bros. had bought the rights to her life. The star was not asked to play herself—a role intended for Leslie Caron—and, since the film was never made, may not have profited from the sale. About this time, she agreed to tell Jean Noli the story of her life, to be published in *France Dimanche* at ten thousand francs (about two thousand 1960s dollars) an installment. Blending Zola and *True Confessions,* she stressed her impoverished youth, then gave a sensational account of her travails with drink, drugs, and men. While relating her cures as if they had happened to someone else, she became agitated when recalling the most recent one: "While I was racked with pain on my bed, a face suddenly appeared to me: that of my mother, who had abandoned me when I was two months old, whom I found again fifteen years later in a tawdry room in Pigalle, gasping, 'My fix, I want my fix!' . . . It was her face, the memory of her, that saved me."

Piaf had ample time to draw up the balance sheet of her life during her convalescence. It might have been comforting to hear from Takis Horn a decade after their romance, when—in hopes of speeding her recovery—the actor sent her the Saint Thérèse medal she had given him before leaving Athens. But she was plunged into despair on October 12, when she learned of Monnot's death, from a ruptured appendix for which the composer refused treatment. Blaming herself for their estrangement after so many years of close collaboration, Edith agreed to speak about the composer on a national broadcast. "It's very hard," she began, "to talk about Marguerite Monnot, since, as everyone knows, she was my best friend. I won't even mention her talent; it's what helped me to be Edith Piaf."

Piaf was too distraught about Monnot's death to pay attention to the increasing civic unrest. On October 17, the Algerian separatists called on their compatriots in Paris to demonstrate against recent curtailments of their rights. Many demonstrators were beaten as they marched down the Champs-Elysées; those who died as a result of their injuries were thrown into the Seine. Even if Piaf knew of the massacre (it was not officially recognized until 1997), it is unlikely that she would have joined the artists and intellectuals who protested the police actions along with the increased presence of the OAS. Still too weak to do much but rest, she sought guidance in the work of Teilhard de Chardin, a Jesuit philosopher whose attempt to reconcile religious faith with science, *The Phenomenon of Man,* became required reading for her friends. Not sharing her enthusiasm for the book, they were heard to mutter that it was too esoteric, or to joke about having to take "tea in the garden," a play on the author's name.

During Edith's enforced respite, Coquatrix wrote that he missed her: "I spent a tête-à-tête with you one evening recently. Alone at my place, I kept playing the old records you made after the war—marvelous. And then I listened to the latest songs—even more marvelous. I'm waiting for the new ones, and then more; they are so badly needed, we all need you so much. If you knew how dull the 'profession' (our profession) has become without you!"

In actuality, the French music scene was far from dull that year. The National Assembly almost managed to ban rock-and-roll concerts altogether, then gave up the attempt. In the autumn, Coquatrix hired Johnny Hallyday to sing at the Olympia for three weeks, despite his doubts about the French Elvis. Resplendent in a dinner suit, the eighteen-year-old danced the new trans-Atlantic craze, the twist, sang a French version of "Let's Twist Again," and generally took young people's minds off the crisis (men his age were being sent to fight in Algeria). For some, Hallyday's blend of agitated syncopation with the emotional urgency he had absorbed from Piaf created a new style in popular music, one that appealed to teenagers craving a culture of their own. For others, it was a betrayal of the great *chanson* tradition. Piaf was the end of *music-hall*, Noli believed. After her, there was only show business.

Soon after a national radio program entitled *Rock Has Landed in France* ran a debate on the subversive new music, Hallyday's performances were banned in several provincial cities. When he *was* allowed to play, the police used tear gas to control the crowds. Within a few months of these disturbances, the OAS, oddly attuned to the younger generation's rebelliousness, would launch a violent attempt to sabotage De Gaulle's plans for a cease-fire under the code name "Operation Rock and Roll."

The year 1962 began with Dumont's disgrace. After fourteen months of devoting his life to Piaf, he needed a vacation. A trip to the Alps would restore his health, he believed. If Edith joined him, both would benefit from the air and the healthy way of life. Reluctantly, she made plans to accompany the composer in January but changed her mind at the last minute. The Paris air suited her perfectly, she told Noli; now that Dumont had left without her, he was not welcome at the Boulevard Lannes. Up to this point, the composer had exercised a positive influence over Edith, despite what she saw as his most serious flaw—the family he refused to sacrifice to be at her service.

A few days after Dumont's departure, Claude Figus wangled his way back into Piaf's good graces. As her protégé, Figus had been promised a gig at Patachou's Montmartre cabaret, where the well-known singer and her friends—Aznavour, Brel, Brassens—all performed. Knowing that the best way to Edith's heart was through music, Figus sent her a copy of his first single, "A t'aimer comme j'ai fait." The lyrics were bound to please her: "*Je t'aime comme un chien / Peut adorer son maître*" ("I love you as a dog / Adores his master"). Piaf succumbed to his flattery; Figus rejoined her as her secretary and drug provider.

One night, Figus brought with him a tall, good-looking twenty-six-year-old of Greek extraction named Théophanis Lamboukas. A hairdresser who worked at his family's salon in the Paris suburbs, Théo had always wanted to sing; though attracted to him in his own right, Figus also saw him as a companion for Edith, now that Dumont was out of the picture. At first, intimidated by her fame, Théo hardly spoke a word—until the night he spent at the Boulevard Lannes after missing the last train home. Recalling her idyll in Athens with Takis Horn, Edith baptized the coiffeur Théo Sarapo—a surname, she said, that in Greek meant "I love you."

Edith explained to friends that as her new secretary, Sarapo handled her correspondence, and Figus her appointments. The two men were her only visitors when she was again hospitalized in March after a bout of bronchial pneumonia, which required long hours in an oxygen tent. Noli pried the clinic's address out of her entourage and, with Vassal, turned up to find Edith sipping tea while Figus and Sarapo drank champagne. When Piaf introduced Théo, the young man did not make a strong impression on Noli: "He was too gentle, too soft, too attentive." Moreover, his manner seemed effeminate. Piaf asked the journalists to return the next day, when she would arrange to be in the oxygen tent for Vassal's photograph: "In this kind of calculation she was infallible, relying solely on artistic instinct and her prodigious knowledge of her public."

Two days after Piaf's release from hospital, the French and the Algerians signed the Evian Accords, ending the war. More preoccupied with getting back to work than with politics, she decided to forgive Dumont. Soon she began rehearsing his new songs for her, including "Toi, tu n'entends pas," a woman's complaint to a lover who is deaf to her passions (circuses, carousels, crowds, poets), and whom she admonishes, "*Tu les entendras / . . . / Le jour où tu m'aimeras!*" (You will hear them / . . . / When you love me!"). Together they sang his "Inconnu excepté de Dieu," a meditation on the burial site of one "known only to God"—the phrase on the graves of countless unknown soldiers—with the words intoned by Piaf in the background.

In 1962, in addition to five more of Dumont's compositions, she recorded Mikis Theodorakis' songs for the dance film *The Lovers of Teruel* (including the operatic title song and "Quatorze Juillet," a bittersweet waltz), along with her one overtly political song, "Roulez tambours"—which she wrote about this time, perhaps thinking of all those unmarked graves. "Roll the drums," it began: "*Pour ceux qui meurent chaque jour / Pour ceux qui pleurent dans les faubourgs / Pour Hiroshima, Pearl Harbor.*" ("For those who die each day / For those who weep in the slums / For Hiroshima, Pearl Harbor.") To a litany of wars, the singer opposed her arms: love and music.

Théo's accounts of military service in Algeria as a twenty-year-old made it clear that this experience had left scars. His vulnerability moved Piaf in the same way that Doug Davis's similar nature had won her heart. Since leaving Edith, the American had remained in France and painted portraits of Rex Harrison, Vivien Leigh, Alice B. Toklas, and his old friend the singer Rod McKuen; he had hopes for exhibitions in both Paris and Atlanta. In April, when Doug and Edith were reconciled, she invited him to stay at the Boulevard Lannes and commissioned portraits by him of her two secretaries. One can only imagine the emotional dynamics in the apartment, but having three male companions gave Piaf the energy she needed. And if Figus and Sarapo were still lovers, Théo's affection for Edith was obvious to all.

"Aren't I lucky to have had so many beaux," Piaf teased at a press conference. "They're all young, handsome, charming, and, after knowing me, brimming with talent." Théo was not her lover, she said, but in a few years he too would be singing at the Olympia. The *music-hall* tradition was in her debt: "There aren't enough stars? Well, I know how to make them." Each new discovery needed only to be photographed at her side to be known as her lover, a publicity coup worth millions. She had helped Dumont, Marten, Figus, Moustaki, and others this way. But where her private life was concerned, "people know only what I want them to."

She kept her sadness to herself after learning of Doug Davis's death in a plane explosion on June 3, just after his embarkation with a group of art students bound for Atlanta. (McKuen wrote a poem entitled "Orly Field" as a memorial to Davis.) Mourning his death, which brought back that of Cerdan, Edith threw herself into preparations for the future. She rehearsed nonstop with Figus and Sarapo after persuading both Dumont and the young composer Francis Lai to set the lyrics she had written for her protégés. When Figus began singing at Chez Patachou, she worked exclusively with Théo, teaching him to support a song's meanings with body language and gestures, often making him rehearse until he was near exhaustion.

By June, Théo was ready to sing Emer's love duet "A quoi ça sert, l'amour?" with Edith, the composer having rewritten it for them at her request. They appeared on national television as a couple who ask each other questions about love's purpose. "What is love good for?" Théo crooned, gazing down at Edith. The reason for living, she sang, looking up into his eyes: "*A chaque fois j'y crois / Et j'y croirai toujours / Ça sert à ça, l'amour.*" Once again, *amour* rhymed with *toujours*. Willing herself to believe that this would be the case with Théo, she smiled: "*Mais toi, t'es le dernier! / Mais toi, t'es le premier! / . . . / Toi que j'aimerai toujours / Ça sert à ça, l'amour.*" ("Each time I believe / And I always will / . . . / But you're the last one! / You're the first one! / . . . / I'll love you always / That's what love is good for.")

In June, Pierre Desgraupes began his third televised interview with the star by asking, "Edith Piaf, are you happy?" "I'm happy when I'm singing," she replied, "very happy." To his query about the source of her strength, she said, "It's a question of faith." When he asked if she believed in chance, she smiled and said, "I simply believe." Love had never disappointed her; it had given all that she desired. When Desgraupes asked why she always gave so much to younger singers, she said that she could see into people: "I have a kind of second sight. Even if no one else sees, I do. I see what a person will be in two years' time." As for Sarapo, she continued, "He's exceeded my expectations; he's learned with remarkable speed."

Edith toured the north of France with her two secretaries turned singing partners at the end of June; in July, she and Théo vacationed in Cannes, where they also gave several concerts. After an affectionate onstage reunion with Les Compagnons in Nice, she introduced Théo as her fiancé. "To be able to sing, you must be in love," she added—a comment that made clear how closely their engagement was tied to her vision of the future. Though traditionalists might call them "the most dissimilar, astonishing, touching, ridiculous, irritating, *sympathique*, immoral couple," the public loved the idea that la môme had found happiness.

On her return to Paris, Piaf prepared six new songs, including "Roulez tambours," "A quoi ça sert, l'amour," and "Le Droit d'aimer"—whose lyrics proclaimed her right to love and be loved, "no matter what they say." On September 25, she chanted "Le Droit d'aimer" from a platform on the Eiffel Tower to the huge audience gathered for the opening of Darryl Zanuck's film on the Normandy invasion, *The Longest Day.* Terrified by the height, she nonetheless followed the new song with the previous year's anthem, "Non, je ne regrette rien"—that night embodying the twin aspects of her persona as France's eternal *amoureuse* and as she who rises above adversity to triumph. "To attain this altitude," the writer Joseph Kessel said, echoing popular sentiment, "Piaf paid the price, every kind of price: poverty overcome, frailty and anxiety mastered, a merciless artistic standard, incredible courage."

At the end of September, some twenty-five hundred spectators applauded wildly when Edith sang with Théo at the Olympia. Seated in the front row at the gala performance, Hallyday was moved to tears, unaware that Edith was terrified after learning that Signoret and Montand, the singers Sacha Distel and Serge Gainsbourg, and the actress Michèle Morgan were in the audience. Piaf was clearly exhausted, an observer wrote; "her ravaged face resembled her most dramatic, most painful songs, her arms and body showed the stigmata of illness and suffering." Yet she had triumphed again. She had made Théo into a singer and found the courage to envision marriage with a man twenty years her junior. The press, more cynical in their judgments, noted that her voice was harsh and had lost some of its power. Others commented on the tasteless display of Théo's health when he sang barechested—a cruel contrast to Edith's frailty.

In private, confiding her doubts to Noli, she said that though marrying Théo made no sense given the age difference, with him she felt "not only the love of a woman for a man but also another feeling that life has denied me until now: maternal love." In the end, she thought, "only those who see wrong in everything will be offended." Piaf knew that she did not have long to live, Dumont reflected years later: "Her marriage to this young man shocked the press and the commentators but not the people, who adored Edith and Théo. She wanted to do something mythic . . . to show that right to the end, she embraced love, youth, beauty. It was hugely romantic."

Dumont was right about Edith's public. On October 9, her wedding day, thousands of fans lined the streets of the sixteenth arrondissement to catch a glimpse of their idol, unaware that, until very recently, she had thought of changing her mind. That morning, the star's romanticism won out over her sense of the ridiculous. With Barrier as their witness, the couple were wed in a civil ceremony by Robert Souleytis, the local mayor: "You are a great artist and a great Frenchwoman," Souleytis told her. Then, at the Greek Orthodox church nearby, they took their vows while a chorus chanted and hundreds of candles flickered—the kind of wedding Edith had always wanted in the only church that would marry a divorcée. Théo (in a black suit and tie) kissed his wife (in a plain black dress) and smiled for the reporters, who outnumbered the guests. Prominent among them were Vassal and Noli, who took credit for talking Edith into marrying Théo for the benefit of the publicity they would receive in *France Dimanche*.

When the newlyweds emerged from the church, they were showered with rice from nearby windows as paparazzi struggled to record the event and the crowd shouted "bravo." The hordes of Parisians, monitored by six busloads of police, rivaled the crowds that greeted De Gaulle or Brigitte Bardot, *Paris-Jour* noted. It was a case of Lolita in reverse, *L'Aurore* wrote, Nabokov's novel having recently caused a scandal in France: "That Edith Piaf arranged the saddest kind of publicity for her new union with a young man who was in diapers when she was singing 'Le Fanion de la légion' suggests either a lack of awareness or an obsession. It's true that artists need their public. But it's too bad that an artist of her caliber decided to invite the public into her bedroom." Refraining from personal remarks, an American television commentator noted that "the legendary singer of torch songs . . . has never lived by convention."

The next night, the newlyweds returned to the Olympia, where they were booked until October 24. Unmoved by the bravado of their union, some critics wrote scathingly of Piaf's performance. Her new songs were preachy; what was worse, she sang off-key. "Marie-trottoir," a revamped lady-of-the-night number by Vaucaire and Dumont, was a tiresome form of recrimination, one reporter said. Piaf was obviously ill, he continued, "and her remarkable voice is not the one that enchanted me when I listened to her records. The words waver; the notes quaver; the tunes are tuneless." More charitably, the writer André Brink said that Piaf "was extending the range of music in a completely different direction." Standing in the spotlight "like a dying moth," she gripped the microphone and sang "in a voice like a shout from a tomb . . . the voice of life itself, refusing to die, refusing to be silenced, the voice of humanity itself."

Piaf's appeal to humanity in general was well received by the throngs who came to applaud when she and Théo toured Belgium and Holland that winter. Each night from November 17 to the end of the year, the star walked gingerly onstage to "Non, je ne regrette rien."

Her repertoire did not vary, but she was sometimes barely able to complete the program. At Nijmegen on December 14, she sang off-key in the opening number—"Le Chant d'amour," set to music by Dumont to suit the poignancy of Piaf's lyrics about her "ordinary" love song. "*Si vous voulez bien écouter / Je vais chanter un chant d'amour,*" it began—"If you wish to listen / I'll sing you a love song," one that was based on her belief that those who truly loved each other met again after death. The crowd cheered in spite of her substandard performance, moved by the sentiment and her will to survive.

Piaf's hoarse, almost nasal tone was better suited to her protest song "Roulez tambours," which she performed at each concert that winter. As the tempo slowed, she sang more softly: "*J'ai vu tant de misère / Et tant souffrir autour de moi / Que je ne me rappelle guère / Si la douleur était pour moi / J'ai souvent vu pleurer ma mère / Je crois bien que c'était pour moi / J'ai presque vu pleurer mon père / Il ne m'a jamais dit pourquoi.*" ("I've seen so much misery / So much sorrow all round / I can't recall / If it was for me / I often saw my mother cry / I think she cried for me / I almost saw my father cry / He never told me why.") Audiences sensed that the song linked personal grief to the world's pain. But they could not know that in naming the ghosts who haunted her dreams, Piaf made her song an act of forgiveness.

Many listeners took another song on the program, "Emporte-moi," as an expression of the star's wish to transcend her sorrows. Painting a lurid picture of the Pigalle she had known in her youth, Piaf implored, in a voice that was harsh and sometimes flat: "*Emporte-moi bien loin, bien loin d'ici / Emporte-moi là-bas dans ton pays.*" ("Take me away, far away from here / Take me over there to your country.") Despite her vocal weakness, the audience also grasped the spiritual dimension of "Le Droit d'aimer," concerning her need to give herself completely: "*Quoiqu'on dise ou qu'on fasse / Tant que mon coeur battra / Quelle que soit la couronne / Les épines ou la croix.*" ("Whatever they do or say / As long as I live / Despite the crown / The thorns or the cross.") Piaf as Christ-figure required a stretch of the imagination, but the religion of love espoused in her songs struck a chord in her admirers.

Edith and Théo were interviewed on television in Lyon three days after her forty-seventh birthday and just before Christmas, dates that were connected in her mind. Piaf said that the secret of her strength was her faith. Always an optimist, she was full of hope for the future; she sang about love because "that's the basis of everything." Théo would become a first-rate singer in time, she continued, though he confessed that his stage fright grew worse each night. The press did not agree. One journalist replied to the question posed by their duet, "A quoi ça sert, l'amour?" ("What is love for?"), by writing acerbically, "To make you blind, of course, though under some circumstances love would do better to be silent." Even if many said that Théo lacked lung power, Piaf's public embraced her despite the critics' reservations.

The star put on a brave front throughout the tour but was barely able to cope with the rigors of two shows daily over the course of six weeks. Her intimates wondered how much longer she could go on, even with stimulants. Her health was deteriorating before their eyes; her marriage was not a source of strength. "I won't do any harm," Barrier said decades later, "by telling you that there was no longer anything between her and Théo. 'It's been over for some time,' she told me. She married him because it was too late to call it off vis-à-vis the press, the public, and maybe also Théo."

Although hugely romantic, their marriage had come too late, Dumont believed—when Piaf was too ill, too diminished in her sense of herself, to enjoy it. By this time, her mind was on final things—how to transmit to her public her faith in love as their shared reason for being, for the intense spiritual bond that they felt with each other.

CHAPTER SIXTEEN

1963

Piaf knew that her public was more forgiving than the critics who caviled about preachy lyrics and quavery performances. About this time, she recorded a talk meant to reveal all that she had learned from her tumultuous life. Music had long been her soul's conduit, but she wanted to speak to her audience as friends—"because you *are* my friends," she began, her voice full of warmth as she visualized them.

"I've never regretted anything," she continued, paraphrasing her famous song. "Each experience brought something . . . that helps me to express all sorts of feeling and emotion." First she would speak about friendship. Having hurt many of her friends without meaning to, she said that one must put oneself in the other's place rather than exercise judgment—a principle that also applied to social problems. For example, instead of rejecting the unruly fans of rock and roll, people should try to understand them: "They want to prove something. . . . There's always this threat hanging over us—war, the aftermath of war, the next war. That takes the romance out of life. But the young want to have fun, to make noise, to be part of their century."

What mattered most was love. "Everything comes down to that, love for humanity, for work, for the things one loves, just plain love between two beings." To live fully, people needed to find the love within, "to reveal it to yourselves." One understood the meaning of experience, she thought, by paying the price for it and by being unselfish: "It's extremely difficult to enjoy love to the utmost without asking for more. It's already something to have had a little." What was more, love, "the only emotion that money can't buy," existed in its own right long after the loved one's death. Piaf ended this unusually direct talk by singing her hymn in memory of Cerdan, "La Belle Histoire d'amour"—confounding earthly and divine love in its address to the beloved who awaits her in heaven.

Whatever reservations Edith had about her marriage, she adopted Théo's family as her own. Her sisters-in-law Cathy and Christie taught her the twist; their mother asked Edith to call her Maman, though they were nearly the same age; Edith invited twenty-year-old Christie to live with her and Théo in Paris. On the advice of Loulou Barrier, she rewrote her will to leave everything to her husband, an act that she accomplished with difficulty given her arthritic hands. To celebrate Théo's twenty-seventh birthday, Edith shared the stage with him for a benefit performance in January in the Lamboukases' suburb—to the delight of their friends and neighbors, who saw the star's marriage to the coiffeur as something like a fairy tale.

The couple spent weeks rehearsing for their February engagement at the Bobino Theater in Montparnasse, where Edith first sang in 1938. Intimidated by her sister-in-law, Christie sat quietly as they went over each song in Théo's repertoire, including several composed for him by Edith. When the young woman said that she too wanted to sing, Edith began teaching her along with Théo. As Christie Laume (a surname chosen for her by Piaf), she was to introduce the program and sing three tunes of the sort called *yé-yé*, the youth craze being marketed with songs that wed adolescent yearnings to the intoxicating beat of rock and roll. This new style was light stuff compared with her tradition, Piaf told Noli. But, in accordance with her belief that the young should do things their way, she inspired Christie to become a practitioner of *yé-yé*—which suited her youthful looks better than the theatrical *chanson*.

That winter, as the radio program *Salut les copains* (*Hi, Guys and Gals*) pumped out *yé-yé* hits by sprightly young women—France Gall, Françoise Hardy, and Sylvie Vartan, who later married Johnny Hallyday—Piaf's fans awaited her return. "A newlywed is coming back to the *music-hall*," a critic wrote with tongue in cheek. "Edith

Piaf hasn't ceased to amaze us," he continued, noting rumors that considerable progress had been made by "Monsieur Piaf."

Meanwhile, Edith and Théo sang at a succession of Paris movie theaters, her preferred way to prepare for new engagements. "Edith loved to work like this," Danielle Bonel explained. "She went home each night after singing to people who couldn't afford the great Parisian theaters. It was her way of keeping in touch . . . since, in those days, working-class families didn't have televisions." It was also her way of teaching her husband the difference between the overnight-success stories of the new music business and the slow growth of singers' reputations in the era of *chanson*.

Piaf's decision to appear at the Bobino, which had seen better days, was another way of keeping in touch with the great numbers of her followers who had modest resources. On opening night, the Bobino was full of working-class couples from the neighborhood (Montparnasse was then less fashionable than today). Holding Sophie, the poodle that was Théo's gift to Edith, in her arms, Christie introduced her brother, the opening act, then Edith, who sang fifteen songs, including several new ones inspired by her old themes—streetwalkers ("Margot coeur gros") and sailors ("Tiens v'là un marin")—and the "ordinary" love song she had composed with Dumont, "Le Chant d'amour."

One of the most poignant songs on the program, in that its lyrics had Piaf look back at her life, was "J'en ai tant vu," by Emer and Rouzaud. To a brisk accordion accompaniment, she began softly, "*Quand je colle le nez à la portière / Je vois passer ma vie entière / Au fil de mes peines, de mes joies / Et j'en vois beaucoup, croyez-moi / Mais pour toujours recommencer.*" ("When I glue my nose to the window / I see my whole life pass by / To the tune of my joys and sorrows / There are lots, believe me / But I always start again.") In a nod at the miraculous effect of "Non, je ne regrette rien," the lyrics emphasized both Piaf's gift for self-renewal and her sense that she had often walked the tightrope without a net.

That night, the *New York Times* found Piaf "in stronger and better voice than she has been for a long time." *Le Monde* agreed. The star was "in full bloom, radiant, savoring to the full measure the cheers, as if brought to life again by the well-earned enthusiasm of the public" and their love tokens, the small, inexpensive bouquets that covered the stage. (A sailor threw his hat when she sang of a mariner "as handsome as a god in uniform.") Only *Le Figaro* reverted to the gossipy tone of previous months when it came to Théo and Christie: "Like Napoleon, our empress of song practices a kind of family politics, which . . . seems to work well for her."

Buoyed by her nightly communion with "her" public, Piaf looked to the future. To aid the UN High Commission for Refugees, she agreed to participate gratis in a group recording meant to raise money worldwide, along with Maurice Chevalier, Louis Armstrong, Nat "King" Cole, Bing Crosby, Ella Fitzgerald, and Mahalia Jackson. The Mark Hellinger Theatre was planning a Broadway show for her in the fall: to be called *Piaf!*, it included a role for Théo. And even though impresarios from Germany, Canada, and Japan also hoped to book her, it was the United States that mattered. "You know," she told Noli proudly, "the only French stars who are a success there are Chevalier and myself." In the meantime, she performed without incident through the end of her Bobino engagement in March, when the audience applauded for twenty minutes and admirers congratulated her with the sense that they might be saying farewell.

Though in excellent spirits, Edith seemed even smaller—"as if she had shrunk back into her illness," Noli wrote. Only close friends knew that each night Lucien Vaimber waited backstage to manipulate her spine between numbers, Danielle Bonel brewed the teas that kept her in voice, and Simone Margantin, the private nurse who lived at the Boulevard Lannes, stood by. To control her digestive disorder, Edith ate only dishes made at home or the unvarying menu prepared at the theater by Danielle (noodles, chopped steak, and canned apricots). Margantin, Noli's source for news, told him that, in addition to arthritis and acute liver damage, Piaf was suffering from insomnia, for which she took sleeping pills that had to be counteracted by injections the next day. "Edith is using herself up," Margantin believed. "She still has enough nervous energy, but one day, . . . she'll find that she is totally empty."

Still running on nervous energy, Piaf gave an impromptu concert with Théo at Chez Patachou, in Montmartre, on March 24, which no doubt recalled her stints in the local dives thirty years earlier. The couple performed together at cinemas in Paris and Amiens while Edith suffered a bout of bronchitis. Still coughing, she went with her entourage to Lille, the capital of northern France, where she had lived like a Gypsy with her father. Four decades later, she was to sing at the Opera House, but because of a transport strike it was half empty for her recitals at the end of March. "Lille is a horrible memory," Danielle recalled. "Very few people in the theater, Edith exhausted. We didn't know that she would never appear onstage again. Lit by the projectors, she stood there like a brave little soldier to receive the last applause from the public that she loved so much and served so well."

Piaf recovered in time to record what would be her last song, "L'Homme de Berlin." Michèle Vendôme, the lyricist, recalled that the original title, "The Man From Bilbao," was changed at Piaf's insistence, because, she told Vendôme, "Nothing happens in Bilbao but there's a lot going on in Berlin." The young woman continued: "When I was writing for her, I felt I understood her. I felt as if I were speaking through her. . . . Being close to this woman who was very funny, sometimes very cruel, inspired me. At the same time it was nightmarish, a terrible worry to see her at the end." "L'Homme de Berlin" ended on a defiant note tinged with sadness: to her unfaithful lover Piaf sang over and over, "*Il n'y a pas que lui*" ("He's not the only one"), until these brave words faded to the poignant final "*que lui*" ("the only one").

In April, Piaf was rushed to a clinic in Neuilly for a blood transfusion when it was learned that her red-blood-cell count was dangerously low. Only semi-conscious, she sang her entire repertoire over her first few days there, before lapsing into delirium and another hepatic coma. Théo donated his blood, type A positive, like Edith's; Barrier canceled all engagements; her entourage tried to hide her illness from the press by claiming that it was Théo who needed medical attention. By May 1, when the Bonels brought her the traditional bouquet of lilies of the valley, she weighed only thirty kilos (sixty-six pounds), yet had regained her spirit. They were to spend the summer on the Riviera, where she would start rehearsing again once she had made a full recovery.

Before leaving for La Serena, the seaside villa that Edith had rented for June and July, she received a note from Cocteau, who had himself just recovered from a serious illness. It read: "My Edith, Released from death I don't know quite how (that's what we do, you and I) I embrace you because you are one of the seven or eight people to whom I send tender thoughts daily."

On May 3, Edith, Théo, and her entourage—Simone Margantin, the Bonels, Francis Lai, Noël Commaret, Suzanne, Christiane, and the chauffeur—flew to Nice, then drove to Saint-Jean-Cap-Ferrat, a sheltered site on a peninsula jutting into the Mediterranean that had, since the start of the century, attracted the rich and famous. Cocteau had wintered there for a decade, at the home of a wealthy patron. Though this magnificent residence was in sight of La Serena, Piaf was content to be where she was, she told a visitor: "Vacations are great! This is the first time I've ever had one. You can imagine how happy I am. . . . Of course it isn't ours. But I hope that if we work hard, my Théo and I, next year we can have one like that."

Though less grand than Cocteau's villa, La Serena was not lacking in distinction. The twenty-room house, which had gardens, a swimming pool, and a view of the sea, also came with a staff. Théo's family came for an extended visit; Suzanne made sure that meals were available at all hours. Soon many of Edith's acquaintances also showed up to enjoy her hospitality and sample the luxurious local lifestyle chronicled in *Paris Match*.

By mid-June, she had recovered sufficiently to start rehearsing, her voice having regained its strength and timbre. Piaf's spirits were high when Vassal and Noli visited, even though she was restricted to a diet of noodles and boiled fish for the sake of her *foie*. (Edith's liver barely functioned, Margantin explained: her doctors warned that the slightest excess would send her back into a coma.) Still, she posed for Vassal, picking flowers in the garden, watching Théo in the pool, and pretending to play Ping-Pong.

When a new inmate of La Serena urged Edith to enjoy herself as he was doing, she indulged in rich dishes that had exactly the effect Margantin was trying to prevent. On June 20, she went into a coma that lasted eight days, enough time for the hangers-on to decamp. On Piaf's return from the hospital, she asked to see her friends. Those who rushed to her side—Bourgeat, Emer, Contet, Dumont, and Asso, whom she helped financially—all feared that their visits might be the last. Cocteau telephoned regularly from his château outside Paris. Denise Gassion appeared unexpectedly but was sent away after she too asked for money. Aznavour visited often, on one occasion performing Russian dance steps to amuse Piaf and offering her financial help, since Barrier had canceled her engagements, including the Broadway musical. To boost Edith's morale, the household put on a show for Bastille Day. Marching into her bedroom with saucepans on their heads, they clanged the lids and sang "La Marseillaise." She roused herself to sing an old favorite, the nose-thumbing Montmartre tune "Nini peau de chien."

Their euphoria did not last long. Margantin told Noli that the next time he came they would be in a smaller house with no room for hangers-on: "The doctors . . . said quite clearly that if she made it through the next six months without going into a coma, she might survive. But if she relapsed, it was hopeless." Projecting her fears onto Théo, Edith watched over him with maternal solicitude. He must not swim in the sea (to keep from drowning); he must avoid the local temptations—drink, drugs, fast cars, gambling—indulged in by the younger generation of stars. To this end, she rented film after film to show at home while he sat by her side.

In August, Edith, Théo, and their inner circle moved to La Gatounière, a rental property near Mougins. There she kept to her diet, strolled in the garden on Théo's arm, sipped iced tea under a parasol, and talked of the future. She would have liked to perform in *The Threepenny Opera*, she told the Bonels, but when she sang for them, they saw that her memory was failing. During an impromptu call by Noli and Vassal (in the area for an article on Hallyday), she spoke only a few words at a time. "I had the impression that she had ceased to think about new projects," Noli noted. Only Théo's plans were of interest. Since he would soon go to Paris to act in a remake of the

Edith in Neuf garçons, un coeur (1947): *the film features her singing her compositions* "La Vie en rose" *and* "Sophie," *originally written for Yves Montand.*

Edith and Yves Montand after a joint concert, 1945

Jean-Louis Jaubert (then Edith's current beau, far left), Maurice Chevalier (center), Piaf, and friends in front of the Metropolitan Museum of Art, November 1947

Edith performing with Les Compagnons de la Chanson, 1947

Drawings of Edith and Les Compagnons illustrating
the Herald Tribune *review in which Virgil Thomson*
calls her the embodiment of French song

Edith reading the newspaper in her dressing room at the Versailles Club, her favorite New York venue, 1947

Tony Zale taking a right jab from Marcel Cerdan during their September 21, 1948, match at Roosevelt Stadium, Jersey City, which ended with Cerdan's becoming world middleweight champion

Edith, Marcel Cerdan, and Simone Berteaut, aka Momone, New York, 1948

Edith and Lena Horne, c. 1948

Franchot Tone and Edith during a radio broadcast linking New York and Paris, 1950

Edith's wedding to Jacques Pills, New York, September 16, 1952, with Loulou Barrier, Marlene Dietrich, and Nicholas Prounis, manager of the Versailles

Paris police protecting Théo Sarapo and Edith from admiring fans after their wedding at the Greek Orthodox Church, Paris, October 9, 1962; on Théo's left, Claude Figus

Edith strikes a saucy pose at the Rosicrucian Temple in San Jose, California (1956), with her entourage and members of the Order. Standing, left to right: Orlando Perrotta, Marc Bonel, Jacques Liébrard (her guitarist-lover), and Albert Doss. Seated to Edith's right is Danielle Bonel, and to her left is Lysanne Coupal, her secretary, whom she dismissed when she learned of Coupal's affair with Liébrard.

FELIX G. GERSTMAN presents

Edith Piaf

assisted by
an Orchestra and Chorus

CARNEGIE HALL
WEDNESDAY, MARCH 25, 1959
Tickets: $4.80, $4.20, $3.75, $3.05, $2.50
at Office Felix G. Gerstman, 140 W. 42nd St. (LO 4-6990)
and Box Office Carnegie Hall

FACING: *Piaf's second recital at Carnegie Hall, January 13, 1957, when, despite severe bronchitis, she sang twenty-three songs in French and English for the three thousand spectators*
LEFT: *Flyer announcing Piaf's third engagement at Carnegie Hall. (It had to be canceled when she collapsed from bleeding ulcers requiring repeated surgeries and a prolonged stay at New York's Presbyterian Hospital.)*
BELOW: *Edith gathering wildflowers in the fields during a period of convalescence in Dreux, 1958*

Edith coaching her protégé-lover Félix Marten in her Boulevard Lannes apartment, with Michel Rivgauche at the piano, 1958

Edith feeding her new companion, artist Douglas Davis, whose portraits of her were used on her record covers, 1959

Sheet music for "Non, je ne regrette rien," the song that brought Piaf back to life after her "suicide tour" (portrait by Douglas Davis)

Charles Dumont and Edith, Christmas 1960

Théo and Edith walking in the woods in Belgium, 1962

Mourners traversing Père Lachaise cemetery to reach Edith's grave on October 14, 1963, the day of her funeral, when her cortege stopped traffic all the way across Paris

silent film classic *Judex,* Piaf asked Noli to write about his role: "People don't like him," she said. "They think unpleasant things about him. . . . Please be kind and help him."

Two weeks later, her condition worsened when a local doctor, unaware of her medical history, prescribed a diuretic that sent her into another coma. The star was rushed to a nearby clinic, where she remained for ten days, gradually regaining consciousness on a regimen of liver extracts, vital serums, and rest. For the next month, she was taken there twice a week to receive the implant treatments that kept her alive. At this point, the distrust between the two camps of her entourage—the Bonels, who had cared for her at home and abroad for many years, and Margantin, Vassal, and Noli, who saw themselves as better qualified to understand her—became open hostility after Vassal photographed her in a comatose state, a scoop for *France Dimanche.* Though no longer welcome at La Gatounière, the journalists kept in touch with Simone Margantin, who told them of the household's next move, to a village near Grasse where Edith would be in peace.

Piaf's entourage moved to Plascassier, in the wooded hills high above the Riviera, on September 1. The house, which mingled different architectural styles—Baroque, Provençal, and Norman—would have been enjoyable under happier circumstances. It had a neglected garden full of leaves, an unkempt swimming pool, and the quiet that came from being set back from the road. Edith said that its gentle atmosphere suited her. Strolling in the garden, she seemed absent, as if in a dream. To a journalist who called one day she said that Théo was now the family breadwinner. "It doesn't keep him from phoning three times a day and spending weekends with me," she continued, putting his absence in the best light, though in private she said that she was tired of him.

During the week, Edith spent mornings in bed and afternoons in the garden, knitting and chatting with Simone, who became her confidante as well as her nurse. Together they read a weighty tome on French history. Soon the star began supervising the education of her new protégée, Clarine, a teenager from the village who helped in the household. The girl, she insisted, must make something of herself. Her parents, the village grocers, may have sensed that their famous client saw Clarine as a substitute daughter—or a version of her young self. "I suffered too much from the lack of an education," Edith said. "We must help her." Once Simone, who wrote poetry, began to impart her feeling for literature to the girl, and Edith made her practice English for hours each day, Clarine rarely picked up a broom.

Few people came to Plascassier. One day Dumont phoned from a bar in Marseille; he and Jacques Brel had just written a song for Edith, "Je m'en remets à toi" ("I Defer to You") and wanted to show it to her. They could not see her in her current state, she said: Dumont should sing their composition over the phone. He did so. She approved of Brel's lyric—"*Pour ce qui est d'aimer / Pour une part de chance / Pour ce qui est d'espérer / Ou de désespérance, / Je m'en remets à toi.*" ("When it comes to love / When it comes to luck / When it comes to hope / Or to despair / I defer to you.") She asked Dumont to bring her the song when she returned to Paris. "I was happy to be in touch with her," he said years later, "but I wish I had gone up there anyway."

Despite their bad behavior in August, Vassal and Noli were welcomed when they drove to Plascassier on October 5. Edith received them in the garden. Did Noli know the Rosicrucians' philosophy? she asked. One could be both a Christian and a member of their order, she explained. "They believe in reincarnation, and I do too. For a long time I've wondered what becomes of us. It can't be true that once we're dead we're nothing but dust." As for herself, she would have liked to spend more time on earth while awaiting the Last Judgment. When Edith fell asleep in her chair, Noli asked Margantin for a prognosis. "She goes from exaggerated gaiety to dark despair," the nurse replied. "When she's depressed, she keeps saying, 'I paid a great price for my stupidity.' I fear she's lost her will for the first time in her life."

After Théo and Loulou Barrier left for Paris at the end of the weekend, more impromptu visitors arrived—Simone Berteaut and her daughter Edith. When Momone had telephoned earlier that day to ask if she might come to Plascassier, Piaf told Danielle to say that she was too tired. Her old friend came anyway, hoping for a reconciliation that did not take place. Edith was too weak to see her and her namesake for more than a few minutes. (In her 1969 life of the star, Berteaut would invent a touching reunion scene to exonerate her misdeeds.)

On October 9 (the anniversary of her wedding to Théo), chills and dizzy spells kept Edith in bed. Sure that she would never sing again, she listened to all of her recordings. Cocteau phoned to say that he would come to see her very soon. Later, as her voice began to fail, she told Danielle, "My dear, we'll go on more splendid trips together."

In Simone Margantin's account, Edith asked the nurse to lie next to her on the bed while she napped. After she went down to eat dinner, she heard Edith calling her and rushed upstairs. Barely able to speak, Edith said she was afraid. With Simone's help, she knelt on the floor to whisper her prayers. During the night, when the nurse went to Edith's room to check on her, she was shocked to find her face the color of straw. She called the local doctor, who came early the next morning and said that it was a matter of time. Unaware that Edith was hemorrhaging internally, Simone tried to make her comfortable, wiping her forehead and lips, holding her hand. Danielle took turns at Edith's bedside and called in vain for a priest to administer the last rites. That afternoon, Edith sat up, her brilliant blue eyes fixed on something in the distance. Then she fell back down, death having claimed her.

Just as the legends surrounding Piaf's birth make it difficult to establish the truth, rival accounts of her death by those close to her give the biographer pause. One can see that life at close quarters with a luminary whose last days were under relentless surveillance by the press would set the household on edge, and that differences in background and temperament would be exacerbated under pressure. Decades later, Danielle Bonel contradicted Simone Margantin's account of Piaf's final hours: it was she, Danielle, the devoted long-term companion rather than the recent arrival, who had been with the star at the end.

With hindsight, we can see disagreements over Piaf's death as competing stories about the passing of her spirit—the transmission to her intimates of her blessings. On October 10, the day she died, the two clans worked together to honor her wish to be buried beside her father and her daughter at Père-Lachaise. Danielle rushed to the clinic where Edith had last been treated and, with the mother superior's help, found an ambulance to take her body to Paris—a move that was, strictly speaking, illegal, but one that allowed them to elude the reporters gathered outside the villa. Théo and Loulou arrived that afternoon from Paris. The ambulance left a few hours later, with Simone and Théo on either side of Edith, as if she were asleep. Danielle and Loulou closed up the house and flew to Orly the next day as headlines in extra-bold type announced Piaf's death at seven that morning, her doctor having agreed to sign a certificate giving the date of her demise as October 11, and the place as Boulevard Lannes.

Alerted to the news, Cocteau delivered an impromptu eulogy on the state radio. "Edith Piaf burned herself up in the flames of her glory," he began. "I never knew anyone who was less protective of her spirit. She didn't dole it out, she gave everything away. . . . Like all those who live on courage, she didn't think about death; she defied it. Only her voice remains, that splendid voice like black velvet that enhanced whatever she sang. But if I still have her voice, I have, alas, lost a great friend." An hour later, the poet died—giving rise to the myth that France had lost two of its brightest stars on the same day.

Once in Paris, Danielle and Loulou dealt with practical matters. Embalmers were summoned; Edith was robed in one of the black dresses she had worn onstage. A rose in one hand and an orchid in the other, she was placed in her bed in the library, the makeshift chapel where friends came to say adieu. Robert Chauvigny, who had been too ill to keep working with her, paid his respects; Dédée Bigard came, holding on to her son's arm; André Schoeller lamented her spirit's passing; Tino Rossi, Yves Montand, and Charles Aznavour each sat for some time with their old friend. Other well-known figures filed past her—the Boyer family with Jacques Pills, Suzanne Flon, Paul Meurisse, Félix Marten, Marcel Cerdan, Jr. The French national radio canceled regular broadcasts to present programs dedicated to the star.

Devastated by grief, Théo could not rouse himself to receive visitors, though he did manage to do Edith's hair one last time. "This tragedy was too much for him," Danielle said. "He was still so young and had never gone through anything so cruel." That weekend, Théo opened the apartment to the hordes of admirers who filled the street outside, a decision he came to regret when objects that had belonged to

Edith disappeared in the confusion, even as security guards tried to control the throngs. If some made off with what they saw as holy relics, others pocketed what were at best souvenirs or, more cynically, items that would acquire commercial value given the magnitude of her reputation.

The Archbishop of Paris showed no ambivalence when Danielle requested a mass for Piaf, who, she explained, had always been pious despite her divorce and remarriage. Her notoriety made this impossible, he replied. *L'Osservatore Romano,* the organ of the Vatican, had declared that she lived "a public life in a state of sin," that she was, moreover, "an icon of false happiness." The Archbishop offered a compromise. The chaplain appointed to minister to artists would officiate at the funeral on October 14. The night before, a priest who said that in the past Edith had restored his faith defied the Vatican and blessed her body.

Piaf's funeral procession, the only occasion since World War II to bring Paris traffic to a halt, began in the morning. More than forty thousand mourners accompanied the black limousines from the plush sixteenth arrondissement to the modest streets of Belleville and, finally, Père-Lachaise. The throngs, made up of ordinary Parisians, poured out their love for the star who, they felt, had given voice to their lives. Thousands crossed themselves and stood in silence as the procession passed.

Once at the cemetery, things got out of hand. Women wept and fell to the ground; spectators climbed onto tombs for a better view; people threw themselves at the celebrities in attendance, for autographs. The police were barely able to keep order as the official mourners—Théo and the Lamboukas and Gassion families, Barrier, Coquatrix, Margantin, the Bonels, and Piaf's friends, including Aznavour, Pills, Dumont, and Dietrich—threaded their way along the cobblestones. At the graveside the chaplain made up for the lack of a mass with ritual blessings and absolution. When Edith was laid to rest, the president of the SACEM, the organization that had once refused to admit her to its ranks, pronounced an oration that concluded simply, "A type of French song comes to an end with Edith Piaf."

"She had a burial fit for a queen," Noli's taxi driver observed as he and Vassal rode through the city that day. Though it seemed fitting that she had been buried with her statue of Saint Thérèse and holy images along with her stuffed animals, Noli was shocked by the chaotic circumstances surrounding the event. "You know," Vassal replied, "I'm sure that Edith would have loved to be present. It was another triumph!" The crowd's fervor had turned the occasion into a state funeral.

"The final curtain has come down," *Paris Match* began the first of two special issues devoted to the star. Reviving the legend of Piaf as suffering artist, the article continued, "She was just a bit of sorrowful flesh in an orphan's black dress. . . . an atmosphere in which the common people, those who came from the streets, saw themselves. . . . Today in Paris there is someone missing." Yet the "dark legend" of Piaf's life had been counterbalanced by her faith. Blending popular mythology and saint's life, the twenty-two-page feature ended with Cocteau's last letter to Piaf—as if their friendship, and their nearly simultaneous deaths, established her place in French history.

A week later, *Paris Match* published a second issue, entitled "Her Voice Will Never Die." After noting more than three hundred thousand of her records had sold the weekend following her death (proof that there existed "an electricity of the heart" between Piaf and the people), the magazine printed an interview with Jacques Bourgeat. As her confidant, mentor, and spiritual father, he told the story of her desire to better herself. The interview closed with his pupil's last words to him: "Our friendship will never end. Even in the Beyond, it will continue right to the end of always."

More prosaically, the *New York Times* observed that France had suffered a "double loss." The article quoted Cocteau's last words: "The boat is going down," he had said soon after commenting on Piaf's death and shortly before his own. "It was a poetic image of a vanished world of people he had known who had worked with him and around him to add luster to contemporary French culture," the reporter explained for the benefit of American readers.

Whereas the *Times* accorded greater significance to the death of the poet, the French press kept publishing special features on the singer. Ten days after Piaf's funeral, *France Dimanche* published an edition that included a letter said to be her "last confession." It reads: "Suddenly I feel the need for purity, the desire to weep that used to overtake me when I was a little girl. The desire to rest my head on a friendly shoulder, to close my eyes and, finally, to rest. When I think of my life, all that debauchery, that waste of strength, I'm ashamed. When I look back on that little woman in her fur coat dragging her loneliness and ennui through the night, I think that that's what Piaf was. I ask everyone's forgiveness. When you read this letter, to be published after my death, do not cry."

Piaf's "confession" has never been authenticated. If she did write it, she failed to see what her life meant to those whose forgiveness she requested. Like her public, she thought in terms of saints and sinners—the Madonna and the Magdalene—when it came to judging a woman. Yet her refusal of self-pity also shows what Piaf was: a people's diva whose courage matched her extraordinary gifts, a soul who gave of herself until there was nothing left but her voice and the echo of her laughter. It was her deep-throated laugh, Aznavour believed, "that freed her from anguish, sorrow, and fear—her only fear, of being unable to go onstage to win over the crowds who loved her." Decades later, he still missed her anarchic laughter. More than anything, he thought, it expressed her life's hectic drama, its boundless joie de vivre.

Coda

As one might expect, Piaf's admirers and music-business colleagues showed their bereavement in different ways. Marcel Blistène's farewell to her, *Au revoir Edith*, was written in great haste the weekend after her death; it reached bookstores a week later. By this time, her records had sold out all over France; Pathé and Philips rushed to replenish their stocks while the mass mourning continued. Tributes with titles like "Ils parlent d'elle" ("They Talk About Her") were shown before feature films at Gaumont cinemas throughout the year.

On the first anniversary of her death, Pierre Desgraupes presented a television special—*La Mort d'Edith Piaf*, a documentary including Marc Bonel's movies of Edith recuperating from an illness months before her 1960 Olympia triumph. Almost immediately a controversy broke out in the press, which accused Desgraupes and the Bonels of morbid sensationalism. ("There could be no better way to betray the memory of the departed," *Arts* magazine protested.)

This controversy marked the start of a struggle over the meaning of Piaf's life. She had occupied such a large place in the national imagination that it needed to be filled or, more cynically, exploited as soon as possible. Her intimates were drawn into rival attempts to claim her heritage. For the next six months, with the aid of Danielle Bonel, Théo tried to settle matters. His return to the stage less than two months after Edith's death was criticized by journalists, who called it a lack of respect while noting that his performance could not help evoking her, as if she were still by his side. Théo's attempts to obtain a share of Piaf's royalties were met with opposition from Pathé, for whom she had been the "interpreter" of her best-known songs but not their author. Meanwhile, his career faltered as his debts accumulated—until the end of the 1960s, when he was offered spots in films and on television. In 1970, when it seemed that Piaf's widower had at last earned his place in the entertainment world, he died in a car crash. A memorial service was held at the Byzantine church where they had been married, before his burial beside Edith at Père-Lachaise.

During these years, her entourage made peace with their loss as well as they could, though not always with one another. The Bonels continued to be blamed for what some called a venal interest in making their movies and other souvenirs of their time with Piaf available to the media. (When *France Dimanche* asked to publish their memoirs, the couple accepted a sum large enough so they could retire, but only after consulting with Théo and with Loulou Barrier, who said that this was their due, given their years of loyal service.) In the other camp, or camps, Ginou Richer would accuse the couple of exploiting their years with the star, Jean Noli would publish his version of her last years, and Hugues Vassal would write three books on his time with Edith, with the emphasis on her importance to him as a source of artistic and spiritual guidance. Pierre Lacotte's ballet *La Voix* was produced on French television in 1965, with Edith's voice heard in the background while the hero and heroine danced the story of their *amours*.

As the singer's intimates dealt with the aftermath of her death, the entertainment business searched for "the new Piaf." There were several candidates, including Juliette Gréco and Catherine Sauvage. But Gréco was already a star in her own right, and Sauvage was well known in France as a mordant interpreter of lyrics by Brassens and Ferré. This left two young singers discovered on a 1965 television talent show, Georgette Lemaire and Mireille Mathieu. Lemaire, who like Piaf came from Belleville and performed *réaliste* classics at local dance halls, had a richly resonant voice that recalled Piaf's register. But the music business had other plans. Mathieu, the younger of the two, was more amenable to taking direction from an industry that quickly chose her as Piaf's successor, arranging for her to sing at official events and ensuring that her fame would eclipse that of her rival, despite Lemaire's more "Piaf-like" voice.

A fresh scandal erupted in 1967, by which time Mathieu had been crowned as Piaf's successor. Léo Ferré, whose songwriting career Piaf had jump-started by urging him to move to Paris, declared the star irreplaceable in his new song, "A une chanteuse morte" ("To a Dead Songstress"). Piaf had a bird's name, he began, but she sang with such power that she conjured multitudes. Hailing her as if she were still alive, he called her *"un Wagner du carrefour, un Bayreuth de trottoir"* ("a crossroads Wagner, a Bayreuth of the streets"). Ferré continued, *"Tu aurais chanté France-Soir comme de l'Apollinaire"* ("You could have sung *France-Soir* like a poem by Apollinaire"), but the campaign to replace her by the industry's "shit merchants" (*"auteurs de la merde"*) was all about money. In the last line, Ferré called out for an end to this travesty: *"Arretez! Arretez la musique!"* he yelled, quoting the last line of "L'Accordéoniste." This fierce denunciation of the Mathieu phenomenon was omitted from Ferré's next album by his record company, the same label that handled Mathieu.

Two years later, another exploitation of Piaf's heritage appeared under the name of Simone Berteaut, who hired a ghostwriter to produce *Piaf,* a book that would achieve international success, thanks to its luridness and to the author's claim to be Piaf's half sister. Momone's garish portrait of Edith's "debauchery," coupled with her promotion of herself to equal standing with the star (supported by "eyewitness" accounts of events at which she had not been present), so enraged Edith's actual half sister, Denise, and brother, Herbert, that they sued Berteaut and her publisher for damages and called for the book's suppression. Their suit was joined by legal action on the part of Marinette Cerdan concerning Berteaut's accounts of the boxer, but their efforts came to nothing. Shortly before his death, Théo Sarapo said of the affair, "I wish Edith's memory could be left in peace."

As Léo Ferré foresaw, Piaf would remain a living presence in France. Since 1963, the French media have churned out magazine features, books, television specials, and films about the star, often coinciding with the anniversary of her death or the appearance of new interpreters of her repertoire. Ten years after her death, the Association of the Friends of Edith Piaf was formed and a museum of Piaf memorabilia opened: it continues to attract thousands of visitors each year. In 1981, Jacques Chirac, then mayor of Paris, inaugurated the Place Edith

Piaf in Belleville. In 2003, six lost Piaf recordings were found in the Bibliothèque Nationale, an event hailed in the press as a major cultural discovery. That same year, the city of Paris held a massively attended exhibition, *Piaf, la môme de Paris*, and erected a statue of the singer on the square named for her, near the Edith Piaf bar, itself a miniature museum of sorts. A few streets away, her grave (which lacks an epitaph) is regularly covered with bouquets from admirers whose numbers exceed those drawn to other famous graves at Père-Lachaise.

Given the mounting expressions of Piaf-worship in the years following her death, it was inevitable that film projects would be aired. Warner Bros.' plans for a feature film with Liza Minnelli as Piaf were announced in 1973, and Minnelli was quoted as saying that the singer reminded her of her mother, Judy Garland. This project was dropped because of the cost of filming in France, then turned over to the French company that produced *Piaf: The Sparrow of Pigalle*, in 1974: a commercial failure in France, it was not distributed in the United States. Ten years later, Claude Lelouch's *Edith and Marcel*, with Marcel Cerdan, Jr., as his father, suffered a similar fate outside France. The third attempt to film the star's life won international recognition and an Oscar for Marion Cotillard, the actress who played Piaf—despite its focus on the dark side of her life and its jumbled chronology. ("It wasn't Cotillard who was being honored," one of Edith's intimates quipped. "It was Piaf.")

Tributes to Piaf by kindred souls are found in the work of generations of songwriters whose compositions she inspired. In addition to her intimates, such as Aznavour, Moustaki, and Dumont, who all acknowledge her role in shaping their careers, younger composers have also found her life and repertoire to be rich sources for their own. Elton John's 1976 "Cage the Songbird" declares in no uncertain terms: "You can trap the free bird / But you'll have to clip her wings." Piaf would be a rock star if she were still alive, Céline Dion chanted in "Piaf chanterait du rock" (1991). The following year, a gathering of punk-rock groups proved the point with an album of songs first sung by Piaf and Fréhel, *Ma Grand-Mère est une rockeuse* (*My Grandmother Is a Rocker*).

Piaf's story has also inspired playwrights and performers in France and around the world. As of this writing, Jil Aigrot continues to tour France as the "voice" of Piaf in the biopic starring Cotillard; the musical comedy *L'Empiaffée* wryly updates Piaf's repertoire to show the travails of a "song-worker"; television talent shows feature aspirant stars trying to improve their luck by singing Piaf standards. Presentations based on her life produced elsewhere have included recitals by Juliette Koka and Raquel Bitton in the United States, Jane Lapotaire's play *Piaf* in the U.K., and Caroline Nin's one-woman shows in Europe and Australia. The singer's heritage is currently being reinterpreted by Gay Marshall, who emphasizes Piaf's high spirits; Ziaf, a rock-inspired band that plays in France and the United States; and *Piaf, une vie en rose et noir*, a cabaret-style revue that has performed in France, the Middle East, and China. Nathalie Lhermitte, who plays the singer, told the press recently, "Piaf has been our lucky star."

While I was writing this book, people often spoke of Piaf's fame in countries as distant from, or as unlike, the one with which she is so thoroughly identified—for instance, in Japan, where her songs are thought to convey the essence of that country's aesthetic, the urge to enjoy what is fleeting as it passes, or in Russia, where they are available in Cyrillic and the young singer Pelageya is called "the Russian Piaf." It was pleasing to learn that though Piaf never made the trip she envisioned in 1962 to perform in the Soviet Union, decades later the Russian astronomer Lyudmila Karachkina decided to name a small planet after her: 3772 Piaf. Since then, the diminutive star has been part of the solar system, her incandescence illuminating our lives below.

On a return trip to Père-Lachaise, where I again met many of her admirers, it was clear to me that Piaf lives on, although differently from the way she imagined. The famous cemetery, the *chansonnier* Allain Leprest sings in "Edith"—a moody ballad that perpetuates her heritage—is a full house whose audience is arranged in rows: "Her spirit haunts a strange *music-hall* / The leaves of the trees cry *encore*." This allusive tribute asks the listener, "Do you know what artists do / To make death no sadder / Than saying *au revoir*. . . ?" Its reply could serve as Edith's epitaph: "Millions of anonymous lovers / Come to leave their bouquets / In the back of Père-Lachaise / Section ninety-six / Where she found her last nest / Madame Edith Lamboukas / Known as 'Piaf' . . ."

ACKNOWLEDGMENTS

This life of Edith Piaf could not have been written without the gracious participation of many of her friends, lovers, and collaborators, the archivists and collectors who granted me access to important new material, and the fans still imbued with her spirit nearly fifty years after her death. Together they helped me grasp her immense impact in her own time and her unstinting generosity—the openheartedness that to this day reaches across cultural divides to give listeners goose bumps when they hear her voice.

I am more grateful than I can say to Mme Catherine Glavas and to Maître André Schmidt for permission to consult and quote from Piaf's letters and unpublished writings, but also for the invaluable help I received from him and Mme Annie Rooke in negotiations with the publishers of songs quoted in the text, which was greatly enriched by the inclusion of these materials.

Others whose help was invaluable include members of the Association des Amis d'Edith Piaf, especially Bernard Marchois, who provided introductions to many of Piaf's friends and included me in memorial services for her at Père Lachaise, where I first felt that I might write a life of the star in accord with her spirit.

Archival research for this book at the Bibliothèque Nationale de France could not have been conducted without the help of Laurence Le Bras of the Manuscripts Division, who allowed me to read Piaf's correspondence with Jacques Bourgeat, and the supportive staff of the Département des Arts du Spectacle. I am also profoundly grateful to Geneviève Morlet and Claudine Boulouque of the Bibliothèque Historique de la Ville de Paris, as well as to the staff of the Bibliothèque Marguerite Durand, whose Piaf dossiers deepened my sense of her as a French national icon, and to the interlibrary loan staff at the University of California, Santa Cruz.

I am indebted to Giselle Tellier for arranging my tour of Bernay with local historians Philippe Le Turcq and Marie Caruel of the Bernay Office de Tourisme, where I was granted access to hitherto unavailable documents on Piaf's childhood. My Belleville chapters were enriched by touring the area with Margo Berdeshevsky and with Patrick Dewarez, whose images perpetuate the tradition of Willy Ronis, an important visual source for my writing.

It was a great pleasure to work with Jean-Paul Mazillier and Anthony Berrot, whose archive of documents, memorabilia, and photographs is the major private repository of Piafiana, much of it having been passed to them by Danielle Bonel. Without their help I could not have documented Piaf's life as fully or illustrated it with some of the thousands of photographs in their extensive collection.

I also want to express my thanks to Hugues Vassal, who documented the star's final years and gave me access to his own collection of images, which enabled me to grasp the drama surrounding her illnesses and last days. I am also indebted to Solène Vassal, who is carrying on the work of the Vassal archive.

Interviews conducted with the following witnesses in France, and the materials they gave me, added inestimably to my portrait of Piaf: Edmonde Charles-Roux, Françoise Asso, Micheline Dax, Georges Moustaki, Charles Dumont, Irène Hilda, Serge Glanzberg, Fred Mella, Annick Taillière, and the late Erik Marchal de Salm. Jeanne McDonagh vividly recalled Piaf's performances at the Versailles; Darlene Baker told me about the star's relationship with her brother, Douglas Davis; Gene Lees's comparison of French and American song styles informed my understanding of Piaf's reception in her adopted homeland.

In addition, David Gullentops shared materials that illuminate Piaf's friendship with Jean Cocteau; Julia Panama located unpublished correspondence between Piaf and Toto Girardin; Anne Bramard-Blagny gave me documents, including her film, on the friendship of Piaf and Marguerite Monnot; Frédéric Brun explained the chronology of Piaf's adherence to the Rosicrucian Order and her relations with his father, Jean Dréjac; Andrew Solt and Mary Sherwood gave me film clips of Piaf's performances on the Ed Sullivan show; Rob Hudson made available documents concerning Piaf's recitals at Carnegie Hall; Ann Holsberry discovered old French tabloids for me at various *marchés aux puces*.

I want to express my profound gratitude to those who encouraged me to write this book and guided me in the process: my wise and witty agent, Georges Borchardt; my research assistant, Kristina Valendinova; my inventive image wrangler, Lance Sprague; and many people both known and unknown to me at Knopf, especially my sagacious editor, Robert Gottlieb, and his scrupulous assistant, Sarah Rothbard. I am profoundly indebted to all of them.

I give a deep bow of thanks to both my immediate and extended families—Valda Hertzberg, Garance Burke, and Terry Burke, who kept me going throughout the writing of this book, and the sanghas of the Santa Cruz and San Francisco Zen Centers. I am also grateful to the following, for comfort, hospitality, references, refuge, and for reading and critiquing my manuscript:

Pico Iyer, Hiroko Takeuchi, Michael Wolfe, Cathy Suma-Wolfe, Marc Lambron, Anne Bast, Patricia de Fougerolle, Pauline de Boisfleury, Gérard Gagnepain, Michèle Jolé, Marilyn Goldberg, Louise Bernikow, Joan Schenkar, François Lévy, Michelle Lapautre, Bertrand Lacarelle, Russell Porter, Jacques Primack, Edwige Belorgey, Stephen Pollard, Mary Nelson, Alexandra Pringle, Didier Pascalis, Allison Anthony, Peter Myers, Edith Kunz, Dominique Gérard, Marco Tugayé, Linda Gardiner, Marilyn Hacker, Bette Taxera, Naomi Sawelson-Gorse, Rita Bottoms, Jay Olson, Georges Van Den Abbeele, Marty Michaels, James Robinson, Rita Robinson, Christa Fraser, Tom Honig, Drew Miller, Jerry Kay, Lucie Mazalaigue, Christine Zuffery, Gena Foucek, Pnina Green, Marlene Nanus, Candace Calsoyas, Susan Maresco, Denis Gallagher, Kathryn Stark, Reb Anderson, Katherine Thanas, Kokyo Henkel, Scott Bongiorno, and Carter Wilson.

Finally, I want to thank the impassioned Piaf fans who buoyed my spirits with their encouragement and insights, often accompanied by a meal or a glass of wine. I wish that they had been with me at a recent musical evening in Ménilmontant where the crowd joined in while songwriter Allain Leprest, accordionist Jean Corti, and singer Francis Lalanne performed songs by Piaf and Brel along with their own compositions: they would have been moved, as I was, to see *la chanson française* alive and well in the same Paris neighborhoods where Edith's remarkable life began.

NOTES

The bulk of Piaf's personal papers and correspondence is held in private collections, with one important exception: the unpublished correspondence between
the star and her mentor, Jacques Bourgeat, at the Bibliothèque Nationale de
France. Other Piaf materials in archives or private collections are denoted by
the name of the archive or collection. All quotations from letters are referenced
in the endnotes by date, and where needed, place; "no date" is indicated by
"n.d."; "no page number" by "n.p." All translations from the French are my
own except for works in the bibliography for which the only listing is the English
translation.

To minimize repetition, references to works cited more than once have been
kept brief. When more than one work by an author has been cited, the short
title as well as the author's name is given; when only one work by an author has
been cited, the author's name is given. Published works are listed in full in the
bibliography.

Archives and private collections are abbreviated as follows:

AMORC   Rosicrucian Archives
BMD   Bibliothèque Marguerite Durand
HVA   Hugues Vassal Archives
MBA   Mazillier/Berrot Archives

Frequently used names are abbreviated as follows:

EP   Edith Piaf
JB   Jacques Bourgeat
JC   Jean Cocteau
MC   Marcel Cerdan
RA   Raymond Asso

PRELUDE

xi   "Edith Piaf knocked": Joni Mitchell quoted in "Joni Mitchell Gets Angry,
      Hugs It Out," *New York*, Sept. 26, 2007. Piaf and Billie Holiday were major
      influences on Mitchell's career as a songwriter and performer.

xi   "complete vocal abandon": Martha Wainwright quoted in Louise Cohen,
      "Martha Wainwright: 'Edith Piaf became the ghost behind all that I sang,'"
      Times Online, Oct. 30, 2009.

CHAPTER ONE • 1915–1925

4   "the capital of": Maurice Chevalier, *The Man in the Straw Hat*, p. 8.

4   "My mother nearly": EP quoted in Pierre Duclos and Georges Martin, *Piaf*, p. 63.

4   "She didn't know": Contet quoted in ibid., p. 64.

4   "On the 19th of December": EP birth certificate, quoted in ibid., pp. 62–63.

5   Just before the start: Emma Saîd Ben Mohamed, aka Aîcha, born on December 10, 1876, was the child of Saîd Ben Mohamed of Mogador, Morocco, and Marguerite Bracco of Paris.

6   "I've always thought": EP, *Au bal de la chance*, p. 82.

7   "miniature nation": Clément Lépidis, *Des Dimanches à Belleville*, p. 24.

9   "I got used to": EP quoted in Emmanuelle Eyles, "Grâce aux prières des 'filles' de Bernay, Piaf a retrouvé la vue," *Historia* 601, p. 8.

9   "I always thought": EP television interview with Henri Spade and Jacqueline Joubert, *La Joie de vivre d'Edith Piaf*, April 3, 1954, http://www.ina.fr/video/I00013647/edith-piaf-1-accordeoniste.fr.html, INA archive.

10   "Saint Thérèse performed": "Edith, Thérèse et le photographe," *L'Eveil normand*, March 18, 1999, p. 18.

10   "The day I regained": EP quoted in Duclos and Martin, p. 69.

10   "Edith's eyes": Madame Taillère, quoted in ibid., p. 70.

10   "She was engaging": Madame Taillère quoted in Eyles, p. 7.

11   "She was a good student": Madame Laperruque quoted in Jean-Dominique Brierre, *Edith Piaf*, p. 14.

11   "the girl whose grandmother": Lyliane Carpantier quoted in Duclos and Martin, p. 73.

11   "Sing, little one": Marcel Delamare quoted in "Bernay va dédier une rue à Edith Piaf," *Paris-Normandie*, Jan. 30/31, 1988.

11   "People knew": Jacques Guesnet quoted in "Bernay n'a pas oublié sa 'Môme,'" *Normandie*, n.d.

11   "When I wanted": EP quoted in "Bernay donne une rue à Piaf," *L'Eveil normand*, June 16, 1988.

11   "But my faith": EP, *Ma vie*, p. 63.

12   "We wanted to": Marcelle Lallier quoted in Duclos and Martin, p. 71.

12   "Papa was not": EP, *Au bal*, p. 85.

13   "Gifted athletically": Ibid., p. 82.

13   "I lived in": Ibid., pp. 83–84.

13   A snapshot: See Marcelle Routier, *Piaf l'inoubliable*, p. 12.

13   "I was so afraid": EP interview, *Joie de vivre*, quoted in Duclos and Martin, p. 76.

14   "We kept on traveling": EP, *Au bal*, p. 84.

14   "Father spread his 'hanky'": Ibid.

14   "I had never": Ibid.

15   "rich child's": Ibid., pp. 85–86.

15 "For people": Ibid., p. 86.

15 "I'm not in the business": Louis Gassion quoted in Duclos and Martin, p. 78, and EP, *Au bal,* p. 87.

15 "A handsome man": EP, *Au bal,* p. 87.

16 "I still remember": EP quoted in Duclos and Martin, p. 79.

16 "I had worked": EP interviews, *Joie de vivre,* in ibid., p. 80.

16 "Young woman wanted": Quoted in ibid., p. 81.

16 "the girlfriend": Ibid.

CHAPTER TWO • 1926–1932

18 "A new mother": EP, *Ma vie,* p. 14.

18 "I had gone": Ibid.

19 "My father doesn't": Ibid., p. 88.

19 "While our parents": Herbert Gassion quoted in Duclos and Martin, p. 83.

20 Fréhel had long been famous: Born Marguerite Boulch in 1891, the singer first performed in a well-known Parisian *café-concert* at the age of sixteen. Colette wrote in her novel *The Vagabond* that Fréhel had "the sulky face of a young apache" and sang "like a street urchin" in the years before the war, when she was a celebrated performer. After a disastrous love affair with Maurice Chevalier, Fréhel went into exile in Constantinople and Eastern Europe for eleven years. Addicted to cocaine and badly overweight, she managed to make a spectacular comeback in Paris during the mid-1920s.

21 "mistakes": Herbert Gassion quoted in Duclos and Martin, pp. 85–86.

22 "I bought her": Pierre Hiégel in Bernard Marchois, *Edith Piaf: Opinions publiques,* p. 137.

23 "Everyone kissed": Clément Lépidis, *Belleville au coeur,* p. 59.

25 "I was bowled over": Simone Berteaut, *Piaf: A Biography,* p. 21.

26 "that same voice": Ibid., p. 24.

26 "Saturdays we'd hit": Ibid., p. 28.

27 "alive": Ibid., p. 29.

27 "He looked": EP, *Ma vie,* pp. 14–15.

27 "cutlery or plates": Ibid., p. 15.

28 "She went so far": Denise Gassion, *Piaf, ma soeur,* p. 27.

28 "Edith wouldn't": Berteaut, p. 36.

28 "She had a voice": Odette Laure in Marchois, *Edith Piaf: Opinions,* p. 167.

29 "I felt that something": EP, *Ma vie,* p. 16.

29 "As for the kiss": EP, *Au bal,* pp. 72–73.

29 "And when Edith": Gassion, p. 28.

29 "She interpreted": Rina Ketty in Marchois, *Edith Piaf: Opinions,* p. 147.

CHAPTER THREE • 1933–1935

31 "the most intense": Patrice Bollon, *Pigalle,* p. 18.

31 "I didn't have": Berteaut, p. 38.

32 "It's not easy": Ibid., p. 39.

33 "There is nothing": René Fallet, *Pigalle* (Paris: Dormat, 1949), quoted in Bollon, p. 7.

34 "Edith never spoke of him": Berteaut, p. 43.

35 "I had to look out": EP, *Ma vie*, p. 19.

35 "had a soft spot": Le Breton, *La Môme Piaf*, pp. 12–13.

36 "Her shoes": Ibid., pp. 14–15.

36 "It was a mystery": Maurice Maillet, *Edith Piaf inconnue*, pp. 33, 38.

36 "Life-saving shock": EP, *Ma vie*, p. 20.

36 "the tough guy": Ibid., p. 21.

37 "I had a desperate, almost morbid, need": Ibid., pp. 22–23.

37 "When she tried to reason": Maillet, pp. 40–41.

38 "She took strength": Ibid., pp. 43–44.

38 "she prayed": Marc Bonel and Danielle Bonel, *Edith Piaf*, p. 200.

38 "For eight days": EP, *Ma vie*, p. 120.

38 "Ten francs": Ibid., p. 122.

39 "You're right": EP quoted in Jean Noli, *Edith*, pp. 77–78.

39 "It was a very dark moment": Berteaut, p. 44.

39 "She must have been": EP quoted in Jacqueline Cartier and Hugues Vassal, *Edith et Thérèse*, p. 163.

CHAPTER FOUR • 1935–1936

40 "People have the wrong": Berteaut, pp. 45–46.

41 "the pianist": Ibid., p. 45.

41 "Her songs expressed": Ketty, in Marchois, *Opinions*, p. 147.

41 "Fate took me": EP, *Au bal*, p. 33.

42 "We were so petrified": Berteaut, p. 48.

42 Gerny's portly impresario was himself a habitué: Alternative versions of Piaf's discovery, as unverifiable as the "official" one, have been proposed by some biographers. Brierre quotes a Montmartre regular's claim that his mother, a performer at le Gerny's, took Edith there to meet Leplée (p. 27); P'tit Louis told David Bret that one of Edith's hoodlum lovers, who was "knocking off" Leplée because of his homosexuality, engineered their meeting in order to "screw Edith for more money" (pp. 14–15). I see no reason not to adopt Piaf's account, which is confirmed by Berteaut and upheld by most of the singer's biographers (including Margaret Crosland, Duclos and Martin, and Hugues Vassal): it has the merit of presenting Edith Gassion's "rebirth" as La Môme Piaf from her own perspective.

42 "the tender blue": EP, *Au bal*, p. 34.

42 "I put all my heart": EP, ibid., p. 38.

43 "I was baptized": Ibid., p. 40. *Un piaf* also suggests *piaffer*, the action of a horse stamping its feet, and *piaffer d'impatience*, pawing the ground with impatience or enthusiasm.

44 "I was dressed": Ibid.

44 "Her voice overwhelmed": Ibid., p. 42.

44 "That kid": Ibid., p. 44.

44 "You really had them": Ibid.

44 "When I think": Ibid., pp. 47, 48.

45 "'Chand d'habits" (slang for *marchand d'habits,* old-clothes salesman), drew on the cries of the rapidly disappearing street merchants.

45 "I felt that I was on the path": EP, *Au bal,* p. 56.

45 "I felt a sense of compassion": Jacques Canetti, *On cherche jeune homme aimant la musique,* p. 65.

45 "a singer who lives": "Au Gerny's," *Petit Parisien,* Nov. 1935, reprinted in Bernard Marchois, *Piaf: Emportée par la foule,* p. 9. The reporter recognized in Piaf's songs the nostalgic poetics found in Francis Carco's novels of the lower depths, *Jésus-la-Caille* (1914) and its sequel, *Les Malheurs de Fernande* (1918). On this tradition in relation to Piaf, see Adrian Rifkin, *Street Noises.*

46 "embarrassed at being": Pierre de Regnier, "Toujours au Gerny's," n.d., reprinted in Marchois, *Piaf: Emportée,* p. 9.

47 "She was relaxed": Canetti, p. 69.

48 "He was a simple": Maillet, p. 110. In *Ma vie,* Piaf calls the sailor Pierrot.

48 "incapable of forgiving": EP, *Ma vie,* p. 25.

48 "she had difficulty": Maillet, p. 111.

48 in letters the same size: EP, *Au bal,* p. 55.

49 "How can I describe": Ibid., p. 60.

49 "The man in the street": Marcel Montarron, "Les Quatre Tueurs," *Détective,* April 16, 1936, pp. 2–3.

50 "I had to say": *Éclair-Journal* quoted in Brierre, pp. 35–36.

50 "She died eight months": Marcel Montarron, "La Môme Piaf," *Voilà,* April 18, 1936, p. 6.

51 "I might as well": EP, *Au bal,* pp. 62–63.

51 "If she's good": Ibid., p. 64.

51 as Piaf's "demon": Berteaut quoted in Duclos and Martin, p. 116.

52 "She was attentive": JB quoted in ibid., pp. 109–10.

52 "She never even thought": Ibid., p. 114.

52 "I'm no longer with Jeannot": EP to JB, Aug. 5, 1936.

53 "an impossible dump": Berteaut, p. 79.

54 "She was a wild thing": Asso quoted in Duclos and Martin, p. 125.

54 "devilish girl": Asso quoted in ibid., p. 120.

54 "My situation wasn't great": EP, *Au bal,* p. 65.

54 "I've been doing a lot": EP quoted in Asso, Marchois, *Edith Piaf: Opinions,* p. 15.

54 "I was saved": EP, *Au bal,* p. 66.

CHAPTER FIVE • 1937–1939

55 "It took him three": EP, *Ma vie,* p. 32.

55 "could she submit": Asso quoted in Duclos and Martin, p. 125.

55 "to facet her": Asso, in Marchois, *Edith Piaf: Opinions,* p. 14.

55 "Distorting the words": Asso quoted in Duclos and Martin, p. 125.

56 "My work was": Asso quoted in Brierre, p. 43.

58 "Now do you understand": EP, Radio Europe 1 broadcast, 1961, quoted in Crosland, p. 60.

59 "astonishing progress": *Le Figaro,* April 1, 1937.

59 "The frail street flower": *Paris-Soir,* April 3, 1937, reprinted in Marchois, *Piaf: Emportée,* p. 11.

59 "the voice of revolt": Henri Jeanson quoted in Duclos and Martin, p. 133.

59 "Here is the miraculous": Maurice Verne, *L'Intransigeant,* quoted in ibid., p. 132. Piaf liked Verne's piece so much that she included it in *Au bal* (pp. 69–70), along with the praise of Asso's lyrics quoted in the text.

60 "La Môme is dead!": Duclos and Martin, p. 136.

61 "The 'môme' was charming": Marc Blanquet, in *Le Journal,* Nov. 26, 1937; reprinted in Marchois, *Piaf: Emportée,* p. 11.

61 "She seemed to be standing": Anon., Nov. 25, 1937; reprinted in Marchois, *Piaf: Emportée,* p. 11.

61 jazzy, lighthearted: Trenet, known as *"le fou chantant"* (the singing nut), became an immediate success with songs combining influences from jazz and swing with a popular lyricism and vision of happiness. He and Piaf were seen as the representative singers of their time in their contrasting but complementary ways of renewing *la chanson.*

61 "her perfect diction": Gustave Fréjaville, *Comoedia,* n.d., in Marchois, *Piaf: Emportée,* p. 12.

61 "Edith Piaf has worked": Feral, Granet, Lévy, n.d., no sources given, quoted in Duclos and Martin, pp. 138–39.

63 "Critics who acclaimed": Adrian Rifkin, "Musical Moments," p. 144.

64 "What news of the war?": EP to RA letters, n.d., quoted in Duclos and Martin, pp. 142–44.

64 "I cried a lot": Ibid.

64 "My dear love": Ibid.

65 "For Suzanne": Flon quoted in Duclos and Martin, p. 146.

65 "my best friend": EP, *Au bal,* p. 92.

65 "I think you would be wrong": Asso quoted in Duclos and Martin, p. 153.

66 "Far from the noise": JB quoted in EP, *Au bal,* pp. 191–92.

66 "moral jailer": Asso quoted in Duclos and Martin, p. 151.

66 "the critic Léon-Martin": Marchois, *Piaf: Emportée,* p. 12.

CHAPTER SIX • 1939–1942

68 "We understood that terrible things": Chevalier, p. 172.

68 "My job is to sing": EP, in *Notre Coeur,* Oct. 28, 1940, in Duclos and Martin, p. 174.

68 "It's better than anything": EP to RA, c. Dec. 3, 1939, quoted in ibid., p. 156.

69 "not a word": Paul Meurisse, *Les Eperons de la liberté,* pp. 106–107.

69 "Edith Piaf doesn't": Ibid., p. 110.

69 "She makes her way": Salvador Reyes, in *La Hora*, Nov. 5, 1939, in Duclos and Martin, pp. 156–57.

70 "*Ciel! Mon mari!*": Meurisse, p. 113. Asso's resentment is apparent in his next song, "On danse sur ma chanson": "They're dancing / On my finest memories / On the taste of my desire. . . ."

70 "I won't have to go to the composers'": EP quoted in Meurisse, p. 114.

70 "It wasn't so much that *le savoir-vivre*": Ibid., p. 115.

70 "She would laugh and begin again": Ibid., p. 116.

71 "shit": Ibid., p. 130.

72 "The response was delirious": Emer, in Marchois, *Edith Piaf: Opinions*, p. 103.

72 "Living with him": EP, in *Notre Coeur*, Oct. 28, 1940, in Marchois, *Piaf: Emportée*, p. 27.

73 "regal simplicity": Jean Cocteau, "Je travaille avec Edith Piaf," *Paris-Midi*, April 19, 1940.

73 "at the summit": Meurisse, pp. 136–37.

73 "handsome, indifferent man": Cocteau, "Le Bel Indifférent," in *Théâtre complet*, p. 856.

73 "dream theater": Cocteau, "Je travaille."

73 "Mademoiselle Piaf": *Marianne*, in Cocteau, *Théâtre complet*, p. 1742.

73 "Her acting is": *Le Figaro*, in ibid.

73 "magnificent": *Les Nouvelles littéraires*, in ibid.

74 "Krauts or no Krauts": "Boches ou pas Boches, la capitale de la France, c'est Paris" (Meurisse, p. 148).

74 "It was a terrible shock": Meurisse, p. 150.

75 "At this time": Ibid., p. 152.

75 "the sharp wind": *Aujourd'hui*, Sept. 22, 1940, in Marchois, *Piaf: Emportée*, p. 26.

75 "excessively fearful": EP quoted in Duclos and Martin, p. 174.

75 "Edith Piaf has more": Babette, "Salle Pleyel: Edith Piaf," *Paris-Soir*, Oct. 1, 1940.

76 "On the one hand": Henri Contet, in Duclos and Martin, p. 215.

77 "Everything she did": Jean-Louis Barrault, in Marchois, *Edith Piaf: Opinions*, p. 20.

78 "Je ne veux plus laver la vaisselle": The sheet music for "Je ne veux plus laver la vaisselle" identifies it as a song from *Montmartre-sur-Seine*. Though Piaf recorded the song in 1943, it was not included in any of her records and was rediscovered only in 2003 at the Bibliothèque Nationale.

78 "this false street set": Henri Contet, "Edith Piaf chante dans la rue," *Paris-Midi*, Sept. 16, 1941.

78 "What to do": Henri Contet, "Edith Piaf pleure son amour perdu," *Ciné-Mondial* [1941], in Marchois, *Piaf: Emportée*, p. 28.

79 "that little person": *Je suis partout*, n.d., and *Révolution nationale* [July 15, 1944] quoted in Brierre, p. 55.

79 "that laugh": Meurisse, p. 159.
79 "She knew that because": Norbert Glanzberg quoted in Astrid Freyeisen, *Chansons pour Piaf*, p. 89.
80 "When Edith leaned": Ibid., p. 82.
80 "What could I do?": Ibid., p. 90.
80 "We were opposites": Meurisse, p. 160.
80 "without any question": Léo Ferré, in *L'Eclaireur de Nice* [March 1942], quoted in Duclos and Martin, p. 183.
81 "I'm worried": EP to Glanzberg, Oct. 26, 1942, in Freyeisen, p. 94.
82 "Whatever people say": Andrée Bigard, in Marchois, *Edith Piaf: Opinions*, p. 31; cf. Freyeisen, p. 85.

CHAPTER SEVEN • 1942–1944

83 "easy recipes": *Marie Claire*, May 20, 1942, p. 12.
83 "Edith Piaf is coming": T. Marval, in Marchois, *Piaf: Emportée*, p. 29; cf. Legrand-Chabrier in *Le Nouveau Temps*, Oct. 21, 1942: "Edith Piaf's return to her adoring Paris public is the big event of the week," n.p.
83 "all of Paris": EP to Glanzberg, Oct. 11, 1942, in Freyeisen, p. 91.
84 "in the person": Louis Terrentrov, in *L'Auto*, Oct. 30, 1942, in Marchois, *Piaf: Emportée*, p. 29.
84 "the best *tour de chant*": Legrand-Chabrier, "Rentrée d'Edith Piaf à l'A.B.C.," *Le Nouveau Temps*.
84 "a purity of intention": Françoise Holbane, in *Paris-Midi*, quoted in Duclos and Martin, p. 192.
84 "She no longer looks": Gustave Fréjaville, in *Comoedia*, Oct. 31, 1942, quoted in ibid., pp. 191–92. Fréjaville warned Piaf not to "push" her voice, whose capacity to touch the listener "[was] not in the volume of her sound but in the quality of her timbre."
85 "I'm terribly afraid": EP to Glanzberg, Nov. 27, 1942, in Freyeisen, p. 94.
86 "guide fish": Madame Billy, *La Maitresse de "maison,"* pp. 111, 116.
86 "They all knew her": Ibid., p. 115.
86 Piaf spent her whole life: Contet, letter, in *Témoignages sur Edith et chansons de Piaf*, p. 17.
87 "We writers": Contet quoted in François Lévy, *Passion Edith Piaf*, p. 89.
87 "Her enthusiasm compensated": Contet quoted in Duclos and Martin, p. 201.
88 "nuances of feeling": Gustave Fréjaville, in *Comoedia*, in ibid., p. 197.
88 "What marvelous evenings": Madame Billy, p. 115.
89 "She was very unstable": Ibid., p. 117.
89 "She became the good": Ibid., pp. 126–27.
89 "She was as beautiful": Ibid., p. 127.
89 "She transcends herself": Jean Cocteau, "Edith Piaf," clipping, Jan. 2, 1947; reprinted in EP, *Au bal*, preface.
89 "his closest intimates": Anon. quoted in Jean Cocteau, *Journal, 1942–1945*, p. 347.

90 "You have skillfully renewed": Anon., "L'Art d'Edith Piaf," n.d., in Marchois, *Piaf: Emportée*, p. 30.

90 "keep going to see": Didier Daix, "Edith Piaf à 'La Vie en Rose,'" *Paris-Midi*, May 11, 1943.

90 "like her daughter": "Line Marsa chante avec la même voix et les mêmes gestes que sa fille, Edith Piaf," *La Semaine*, May 9, 1942.

90 "*petite Didou*": Line Marsa, aka Jacqueline Maillard, to EP, in Bonel and Bonel, p. 116.

90 "more upset than indifferent": Madame Billy, p. 117.

91 "enough for several doses": Ibid., p. 119.

91 "Every morning": Manouche quoted in Bret, p. 52.

91 "I'm not a *chanteuse réaliste*!": EP quoted in "Je n'aime pas les chansons réalistes," *Actu*, June 20, 1943, in Duclos and Martin, pp. 201–2.

91 "but they could still": Georges Bozonnat, "Sur le gril," *L'Appel*, Aug. 26, 1943.

92 "Groomed and coiffed": Contet quoted in Duclos and Martin, p. 220.

92 "He didn't seem to feel": Madame Billy, p. 118.

92 "Mademoiselle, that just isn't done": Ibid., p. 116.

93 "with her remarkable intuition": Andrée Bigard, in Marchois, *Edith Piaf: Opinions*, p. 29.

93 "I don't think it would be helpful": EP quoted in H. D. Fauvet, "Edith Piaf va chanter pour les prisonniers," *Paris-Midi*, Aug. 9, 1943.

93 "top-notch": EP quoted in H. D. Fauvet, "Edith Piaf est revenue heureuse d'avoir fait des heureux," *Paris-Midi*, Oct. 3, 1943.

94 "*Ma chanson, c'est ma vie*": EP's lyrics in H. D. Fauvet, "Edith Piaf est entrée à la Société des auteurs," *Paris-Midi*, Jan. 13, 1944.

94 "It's all I could find": Robert Dalban, in Marchois, *Edith Piaf: Opinions*, pp. 80–81, and Duclos and Martin, p. 218.

94 "Edith, the pianist, and I": Andrée Bigard, in Marchois, *Edith Piaf: Opinions*, p. 29.

95 "I loved him": EP to Glanzberg, March 31, 1944, in Freyeisen, p. 163.

95 "She wasn't up to": Gassion, pp. 78–79.

CHAPTER EIGHT · 1944–1946

96 "We said goodbye": Madame Billy, p. 130.

97 "powerful emotions": Françoise Holbane, "Edith Piaf au Moulin de la Galette," *Paris-Midi*, June 6, 1944.

97 "His personality was terrific": EP, *Au bal*, p. 109.

97 "I had fallen in love": Yves Montand, with Hervé Hamon and Patrick Rotman, *You See, I Haven't Forgotten*, pp. 108–9.

98 "Yves never argued": Contet quoted in ibid., pp. 110–11.

98 "Montand, who is beginning": *Midi-Soir*, Nov. 10, 1944, quoted in ibid., p. 124.

99 "Don't be a fool!": EP quoted in ibid., p. 118.

99 "No sanction": Herbert Lottman, *The People's Anger,* pp. 259–60. Cf. Duclos and Martin, pp. 225–26.

100 "some of which were": EP quoted in "Les 118 Evadés d'Edith Piaf," *Ce Soir,* Oct. 21, 1944.

100 "the songs you can't drop": Montand, p. 124.

100 "this tall handsome guy": "Edith Piaf triomphe aux nouveautés," *Victoire Tendance,* Nov. 25, 1944, in Marchois, *Piaf: Emportée,* p. 32.

100 "She was a little shaken": Lydia Livi Ferroni quoted in Montand, p. 125.

102 "Don't try to rise": Serge Weber, in *Francs-Tireurs,* Feb. 15, 1945, in Brierre, p. 67.

103 "*tristesse souriante*": Pierre Francis, "Edith Piaf et Yves Montand au Théâtre des Variétés" [April 1945], in Marchois, *Piaf: Emportée,* p. 43.

103 "When I toured with Yves": EP quoted in Monique Lange, *Piaf,* p. 100.

103 title, lyrics, and music: Because Piaf had SACEM accreditation as a lyricist but not as a composer, she asked Marguerite Monnot to lend her name to "La Vie en rose." When Monnot refused, Piaf turned to her old friend and accompanist Louiguy (Louis Guglielmi), who agreed.

104 "What triggered their shared distress": Montand, p. 128 (these remarks by Hamon and Rotman).

104 shouting "Bravo!": René Bizet, in *Paris-Presse,* Sept. 15, 1945, quoted in Duclos and Martin, p. 242.

105 "small-time hoods": Jean Wiener, in *Spectateur,* Oct. 3, 1945, in Marchois, *Piaf: Emportée,* p. 44.

105 "the strongest personality": Max Favalelli, in *La Dépêche de Paris,* Oct. 28–29, 1945, in Montand, p. 133.

105 "Maybe you're right": Enclosed in EP to JB, Oct. 29, 1945.

105 "A telegram": Ibid.

105 "I shall always be proud": EP, *Au bal,* pp. 112–13.

106 "When Edith managed": Danielle Bonel quoted in Brierre, p. 69, where the author also quotes a contemporary of Piaf's who claims that she engineered the break by telling Montand that he did not need her. It is tempting to think that Piaf's way of provoking the ends of liaisons in some way replayed the dynamics of her abandonment by her mother.

107 "mountains of snow": EP to JB, Saint Moritz, Feb. 19, 1946.

108 "boy-scout-like": EP, *Au bal,* pp. 115–16.

108 "the strange marriage": Jean Cocteau, "Les Compagnons de la Chanson," *Diogène,* May 24, 1946, in Marchois, *Piaf: Emportée,* p. 45.

109 "lessons": EP to JB, June 20, 1946.

109 "Words and music": Henri Contet, "Du Palais de Chaillot au Club des Cinq," *Toujours Paris,* May 23–29, 1946, in Marchois, *Piaf: Emportée,* p. 46.

CHAPTER NINE • 1946–1948

110 "In the troubled post-Liberation": Jean-Claude Klein, *Florilège de la chanson française,* p. 206.

111 "modernize": EP, *Au bal*, p. 117.

111 "Madame Edith Piaf is a genius": Jean Cocteau, text read May 16, 1946, in EP, *Au bal*, preface, and in Duclos and Martin, p. 253.

112 "I cannot allow": Fred Mella, *Mes Maîtres enchanteurs*, pp. 100, 105.

112 "She thought of herself": Jean-Louis Jaubert, in Marchois, *Edith Piaf: Opinions*, p. 144.

112 "Know that all of Paris": EP telegram quoted in Dominique Grimault and Patrick Mahé, *Piaf Cerdan*, p. 34.

113 "It began very badly": EP quoted in Duclos and Martin, p. 260.

113 "the heat": EP to JB, Sept. 4, 1946.

113 "I love you as I have never": EP to Dimitris Horn, in Helena Smith, "Yes, Piaf Did Have One Great Regret," *Guardian*, Dec. 8, 2008, p. 17.

114 "If a song": EP quoted in Henri Spade, "Edith Piaf chante le malheur mais croit au bonheur," *Radio 46*, Nov. 22, 1946, in Marchois, *Piaf: Emportée*, p. 47.

114 a lushly orchestrated ballad: Emer wrote "Si tu partais" for Piaf after she told him of her "platonic" affair with Horn, according to Bret (p. 68).

115 "We're street kids": Charles Aznavour, *Le Temps des avants*, p. 120.

115 "I wasn't in love": Ibid., p. 122.

115 "her sense of humor": Ginou Richer, *Mon Amite Edith Piaf*, p. 20.

116 "When you've been singing": EP, *Au bal*, p. 128.

116 "fervor" was justified: G. Joly, "Edith Piaf à l'Etoile," *Aurore*, Sept. 10, 1947, in Marchois, *Piaf: Emportée*, p. 49.

117 "She didn't just sing": Freedland, in William Laurent, *Edith Piaf*, p. 69.

117 "I don't do things": EP, *Au bal*, p. 129.

117 "during the war": Louis Calta, "Edith Piaf Bows to Rialto Tonight," *New York Times*, Oct. 30, 1947, p. 31.

117 "no sequins": Lester Bernstein, "The Perils of Piaf," *New York Times*, Oct. 26, 1947, p. X3.

117 "a quality that I find commendable": EP, *Au bal*, p. 134.

118 "What a marvelous country": EP to JB, Oct. 25, 1947.

118 "of the kind encountered": George Jean Nathan, "Edith Piaf and Company," in *Theater Book of the Year, 1947–1948*, pp. 124–25.

119 "She is a genuine artist": Brooks Atkinson, "At the Theatre," *New York Times*, Oct. 31, 1947, p. 30.

119 "syrupy melodies": EP, *Au bal*, p. 123.

119 "I've had enough": EP to JB, Nov. 4, 1947.

120 "the art of the *chansonnière*": Virgil Thompson, "La Môme Piaf," *New York Herald Tribune*, Nov. 9, 1947, Sec. V, p. 6.

120 "brightened up her repertory": "Lugubrious Mama," *New Yorker*, Nov. 15, 1947, pp. 26–27.

121 "She had us mesmerized": Jeanne McDonagh interview with the author, Oct. 15, 2007.

121 "quaint but understandable": Nerin E. Gun quoted in EP, *Au bal*, pp. 133–34.

122   "She said that she was dying": Bonel and Bonel, pp. 234–35.

122   "we both have to make our names": EP to JB, New York, Jan. 5, 1948.

123   "She was for ever calling herself": Dietrich quoted in Bret, p. 73.

123   "When she saw me downcast": EP, *Au bal*, p. 137.

123   "Men treated me": EP, in *France Dimanche* [n.d.], quoted in Bret, pp. 73–74.

123   "Edith Piaf has won": "Edith Piaf a conquis Broadway," *Ce Soir*, Feb. 2, 1948.

CHAPTER TEN • 1948–1949

124   "conquered the American public": M.M., in *Le Matin*, March 13, 1948, in Marchois, *Piaf: Emportée*, p. 52.

125   "I've felt all sorts": EP quoted in Robert Bré, "Merci, Marcel, tu es un grand bonhomme," *Paris-Presse*, March 16, 1948, quoted in Grimault and Mahé, pp. 108–9.

125   "With Marcel": Quoted in Mella, p. 154.

126   "I worshipped him": EP, *Ma vie*, p. 44.

126   "Just look at her": Quoted in Jacques Marchand, "L'Affaire Cerdan," *L'Evénement*, April 12, 1983, p. 4.

127   "with things that aren't too complicated": EP to JB, n.d.

128   "When I went outside": EP, quoted in Duclos and Martin, p. 277.

128   "Since his return": *France Dimanche*, May 30, 1948.

128   "Oh, the bastards": EP quoted in Grimault and Mahé, p. 123. Piaf summoned the journalist she suspected of writing the article to her apartment, where Cerdan punched him after he admitted his guilt.

128   "the perfect couple": Edmonde Charles-Roux interview with the author, June 12, 2008.

130   "best propaganda for France": Pierre de Gaulle quoted in Grimault and Mahé, p. 148.

130   "Easy on the sex": Lucien Roupp quoted in ibid., p. 146.

130   "The only thing": EP to JB, Aug. 31, 1948.

131   "Voici M'sieur Cerdan": Herbert Mitgang, "Moroccan Bombardier," *New York Times*, Sept. 12, 1948.

131   "Come on, Tony": EP quoted in Grimault and Mahé, pp. 165–66. See also "Cerdan Captures World Middleweight Title by Knocking Out Zale in Twelfth," *New York Times*, Sept. 22, 1948, Sports, p. 41.

132   "Marcel had never felt": Grimault and Mahé, pp. 170–71.

132   "Hello champ!": Ibid., p. 174.

132   "Like Marcel she wore": Gaston Firnin-Guyon quoted in "Edith et Marcel aux 'States': La Fête," *Les Nouvelles littéraires*, April 7–13, 1983, p. 20.

133   "the happiest moment": EP, *Ma vie*, p. 59.

133   "I love him": EP to JB, Oct. 1, 1948.

133   "there are times": EP to JB, Oct. 8, 1948.

133   "literally obsessed": EP to JB, Oct. 12, 1948.

133   "dark thoughts": EP to JB, Nov. 1, 1948.

133 "I'm going to have him": EP to JB, Nov. 15, 1948.

134 "I had to send Momone": EP to JB, Dec. 2, 1948.

134 "Edith is known": Jacqueline Michel, "La Vie parisienne," *Parisien libéré,* Dec. 21, 1949, p. 2, in Grimault and Mahé, p. 193.

134 "We never tired": François de Roux, "'La Môme Piaf' se métamorphose en princesse," *Figaro littéraire,* Jan. 29, 1949.

135 "violence and illegal detention": "French Boxer Is Sued," *New York Times,* Jan. 21, 1949. Cf. the account in Grimault and Mahé, pp. 204–8.

135 "She's like a sister": EP quoted in Duclos and Martin, pp. 291–92.

135 "I've been made to see": Lucien Roupp quoted in Marchand, "L'Affaire Cerdan."

135 "superior to the circumstances": EP to Geneviève Lévitan, in Grimault and Mahé, p. 185.

136 "Cerdan got up": Tino Rossi quoted in Emmanuel Bonini, *Piaf,* p. 291.

136 "Words are too poor": *Journal d'Egypte Le Caire,* Feb. 25, 1949, in Marchois, *Piaf: Emportée,* p. 53.

137 "I'll be in your gloves": EP to MC, June 13, 1949, in EP and MC, *Moi pour toi,* p. 141.

138 "God's way of letting": EP to MC, July 23, 1949, in ibid., p. 148.

138 "Edith Piaf made her debut": Critics quoted in Félix Lévitan, "Edith Piaf est applaudi chaque soir par les grandes vedettes américaines," *Le Figaro,* Oct. 7, 1949, in Marchois, *Piaf: Emportée,* p. 53.

138 "I'm terribly disappointed": EP to JB [c. Oct. 1949], in Bonini, p. 296.

139 "Does that woman": EP to JB [c. Oct. 1949], in ibid., p. 299.

139 "I have to beat La Motta": Quoted in *France-Soir* and on the radio, in Grimault and Mahé, pp. 253, 260.

CHAPTER ELEVEN · 1949–1952

140 "Why are you hiding?": Quotations and information on EP's reaction to MC's death in Bonel and Bonel, pp. 79–80; cf. Grimault and Mahé, pp. 267–69.

141 "I can think of only one thing": EP to JB [Oct. 31, 1949], in Bonini, p. 302.

141 "I try in vain": EP to "Cel," Nov. 23, 1949, in Marchois, *Piaf: Emportée,* p. 64.

141 "You can take me": EP to Robert Delban, in Duclos and Martin, p. 303.

141 "I would have expected": Philippe-Gérard quoted in Brierre, p. 92.

142 she wanted desperately to believe: Piaf's friend Phillipe-Gérard was of the opinion that Piaf was to some extent a willing dupe; see Brierre, p. 95.

142 "I'll wait a few months": EP to "Cel," Nov. 23, 1949, in Marchois, *Piaf: Emportée,* p. 64.

143 "I know that death": EP, *Ma vie,* p 88.

143 "Our lives do not belong": Ibid., p. 54.

143 "If it had gone on": Simone Berteaut, "Simone Berteaut parle de Piaf," *Dim, Dam, Don* (radio broadcast), 1969, quoted in Brierre, p. 94.

143 "Had he lived": Monique Lange, in Marchois, *Piaf: Emportée,* p. 54. This passage was omitted from the English edition of Lange, pp. 133–34.

144 "She brought to life": Jean Antoine, "Edith Piaf de retour d'Amérique," *Paris-Presse,* March 16, 1950, in Marchois, *Piaf: Emportée,* p. 65.

144 "Piaf is a fallen angel": Jean-François Noël, "Edith Piaf lance face à Dieu le cri même de la terre," *Combat,* March 15, 1950, in Marchois, *Piaf: Emportée,* p. 66.

145 "I need to feel": EP to Tony Frank, May 1, 1950, in Springer, p. 82.

145 "Marinette and I": EP, *Ma vie,* p. 54.

145 "I don't know": EP to Tony Frank, May 4 and May 3, in Springer, pp. 94, 91.

146 "Playing with": Klein, *Florilège,* p. 216.

146 "When she knows": EP to Tony Frank, May 8, 1950, in Springer, pp. 106, 109.

146 "We live in a time": EP to Tony Frank, May 15, 1950, in ibid., p. 114.

146 "I will never": EP to Tony Frank, May 26, 1950, in ibid., pp. 118, 121.

147 her first American album: In July 1950, Piaf recorded "La Vie en rose," "Hymn to Love," "The Three Bells," and "Simply a Waltz" at Columbia's Paris studio.

148 "Edith always needed": Aznavour, pp. 170–71. After sizing up Constantine at the nightclub, Chez Carrère, Aznavour urged the American to introduce himself to Piaf.

148 "Edith Piaf's summer tour": "La Randonée d'Edith Piaf se terminera par un mariage," *L'Aurore,* Aug. 21, 1950, in Marchois, *Piaf: Emportée,* p. 66.

149 "When she turned on": Eddie Constantine quoted in *France-Soir,* Oct. 6, 1969, in Marchois, *Piaf: Emportée,* p. 66.

149 "I should have dealt": EP to JB, Oct. 23, 1950.

149 "Like a Mary Magdalene": JB poem quoted in Catherine Dutheil-Pessin, *La Chanson réaliste,* pp. 299–300.

150 "He's a good dancer": Conversation quoted in Duclos and Martin, p. 313.

150 "[She] is a fine": Roger Nimier, "Triomphe d'Achard," in Marchois, *Piaf: Emportée,* pp. 67–68.

151 "She proved that she": Georges Ravon, in *C'est la vie,* no. 75, 1951, in Marchois, *Piaf: Emportée,* p. 67.

151 "to console her": Henri Spade, in *France-Soir,* Aug. 5, 1977, in Bonini, p. 323.

151 "Edith never knew": Anon., quoted in ibid., p. 322.

151 "Edith liked to laugh": Micheline Dax interview with the author, July 4, 2008.

152 "Edith outdid herself": Micheline Dax, *Je suis gugusse, voilà ma gloire,* p. 53.

153 "It was essential": EP, *Ma vie,* pp. 61–62.

153 Another new song: While continuing to write for Piaf (a total of six songs), Glanzberg also composed the score for Jacques Tati's *Mon Oncle* and several classical pieces, including *Yiddish Suite* and *Holocaust Lieder.*

153 "Edith has found": "Pa-Dam," *Samedi Soir,* Nov. 24, 1951, in Marchois, *Piaf: Emportée,* p. 68.

154 "the George Sand": Maurice Fleury, "Edith Gassion (dite 'Piaf') est-elle la

George Sand du XX siècle?," *Photo-Journal*, Dec. 11, 1952, in Marchois, *Piaf: Emportée*, pp. 69–70.

154 "*ange bleu*": EP letters to Louis "Toto" Gérardin dated Jan. 16, 1952, c. Jan. 26 1952, and June 19, 1952, quoted in Christie's (Paris) press release, communication to the author by Patricia de Fougerolle, June 1, 2009.

155 "extraordinary": René Rouzaud, in Marchois, *Edith Piaf: Opinions*, p. 232. Rouzaud wrote the lyrics for a number of Piaf's songs, including "La Goualante du pauvre Jean."

CHAPTER TWELVE • 1952–1956

156 "especially now": "'Il n'y a que Paris . . . surtout maintenant!," *L'Aurore*, March 22, 1952, in Marchois, *Piaf: Emportée*, p. 68. EP's unpublished letters to Gérardin reveal that she was on intimate terms with the cyclist during the spring of 1952, despite their concern about his wife's jealousy.

157 their latest song: Although "Je t'ai dans la peau" translates as "I've Got You Under My Skin," it is not the Cole Porter song of the same title.

157 "Jacques came back": EP, *Au bal*, p. 155.

158 "Mlle. Heartbreak": *Life*, Oct. 6, 1952, pp. 109–10.

158 "I'm truly happy": EP to JB, Sept. 23, 1952. In this letter Piaf asks Bourgeat for copies of her favorite books, including Erasmus's *In Praise of Folly* and Bergson's *Laughter*.

158 "I don't think she": Philippe-Gérard, in Brierre, p. 114.

158 "In America": EP to JB, Nov. 5, 1952.

158 "Her face was puffy": Gassion, p. 136.

159 "I never thought": Ibid., p. 141.

159 "What a joy": EP to JC, Feb. 28, 1953, in Jean Cocteau, *Le Passé défini*, vol. 2, pp. 64–65.

159 "It was too big": Simone Pills, in Marchois, *Edith Piaf: Opinions*, pp. 199–223, the source for subsequent quotations and information in this section.

161 "I was happy": EP, *Ma vie*, pp. 77–78.

162 "good citizens": Emile Vuillermoz, in *Paris-Presse*, April 24, 1953, in Marchois, *Piaf: Emportée*, p. 70.

162 "conjugated and conjugal": *France-Soir*, n.d., quoted in Duclos and Martin, p. 335.

163 "like a real lady": Simone Pills, in Marchois, *Edith Piaf: Opinions*, p. 211.

164 "Last time I asked": Simone Pills quoted in "Edith Piaf a reçu deux mains d'or," in Marchois, *Piaf: Emportée*, p. 71.

164 "It was easy": Rouzaud, in Marchois, *Edith Piaf: Opinions*, p. 231.

164 "Thank you for helping": *La Joie de vivre*, broadcast Sept. 16, 1955, quoted in *Notes*, p. 62.

166 "After applauding": "Spectacles," *L'Avenir de Bernay*, May 1954.

166 "She's fortunate": Reported by EP in *Radar*, July 1954, in Duclos and Martin, p. 344.

168 "Nothing special": Bonel and Bonel, p. 202.

168 Her new show: Critical tributes in this paragraph are from *Edith Piaf and Her Continental Revue* souvenir program. Angel issued two albums at this time, *Bravo pour le clown* and *Piaf of Paris*.

168 "I was so exhausted": EP to JB, April 20, 1955.

168 "a deeply expressive soul": "Au Her Majesty's Piaf et sa revue continentale," *La Patrie*, May 10, 1955, in Marchois, *Piaf: Emportée*, p. 94.

169 "One needs a heart": EP to JB, June 10, 1955. She added, "I have your friendship, the best of all, as I love you like my father, you're my family, and with Loulou and Marguerite I have no complaints."

169 "because I am passionately": EP, "Demande d'affiliation à l'AMORC," April 12, 1955, AMORC.

169 "a joie de vivre": Anon., 1955, quoted in Bonel and Bonel, p. 249.

169 "When I come back": EP to JB, Aug. 23, 1955.

169 "It was a time": Bonel and Bonel, pp. 66–67.

170 "peace that is profound": "profound peace" is a form of greeting and the aim of life for Rosicrucians.

170 Piaf's repertoire: Piaf recorded both "Soudain, une vallée" and "L'Homme à la moto" on January 3, 1956, at the Capitol Studios in New York.

170 "She's a moving bundle": Maurice Chevalier, *Ma Route et mes chansons,* vol. 7, 1957, in Duclos and Martin, p. 354.

170 "I'll come home": EP to JB, Nov. 17, 1955.

170 "a stark mood": Howard Taubman, "Music," *New York Times,* Jan. 5, 1956, p. 25.

171 "Edith had already noticed": Bonel and Bonel, p. 67.

171 "She always needed someone": Barrier quoted in Duclos and Martin, p. 351.

171 "I'm caught": EP to JB, Feb. 12, 1956.

171 "so I can listen": EP to Jacques Pills, Feb. 21, 1956, BMD.

172 "I found a marvelous country": EP interviewed on *Music-Hall,* June 1956, in Duclos and Martin, p. 359.

CHAPTER THIRTEEN · 1956–1959

174 "I was scared": EP quoted in *France Dimanche,* July 1956, in Duclos and Martin, p. 361.

174 "It was galvanizing": Guillaume Biro quoted in Bonini, p. 387.

174 "the image of a separation": *L'Aurore,* June 7, 1956, in Marchois, *Piaf: Emportée,* p. 95.

175 "We reached this decision": Quoted in Duclos and Martin, p. 362.

176 "to show that existentialist": Aznavour quoted in Duclos and Martin, p. 323.

176 "in which the slightest exaggeration": Gilles Ravon, in *Figaro littéraire* [1956], quoted in Bonini, p. 389.

176 "She had that effect": Marc Bonel quoted in ibid.

177 "something I've never had": EP to JB, Oct. 5, 1956.

177 "It helped her": Bonel and Bonel, p. 218. See also Bourgeat's reply to Piaf's request and account of Rosicrucianism (pp. 219–23).

178   "a sort of confusion": EP to JB, Jan. 3, 1957.

178   "I didn't bring": EP quoted by Danielle Bonel, in Duclos and Martin, p. 365.

178   her best songs: English versions of "Les Amants d'un jour," "Miséricorde," "Heureuse," and Asso's "Un Jeune Homme chantait."

178   "I had the worst": EP quoted in Duclos and Martin, p. 366.

178   science of Spiritism: Kardec, the pseudonym of the French teacher Hippolyte Rivail (1804–69), was known for such works as *The Spirits' Book, The Book on Mediums,* and *The Gospel According to Spiritism.*

179   "study spiritual science": EP to JB, Feb. 16, 1957.

179   "Paname": EP to JB, May 29, 1957.

179   "She was seeking": Bonel and Bonel, p. 224. Bonel alludes to the "profound peace" of Rosicrucianism.

179   "After Jacques": EP, *Ma vie,* p. 81.

181   "you're in charge": EP, March 19, 1958, quoted in Duclos and Martin, p. 373.

181   "an ear-splitting sound": Claude Sarraute, in *Le Monde,* Feb. 8, 1958, in Marchois, *Piaf: Emportée,* p. 97.

182   "the triumph of art": Ibid.

182   "He should sing": EP, radio program, Feb. 16, 1958, in Duclos and Martin, p. 378.

182   "Like so many": Danielle Bonel quoted in Bonini, p. 410.

183   "She was a healthy woman": André Schoeller quoted in ibid., pp. 415–16.

183   "Thanks to this": Hugues Vassal, *Dans les pas d'Edith Piaf,* pp. 57–58.

184   "the Sunday crowd": EP quoted in *Paris-Presse* [April 1958], in Bonini, p. 406.

184   "She wasn't an addict": Barrier quoted in ibid., pp. 407–8.

184   "I was fascinated": Georges Moustaki, *Les Filles de la mémoire,* p. 67.

185   "Edith Piaf Gravement Malade?": *Noir et blanc,* June 13, 1958. A reference on the cover to an article about a nun who left her order because she fell in love underscores the Piaf photo's "spiritual" side, an aspect of her persona emphasized by the weekly, which also ran an article on her career entitled "Trente ans de succès ont épuisés les forces d'Edith Piaf" (pp. 384–85).

185   "It was not exactly": Richer, p. 66.

185   "If one day": EP quoted in *France Dimanche* [June 6, 1958], in Duclos and Martin, p. 385.

185   " 'Milord' was typical": Moustaki, in *Notes,* no. 153, 1998, pp. 69–70.

186   "of knowing how": Moustaki interview with the author, June 29, 2008.

186   "You have to give": Piaf and Moustaki quoted in Brierre, p. 132.

186   "a miracle": EP quoted in *France Dimanche,* Jan. 6, 1958, in Duclos and Martin, p. 390.

187   "She's made a marvelous comeback": Barrier to JB, Jan. 23, 1959.

187   "She could breathe": Georges Moustaki, "Madame Edith Piaf," *Humanité,* Jan. 24, 1978.

187   "It's over": EP to Schoeller, Feb. 2, 1959, in Duclos and Martin, p. 396.

187   "*Loulou, trouve-moi*": Barrier quoted in ibid.

CHAPTER FOURTEEN · 1959–1960

188 "Edith Piaf never lets you down": Anon., "Edith Piaf, Queen of Hearts," in *Waldorf-Astoria Daily Bulletin*, Feb. 24, 1959, MBA.

189 "it was as if homosexuality": Danielle Bonel quoted in Bonini, p. 447.

189 "She's indomitable": Barrier to JB, Feb. 25, 1959.

189 *Noir et blanc*, March 6, 1959.

189 "Our little giant": Chevalier, in Marchois, *Edith Piaf: Opinions*, p. 68.

189 "The greater": "Devenue philosophe en convalescence Edith Piaf chantera à nouveau," *Libération*, March 13, 1959, in Marchois, *Piaf: Emportée*, p. 99.

190 "Edith Piaf's recent": Jack Gould, "TV: 'Springtime in Paris,' " *New York Times*, May 13, 1959, p. 71.

190 "She was very frail": Darlene Davis Baker telephone interview with the author, May 29, 2009.

190 "There was so much love": EP to Monnot, quoted in *Paris-Journal*, June 5, 1959, in Duclos and Martin, p. 401.

190 "What have you brought": *Paris-Journal*, June 23, 1959, in Marchois, *Piaf: Emportée*, p. 100.

190 "that a man": EP quoted in "Elle dit toujours: Ce n'est pas pour cette fois," clipping [Dec. 1959], in ibid.

191 "exactly the kind": EP to Georges Moustaki, read by Moustaki in *Les Hommes de Piaf*, film.

191 "fell literally": Jean-Loup Dariel, in *Le Figaro*, July 12–13, 1959.

191 "It was unbearable": Douglas Davis quoted in *France Dimanche*, Dec. 24, 1959, in Duclos and Martin, p. 404.

191 "a series of deaths": EP quoted by Jean Noli, in *France Dimanche*, July 16, 1959, in ibid., p. 403.

192 "Her laughter": "Elle dit toujours," p. 100.

192 "This is how": Hugues Vassal, interview with the author, March 1, 2008.

192 "abject beings": Michel Rivgauche, in "Jean-Claude Brialy Raconte Edith Piaf," *Europe*, vol. 1 (Aug. 1996), quoted in Brierre, p. 139.

193 "If I can't keep singing": EP quoted in *Détective*, Dec. 10, 1959, in Duclos and Martin, p. 407.

193 imagine *not* singing: *Cinq colonnes à la une*, broadcast Jan. 15, 1960.

194 "the novel of a life": "Edith Piaf, le roman d'une vie," *Paris Match*, Jan. 9, 1960, n.p.

195 "No more injections!": EP's notebooks are reproduced in Bonel and Bonel, pp. 178–80.

195 "There was a pas de deux": Rivgauche, in Jean-Claude Labrecque's film, *67 bis, boulevard Lannes*, 1991, in Brierre, pp. 140–41.

196 "You gave me such joy": Rivgauche to EP [c. May 1960], in Bonini, p. 459.

196 "the most beautiful": EP quoted in "Piaf: L'amour? J'y crois toujours!," *Ici Paris*, June 1–7, 1960, in Lévy, p. 175.

196 "It is hard to say": In Duclos and Martin, p. 413.

197 "If I had to live": EP quoted in *Paris-Jour* [Sept. 1960], in ibid., p. 415.

197 "My life changed": Charles Dumont interview with the author, June 28, 2008.

198 "I always go": *Cinq colonnes à la une*, broadcast Dec. 2, 1960. The last line of "Non, je ne regrette rien" translates as "It all starts with you."

198 "your strong heart": JC to EP, radio broadcast, Radio Lausanne [n.d.], MBA.

199 "At this sad time": Bruno Coquatrix, "Programme Olympia," in Marchois, *Piaf: Emportée*, p. 119.

199 "to be setting out": Michèle Manceaux, "La Semaine, Piaf ressuscitée," *L'Express*, Jan. 4, 1961, p. 33.

200 "I think it's working": For information in this paragraph, see Noli, *Edith*, pp. 48–50.

200 "I adore her": Johnny Hallyday, in *L'Hymne à la Môme*, film.

201 "Edith was the lynch-pin": Dumont interview with the author, June 28, 2008.

CHAPTER FIFTEEN • 1961–1962

202 "It wasn't the dying woman": Juliette Boisrivaud, "Le Double Miracle d'Edith Piaf," in Marchois, *Piaf: Emportée*, p. 118.

202 "This powerful emotive": Klein, *Florilège*, p. 239.

202 "More than ever": Paul Carrière, in *Le Figaro* [c. Jan. 1961].

203 "a cliché": Milton Bracker, "Miracle of the 'Sparrow Kid,'" *New York Times Magazine*, Jan. 22, 1961, p. 9.

203 "There's a new man": "L'Aveu d'Edith Piaf: Cet Homme au piano," *Paris-Presse*, Jan. 21, 1961, in Marchois, *Piaf: Emportée*, p. 119.

203 no longer cared for love: EP quoted in Duclos and Martin, p. 421.

204 "We were very close": Dumont interview with the author, June 28, 2008. All subsequent quotations of Dumont are from this interview.

205 "If you want": EP's physician and EP quoted in Noli, *Edith*, p. 70.

206 "While I was racked": EP quoted in Jean Noli, "Ses Confidences à France Dimanche," *France Dimanche*, no. 3253 [2008], clipping, HVA. There is a similar account of this incident in EP, *Ma vie*, p. 68.

206 "It's very hard": EP quoted in Marchois, *Edith Piaf: Opinions*, p. 187. Raymond Asso wrote of Monnot, after her death, "She came late to all of her appointments but found the way to be early for the final one" (ibid., p. 188).

207 "I spent a tête-à-tête": Coquatrix letter, n.d., quoted in Bonini, p. 481.

207 end of *music-hall*: Jean Noli, *Piaf secrète*, p. 218.

208 "He was too gentle": Noli, *Edith*, pp. 106–7.

210 "Aren't I lucky": EP quoted in "Piaf: Voici comment mes secrétaires font fortune," *Paris-Jour*, March 27, 1962, in Marchois, *Piaf: Emportée*, p. 120.

211 "Edith Piaf, are you happy?": *Cinq colonnes à la une*, broadcast June 1, 1962.

211 "To be able": EP quoted in G.P., "Tout recommence avec lui," in *Paris Match*, Aug. 4, 1962, in Marchois, *Piaf: Emportée*, p. 120.

211 "the most dissimilar": Alain Spiraux, in *La Presse*, Sept. 29, 1962, in ibid., p. 121.

211 "To attain this altitude": Joseph Kessel quoted in Brierre, p. 152.

212 "her ravaged face": Patrick Thevenon, "Victoire, victoire! Edith, tu as encore gagné," *La Presse*, Sept. 29, 1962, in Marchois, *Piaf: Emportée*, p. 121.

212 "not only the love": EP, *Ma vie*, p. 165.

212 "Her marriage": Dumont quoted in Brierre, p. 152.

212 "You are a great artist": Robert Sauleytis quoted in Duclos and Martin, p. 436.

213 "That Edith Piaf arranged": François Brigneau, "Mme. Edith Piaf . . . avec nos regrets," *L'Aurore*, Oct. 10, 1962, in Marchois, *Piaf: Emportée*, p. 121.

213 "the legendary singer": "Edith Piaf and Théo Sarapo Wedding Video," http://vodpod.com/watch/1611937-edith-piaf-and-theo-sarapo-wedding.

213 "and her remarkable voice": Anonymous Swiss reporter cited in Bonini, p. 500.

213 "was extending the range": André Brink, *A Fork in the Road*, pp. 161–62.

215 "that's the basis": Interview with EP and Théo Sarapo, Théâtre des Celestins, Dec. 22, 1962, www.youtube.com/watch?v=nLRH51OjmZs.

215 "To make you blind": Anon., *La Dernière Heure*, quoted in Bonini, p. 511.

215 "I won't do any harm": Barrier quoted in Duclos and Martin, p. 438.

215 when Piaf was too ill: According to Dumont, Piaf's relations with Sarapo were not sexual: "She was in a state in which a woman doesn't want a sexual relation with a young man" (Bonini, p. 488).

CHAPTER SIXTEEN • 1963

216 "because you *are*": EP, radio broadcast c. 1962, "Piaf/Documents, Télé," MBA.

217 This new style: EP quoted in Noli, *Edith*, p. 148. Though less successful than other *yé-yé* stars, Christie Laume would go on to make three record albums.

217 "A newlywed": A.S., in Marchois, *Piaf: Emportée*, p. 122.

218 "Edith loved to work": Bonel and Bonel, p. 302.

218 "in stronger and better voice": Robert Alden, "Piaf Triumphant in Paris Recital," *New York Times*, Feb. 23, 1963, p. 8; this includes the quotation from *Le Monde*.

219 "Like Napoleon": Philippe Bouvard quoted in Bonini, p. 514.

219 "You know": EP quoted in Noli, *Edith*, p. 153. Piaf omitted Patachou, also a great success in the States at this time.

219 "Edith is using": Ibid., pp. 150–51.

220 "Lille is a horrible memory": Bonel and Bonel, p. 303.

220 "Nothing happens": Vendôme, in *Notes*, no. 153, p. 81.

221 "My Edith": JC to EP, April 25, 1963, in *Paris Match*, no. 758, Oct. 19, 1963, p. 70.

221 "Vacations are great!": EP quoted in *France-Soir*, June 7, 1963, in Duclos and Martin, p. 443.

222 "The doctors": Simone Margantin quoted in Noli, *Edith*, p. 192.

222 "I had the impression": EP quoted in ibid., pp. 193–94.

223 "It doesn't keep him": EP quoted in Duclos and Martin, p. 447.

224 "I suffered": EP quoted in Noli, *Edith*, p. 204.

224 "I was happy": Dumont interview with the author, June 28, 2008.

224 "They believe in reincarnation": EP quoted in Noli, *Edith*, pp. 213–14.

224 "She goes from exaggerated": Simone Margantin quoted in Noli, ibid., pp. 204–5.

225 "My dear": EP quoted in Bonel and Bonel, p. 320.

225 rival accounts of her death: Danielle Bonel's version of Piaf's last days, given in Bonini, pp. 530–33, contradicts Margantin's account, as quoted in Noli, *Piaf*, pp. 217–34; it emphasizes the role of the Bonels and devalues the role of the Noli-Vassal-Margantin clan. I have used elements from both when they seem compatible but have preferred Noli, as a source closer in time to the events.

226 "Edith Piaf burned herself": Jean Cocteau quoted in *Le Figaro*, Oct. 12, 1963, p. 54.

226 "This tragedy": Bonel and Bonel, p. 324.

227 "a public life": *L'Osservatore Romano* quoted in Duclos and Martin, p. 449.

227 "A type of French song": Jacques Enoch quoted in ibid., p. 450.

227 "She had a burial": Quotations in this paragraph are from Noli, *Edith*, pp. 236, 239.

228 "The final curtain": "Edith Piaf: Cette Fois le rideau est tombé," *Paris Match*, Oct. 19, 1963, pp. 48, 55.

228 "Her Voice Will Never Die": "Sa Voix ne mourra pas," *Paris Match*, Oct. 26, 1963, pp. 51, 53.

228 "double loss": Henry Giniger, "Double Loss to France," *New York Times*, Oct. 12, 1963, p. 45.

229 "last confession": EP letter published in *France Dimanche*, no. 896, Oct. 24, 1963. Piaf anticipated the language of this (apocryphal?) confession when dictating *Ma vie:* "What I would like is for those who have read my confession, who have heard everything, to say, as it was said of Mary Magdalene, 'Her many sins will be forgiven, for she loved greatly'" (p. 9).

229 "that freed her": Aznavour quoted in preface to Noli, *Piaf secrète*, p, 11.

CODA

230 "There could be no better": Raymond de Becker, in *Arts*, June 1964, quoted in Bonini, p. 559.

232 "I wish Edith's memory": Sarapo to *Le Parisien libéré* [1970], quoted in ibid., pp. 572–73.

233 "It wasn't Cotillard": André Schoeller quoted in ibid., p. 551.

234 "Piaf has been our lucky star": Nathalie Lhermitte quoted in "Piaf est un porte-bonheur," *L'Union*, Nov. 27, 2009.

234 "Edith"—a moody ballad: "*Elle hante un curieux music-hall / Les feuilles des arbres la bissent / . . . / Sais-tu comment font les artistes / Pour ne pas rendre*

la mort plus triste / Qu'un 'au revoir'. . . / . . . / Des millions d'amants anonymes / Viennent y planter leur bouquet / C'est tout au fond du Père-Lachaise / Dans la section quatre-vingt-seize / Qu'elle a trouvé son dernier nid / Madame Lamboukas Edith / Dite 'Piaf'. . ." Leprest changed the actual section number of Piaf's grave, *quatre-vingt-dix-sept* (ninety-seven), to *quatre-vingt-seize* (ninety-six) to rhyme with "Père-Lachaise"—an invocation of poetic license that would have met with Piaf's approval.

BIBLIOGRAPHY

A great many books have been written about Edith Piaf, most of them in French. To grasp her sense of her life, I began by reading everything that Piaf wrote—her correspondence, her song lyrics, and her memoirs, both dictated toward the end of her life: *Au bal de la chance,* published during her lifetime, and *Ma vie,* published after her death. Because Piaf had a storyteller's feel for the presentation of facts, it was necessary to compare these versions of her life (which sometimes contradict each other) with other sources, including her unpublished correspondence, especially the little-known letters to Jacques Bourgeat, her mentor, held at the Bibliothèque Nationale de France.

In the decades following Piaf's death, dozens of memoirs by contemporaries began to appear. The best known, and the most lurid, is a special case: *Piaf,* by Simone Berteaut, her sidekick during her years as a street singer in Paris. Though picturesque, Berteaut's account must be used with caution. It sensationalizes the dark side of Piaf's life, depicting significant scenes as if Berteaut had witnessed them although she was not present, claiming knowledge that she could not have possessed, and stating that Berteaut was not only the companion of her youth but also her half sister—an assertion denounced as false soon after the book's publication, by Piaf's real half sister, Denise Gassion (whose memoir, *Piaf, ma soeur,* unfortunately lacks the kind of vivid details provided by Berteaut). For this reason, I have made judicious use of Berteaut's versions of Piaf's rise to fame and, whenever possible, contextualized them with observations by others.

In this respect, memoirs by those who knew Piaf at different points have been invaluable. Maurice Maillet's *Piaf inconnue* gives a piquant glimpse of her years among the small-time crooks of Pigalle, whose *noir* atmosphere is reflected in her early repertoire. *Les Eperons de la liberté,* by Paul Meurisse, who took Piaf to live in a posh part of Paris, gives a humorous and informative account of their time together at the start of World War II, a period fleshed out by Madame Billy's *La Maîtresse de "Maison,"* on the later war years, when Piaf lived on the top floor of a high-class brothel.

Other reliable sources for this period and the postwar years include the journals of Maurice Chevalier and Jean Cocteau, the memoirs of Charles Aznavour, Micheline Dax, and Georges Moustaki, and, for the end of her life, accounts by Jean Noli, to whom Piaf dictated *Ma vie,* and Hugues Vassal, whom she allowed to photograph her in her most relaxed moments. In addition, recollections of Piaf by such figures as Jean-Louis Barrault included in Bernard Marchois's *Edith Piaf: Opinions publiques* shed light on her life from a variety of angles, as does the compilation of reviews, clippings, and other related documents in Marchois's *Piaf: Emportée par la foule.*

Claimants to the title of Piaf's best friend and confidante arose some years after her death. They include Ginou Richer's *Mon amie Edith Piaf*, which, like Berteaut's memoir, illuminates Piaf's high-spirited behavior with close friends but must also be used with caution, because of the author's tendency to inflate her role in the star's life. Many of Richer's observations are contested by what is, on the whole, a more reliable source, *Edith Piaf, le temps d'une vie*, by Marc and Danielle Bonel, who were part of her entourage for decades and looked after her at the end of her life.

There are also dozens of biographies, both the traditional kind and the *"vies romancées"* (novelized lives) of the star, in French. Since the same stories and interpretations are often repeated from one book to another, I have compared their accounts for historical feasibility or verisimilitude and, when possible, retraced their sources—though this effort was hampered by the lack of footnotes in many French books, including those by Monique Lange, the next biography after Berteaut's to reach an international readership following its publication in English. In the end, I found the most reliable of the many biographies to be Pierre Duclos and Georges Martin's *Piaf*, which not only details sources to a considerable extent but also quotes significantly from her contemporaries, many of whom were alive during the time of its writing. I also relied on Jean-Dominique Brierre's *Piaf: Sans amour on n'est rien du tout*, a useful summary of her place in the *chanson* tradition, which avoids most of the petty gossip found in other biographies. Emmanuel Bonini's *Piaf: La Vérité* appeared when I had nearly completed my own book: a grab bag of information, it lacks notes and, in some cases, attributions, but provides helpful context concerning Piaf's later years.

Like most books about Piaf published in France, the two biographies in English, by Margaret Crosland and David Bret, did not have access to the Piaf-Bourgeat correspondence, or to the letters from Piaf to other lovers that have come to light recently, nor do they appear to have drawn on accounts published in the popular press by her contemporaries. Their lives of the star, though sometimes useful, are hampered, in the case of Crosland, by the author's expressions of disdain toward her subject's lifestyle, and in the case of Bret, by the lack of attributions and the gossipy tone.

I have tried, whenever possible, to reconstruct Piaf's contemporaries' sense of her career by drawing on documents available at the Département des Arts du Spectacle of the Bibliothèque Nationale de France, the Bibliothèque Marguerite Durand, the Bibliothèque Historique de la Ville de Paris, the Bernay Office de Tourisme Archive, the Hugues Vassal Archive, and the Mazillier/Berrot Archive. Popular magazines from the 1930s, 1940s, and 1950s also provided a sense of the changing contexts for individual songs and song styles, their meaning to Piaf's audience, and their role in the development of the myth of the little sparrow as the voice of France.

I was also fortunate to be able to flesh out or confirm my findings in interviews with a number of Piaf's contemporaries, including collaborators, co-performers, and intimates such as Georges Moustaki, Micheline Dax, and Charles Dumont, whose generosity and recall of precise detail added immeasurably to the task I set myself—to tell Piaf's story from her perspective, one that mingled the *rose* with the *noir* in the unlikely tale of the spirited girl from the Paris slums who became one of the greatest voices of the twentieth century.

The following is a selected bibliography of the works that informed my research or appear in the notes.

EDITH PIAF MEMOIRS

Piaf, Edith. *Ma vie: Texte recueilli par Jean Noli*. Paris: Union Générale d'Editions, 1964. Trans. Margaret Crosland, *My Life*. London: Peter Owen, 1990.
———. *Au bal de la chance*. Paris: L'Archipel, 2003. Trans. Peter Trewartha, *The Wheel of Fortune*. London: Peter Owen, 1965.

PUBLISHED CORRESPONDENCE

Piaf, Edith, and Marcel Cerdan. *Moi pour toi: Lettres d'amour*. Paris: Cherche Midi, 2002.
Springer, Anne-Marie. *Amoureuse et rebelle: Histoires d'amour et lettres inédites de Arletty, Edith Piaf, Albertine Sarrazin*. Paris: Textuel, 2008.

BIOGRAPHIES AND STUDIES OF EDITH PIAF

Berteaut, Simone. *Piaf: A Biography*. New York: Harper & Row, 1972.
Bonel, Marc, and Danielle Bonel. *Edith Piaf: Le Temps d'une vie*. Paris: De Fallois, 1993.
Bonini, Emmanuel. *Piaf: La Vérité*. Paris: Pygmalion, 2008.
Bret, David. *Piaf: A Passionate Life*. London: Robson Books, 1998.
Brierre, Jean-Dominique. *Edith Piaf: Sans amour on n'est rien du tout*. Paris: Hors Collection, 2003.
Cartier, Jacqueline, and Hugues Vassal. *Edith et Thérèse: La Sainte et la pécheresse*. Paris: A. Carrière, 1999.
Costaz, Gilles. *Edith Piaf: Une Femme faite cri*. Paris: Seghers, 1988.
Crosland, Margaret. *Piaf*. New York: Fromm, 1987.
Cuesta, Stan. *Edith Piaf*. Paris: Librio Musique, 1999.
Duclos, Pierre, and Georges Martin. *Piaf*. Paris: Seuil, 1993.
Gassion, Denise. *Piaf, ma soeur*. Paris: Guy Authier, 1977.
Grimault, Dominique, and Patrick Mahé. *Piaf Cerdan: Un Hymne à l'amour 1946–1949*. Paris: Robert Laffont, 1984.
Lange, Monique. *Piaf*. Trans. Richard S. Woodward. New York: Seaver, 1981.
Larue, André. *Edith Piaf: L'Amour toujours*. Paris: Editions Carrère/Michel Lafon, 1983.
Laurent, William. *Edith Piaf*. Paris: Loufrani, 1980.
Le Breton, Auguste. *La Môme Piaf*. Paris: Hachette, 1980.
Lévy, François. *Passion Edith Piaf*. Paris: Textuel, 2003.
Lorcey, Jacques, and Joëlle Monserrat. *Piaf et la chanson*. Paris: Séguier, 2007.

Maillet, Maurice. *Edith Piaf inconnue*. Paris: Euro-Images, 1970.

Marchois, Bernard. *Edith Piaf: Opinions publiques*. Paris: TF1, 1995.

—————. *Piaf: Emportée par la foule*. Paris: Vade Retro, 1996.

Noli, Jean. *Edith*. Paris: Stock, 1973.

—————. *Piaf sécrète*. Paris: L'Archipel, 1993.

Richer, Ginou. *Mon amie Edith Piaf*. Avignon: L'Instantané, 2004.

Routier, Marcelle. *Piaf l'inoubliable*. Paris: Renaudot, 1990.

Témoignages sur Edith Piaf et chansons de Piaf. Paris: Métropolitaines, 1984.

Vassal, Hugues. *Piaf mon amour*. Villeurbanne: J.-L. Lesfargues, 1982.

—————. *Dans les pas d'Edith Piaf*. Paris: Les Trois Oranges, 2002.

BIOGRAPHIES AND AUTOBIOGRAPHIES OF OTHERS

Arnaud, Claude. *Jean Cocteau*. Paris: Gallimard, 2003.

Aznavour, Charles. *Le Temps des avants*. Paris: Flammarion, 2003.

Billy, Madame. *La Maitresse de "maison."* Paris: La Table Ronde, 1980.

Caizergues Pierre, ed. *Jean Cocteau 40 ans après*. Montpellier: Presses Universitaires de la Méditerranée: 2005.

Canetti, Jacques. *On cherche jeune homme aimant la musique*. Paris: Calmann-Lévy, 1978.

Cannavo, Richard, and Henri Quiquere. *Yves Montand*. Paris: Laffont, 1981.

Chevalier, Maurice. *The Man in the Straw Hat*. Long Acre, U.K.: Odhamís Press, 1950.

Cocteau, Jean. *Le Passé défini, vol. 1, 1951–1952*. Paris: Gallimard, 1981. Vol. 2, 1953. Paris: Gallimard, 1985.

—————. *Journal, 1942–1945*. Paris: Gallimard, 1989.

—————. *Théâtre complet*. Paris: Gallimard, 2003.

Dax, Micheline. *Je suis gugusse, voilà ma gloire*. Paris: Plon, 1985.

Desneux, Richard. *Yves Montand*. Lausanne: Favre, 1989.

Dietrich, Marlene. *Madame D*. Paris: Grasset, 1984.

Freyeisen, Astrid. *Chansons pour Piaf: Norbert Glanzberg, toute une vie 1910–2001*. Geneva: MJR, 2006.

Mella, Fred. *Mes Maîtres enchanteurs*. Paris: Flammarion, 2006.

Meurisse, Paul. *Les Eperons de la liberté*. Paris: Laffont, 1979.

Montand, Yves, with Hervé Hamond and Patrick Rotman. *You See, I Haven't Forgotten*. Trans. Jeremy Leggatt. New York: Alfred A. Knopf, 1992.

Moustaki, Georges. *Questions à la chanson*. Paris: Stock, 1973.

—————. *Les Filles de la mémoire*. Paris: Calmann-Lévy, 1989.

Steegmuller, Francis. *Cocteau*. New York: Atlantic Monthly, 1970.

CHANSON

Calvet, Jean-Louis. *Chanson et societé*. Paris: Payot, 1981.

Cantaloube-Ferrieu, Lucienne. *Chanson et poésie des années 30 aux années 60*. Paris: A. G. Nizet, 1981.

"La Chanson française." Special issue of *Revue de la Bibliothèque Nationale de France*, vol. 16 (2004).

Chimènes, Myriam, and Josette Alviset. *La Vie musicale sous Vichy*. Brussels: Complexe, 2001.

Conway, Kelley. *Chanteuse in the City*. Berkeley: University of California Press, 2004.

Dauncey, Hugh, and Steve Cannon. *Popular Music in France*. Aldershot, U.K., and Burlington, Vt.: Ashgate, 2003.

Dillaz, Serge. *La Chanson sous la IIIe république 1870–1940*. Paris: Tallandier, 1991.

Dutheil-Pessin, Catherine. *La Chanson réaliste*. Paris: L'Harmattan, 2004.

Hawkins, Peter. *Chanson*. London and New York: Ashgate, 2000.

Klein, Jean-Claude. *Florilège de la chanson française*. Paris: Bordas, 1990.

———. *La Chanson à l'affiche: Histoire de la chanson française du café-concert à nos jours*. Paris: Du May, 1991.

Lees, Gene. *Singers and the Song*. Oxford: Oxford University Press, 1987.

Looseley, David K. *Popular Music in Contemporary France*. Oxford: Berg, 2003.

"Marguerite Monnot dans l'ombre de Piaf." Special issue of *Camosine: Annales des pays Nivernais*, vol. 120 (2005).

Notes: la revue de la SACEM, vol. 153 (1998). Special issue, "Femmes, Histoires d'Ecrire."

"Popular Music in France." Special issue of *French Cultural Studies*, vol. 16, no. 2 (June 2005).

Richard, Lionel. *Cabaret, cabarets*. Paris: Plon, 1991.

Vincendeau, Ginette. "The Mise-en-Scène of Suffering: French chanteuses realists." *New Formations*, vol. 3 (1987), pp. 107–28.

GENERAL

Beevor, Antony, and Artemis Cooper. *Paris After the Liberation, 1944–1949*. New York: Penguin, 2004.

Bernay, Olivier. *Fireworks at Dusk: Paris in the Thirties*. New York: Little, Brown, 1993.

Bollon, Patrice. *Pigalle: Le Roman noir de Paris*. Paris: Hoëbeke, 2004.

Brink, André. *A Fork in the Road*. London: Harville Secker, 2009.

Carco, Francis. *De Montmartre au Quartier latin*. Paris: Albin Michel, 1927.

———. *Rue Pigalle*. Paris: Albin Michel, 1928.

———. *Jésus la Caille*. Paris: Livre de Poche, 1976.

Chevalier, Louis. *Histoires de la nuit parisienne*. Paris: Fayard, 1982.

———. *Montmartre du plaisir et du crime*. Paris: Fayard, 1982.

Clarke, Gerald. *Get Happy: The Life of Judy Garland*. New York: Dell, 2000.

Cobban, Alfred. *A History of Modern France*, vol. 3. London: Penguin, 1965.

Corbin, Alain. *Women for Hire: Prostitution and Sexuality in France After 1850*. Cambridge, Mass.: Harvard University Press, 1990.

Crespelle, Jean-Paul. *La Vie quotidienne à Montmartre au temps de Picasso*. Paris: Hachette, 1978.

Evenson, Norma. *Paris: A Century of Change*. New Haven: Yale University Press, 1979.

Flanner, Janet. *Paris Journal 1944–1965*. New York: Atheneum, 1965.

———. *Paris Was Yesterday, 1925–1939*. New York: Popular Library, 1972.

Gaffney, John, and Diana Holmes, eds. *Stardom in Postwar France*. New York: Berghahn Books, 2007.

Gourse, Leslie. *The Billie Holiday Companion*. New York: Schirmer, 1997.

Griffin, Farah Jasmine. *If You Can't Be Free, Be a Mystery*. New York: Free Press, 2001.

Guesnet, Jacques. *Bernay dans les années 1900*. Bernay: Page de Garde, 2002.

Guillaume, Denis. *La Résistance en France, 1939–1945*. Paris: Berg International, 2006.

Josephs, Jeremy. *Swastika over Paris: The Fate of the French Jews*. London: Bloomsbury, 1990.

Le Boterf, Hervé. *Le Théâtre en uniforme*. Paris: France-Empire, 1973.

———. *La Vie parisienne sous l'occupation, 1940–1944*. Paris: France-Empire, 1975.

Lépidis, Clément. *Belleville au coeur*. Paris: Vermet, 1980.

———. *Des Dimanches à Belleville*. Paris: A.C.E., 1985.

———. *Je me souviens du 20e arrondissement*. Paris: Parigramme, 1997.

Lottman, Herbert. *The People's Anger: Justice and Revenge in Post-Liberation France*. London: Hutchinson, 1986.

Marrus, Michael R., and Robert O. Paxton. *Vichy France and the Jews*. New York: Basic Books, 1981.

Miller, Henry. *Quiet Days in Clichy*. New York: Grove, 1987.

Nathan, George Jean. *Theater Book of the Year, 1947–1948*. Rutherford, N.J.: Fairleigh Dickinson University Press, 1975.

O'Brien, Lucy. *She Bop*. New York: Penguin, 1995.

Paris 1943: Arts et lettres. Paris: PUF, 1943.

Paxton, Robert O. *Vichy France*. New York: Alfred A. Knopf, 1972.

Rearick, Charles. *The French in Love and War*. New Haven: Yale University Press, 1997.

Rifkin, Adrian. "Musical Moments," *Yale French Studies*, vol. 73 (1987), pp. 121–55.

———. *Street Noises*. Manchester: Manchester University Press, 1993.

Ronis, Willy, and Didier Daeninckx. *Belleville Ménilmontant*. Paris: Hoëbeke, 1999.

Rorem, Ned. *A Ned Rorem Reader*. New Haven: Yale University Press, 2001.

Thomson, Virgil. *A Virgil Thomson Reader*. Boston: Houghton Mifflin, 1981.

Vallaud, Pierre. *Les Français sous l'occupation, 1940–1944*. Paris: Pygmalion, 2002.

PERIODICALS

Ce Soir
Détective
France Dimanche
France Soir
Guardian
Historia
L'Avenir de Bernay
L'Eveil Normand
L'Evénement
L'Express

Le Figaro
Le Figaro Littéraire
L'Humanité
Le Monde
Le Nouveau Temps
Les Nouvelles littéraires
Libération
Life
Marie Claire
New York Herald Tribune

New York Times
Noir et blanc
Normandie
Paris Match
Paris-Midi
Paris-Normandie
Paris-Soir
Voilà

INDEX

Page numbers beginning with 241 refer to endnotes and bibliography.

ILLUSTRATION CREDITS

PERMISSIONS ACKNOWLEDGMENTS